Diplomacy in International Law

by

G.E. do Nascimento e Silva

A.W. SIJTHOFF – LEIDEN 1972

To be cited:

Nascimento e Silva, *Diplomacy in International Law*

ISBN 90 286 0282 8

Library of Congress Catalog Card Number: 72-88929

Printed in the Netherlands.

to

my wife

PREFACE

The period following the Second World War witnessed some radical changes in the field of diplomacy, and the emergence of the United States and U.S.S.R. as the two leading powers of the world had an enormous impact in the field of international relations. The role of Great Britain and France, with a long-standing tradition in the art of diplomacy, was taken over by the two super-powers, which were not yet prepared to assume it, for Russia's main concern since the revolution had been centred on the stabilization of the regime, while the diplomatic tradition of the United States suffered from its foreign policy of isolationism.

Among the important changes which occurred we can mention the development of high-level diplomacy and that of multilateral and parliamentary diplomacy, which came to stay, bringing in their wake innumerable radical modifications.

But the outstanding event was the Conference on Diplomatic Intercourse and Immunities held in Vienna in 1961, which codified the rules of law relating to the institution. One can reasonably say that all the innumerable previous works on diplomacy at once became obsolete or demanded a complete revision in order to bring them up to date. In most cases, even taking into account the foremost books on the subject, it would have been simpler to begin the task from scratch. In the case of the Vienna Convention on Diplomatic Relations, for example, the mere reference to an article is not enough, since a complete study of all the preliminary drafts and suggestions and discussion must necessarily be taken into consideration. It was with such an aim in view that this book was written an whenever possible documents of the Vienna Conference and of the International Law Commission were used, to such an extent that some chapters are mostly based on those documents.

Even though the book is of a legal nature it was written primarily for diplomats or members of the foreign service, which explains in part the lack of notes and quotations typical of books on law. The absence of these quotations explains why at certain points in the book the reader may sense a small or even an abrupt change in the language or terminology adopted.

Many friends and colleagues helped me in the preparation and writting of this book, but I wish to make special reference to J.H. Landwehr, for his

decisive encouragement, to K.J. Payne, without whose help the English text would never have been completed, and to my wife, to whom this book is dedicated, for her patience and understanding.

Finally, it must be pointed out that the opinions are purely personal and must not be construed as representing the position of the Brazilian Government, even when based on official documents.

Rio de Janeiro, Summer 1972 G.E.N.S.

CONTENTS

Part I

Diplomacy in General

Chapter I

DIPLOMACY

It is impossible to deny the importance of diplomacy in strengthening a nation's power, not only in external but also in internal affairs. Thanks to an alert and well-structured diplomacy, a government can be kept in touch with the development of other nations and learn from the progress they have made, as long as the rest of the country is in a position to make use of the information so gained.

It is through diplomacy too that the commercial treaties are signed which will bring the new markets within reach of the country's sources of production, markets which will provide the machinery and raw materials indispensable to national progress. The technical assistance of a friendly nation or an international organization is also made available thanks to diplomatic action.

The fundamental importance of diplomacy can be gauged from a consideration of the well-known warning "win the war and lose the peace".

What diplomatic skill can achieve in the face of a deplorable lack of military and economic resources is best illustrated by the example of two Foreign Ministers of the Weimar Republic: one of them, Walter Rathenau, who managed to free Germany from its isolation by signing the Rapallo agreement with the Soviet Union and re-established friendly relations with Britain and France; and the other, Gustav Stresemann, who negotiated the withdrawal of French forces from the Ruhr and the entry of Germany into the League of Nations on favourable conditions. More recently, from 1948 to 1954, diplomacy again played a leading part in the reconstruction of Germany when what is called "the German miracle" came about: in five years, Germany passed from poverty to prosperity, from chaos to order.

Brazil itself owes the consolidation of its vast territory to diplomacy, which succeeded in getting the country's frontiers recognized by its neighbours. Diplomatic action was equally decisive and pressing on the occasion of Brazil's political emancipation, when the first problem was not one of consolidation, but one of security. Having no army, and no navy, and with an immense and poorly populated extent of territory, the Empire was at the mercy of any great European power which might wish to risk a decisive attack. Brazil found her protection behind intense diplomatic action.

In the first works on diplomacy written soon after permanent embassies had become a general feature, the authors' concern with a satisfactory definition of diplomacy was already apparent.

Although the origins of diplomacy are to be found in the remote past, the term itself is a recent one. In 1693 Leibnitz published his *Codex Juris Gentium Diplomaticus* and in 1726 there appeared the *Corps Universel Diplomatique du Droit des Gens*. Both of these were collections of treaties and official documents, but as the matters under discussion had to do with international relations the term began to assume a new meaning. Gallières, whose work is a classic, never used the term diplomat, using instead the word *negotiator*. According to Satow, the expression *diplomacy* was first used in England in 1787.

The word diplomacy is used in more than one sense, but all these senses are connected with each other and are accepted as authentic by lexicologists. It may be used as a synonym for foreign policy, i.e. the international procedure of a particular State, either in a generic sense (e.g. Brazilian diplomacy), or with regard to a particular geographical area (e.g. Middle Eastern diplomacy), or to a particular era (traditional diplomacy or modern diplomacy). In some languages, it is used to mean the foreign service itself, as in the Portuguese expression "ingressar na diplomacia". The third sense, more difficult to characterize, is the one which we shall use in this book and which comprises all the functions performed by a diplomat. Finally, there is the popular sense of the word with the idea of tact, care, courtesy or politeness, as well as the unfavourable connotations of duplicity, astuteness and guile.

Comparing the definitions given by scholars of what we are to understand by diplomacy brings out sharply the existence of wide differences and shows how difficult it is to fit such definitions into the set of characteristics required by a good definition, i.e. that it should be concise, illuminating and generic.

According to Pradier Foderé, "diplomacy brings to mind the idea of international negotiation, the maintenance of external relations, the administration of the national interests of peoples and their governments in their material contact, be it peaceful or hostile. One could almost call it the applied law of nations".[1]

Sir Ernest Satow, giving a more subjective definition, says that "diplomacy is the application of intelligence and tact to the conduct of official relations between governments of independent States, extending sometimes also to their business with vassal States".[2] Often quoted is the definition of Rivier, for whom diplomacy is "the sience and art of representing States and negotiating". Paul Fauchille prefers to avoid a definition and and develops Rivier's

1. "Cours de Droit Diplomatique", vol. I, p. 2.
2. "A Guide to Diplomatic Practice", p. 1.

idea when he tells us that "diplomacy can be regarded as a science and as an art. As a science, its aim is to become acquainted with the legal and political relations between the various States, their respective interests, their historical traditions, and the conditions laid down in treaties. As an art, its aim is to carry on international negotiation: this involves the ability to co-ordinate and direct political negotiations and accompany them with full understanding".[3] Morton Kaplan, thinking in terms of diplomatic planning, says that diplomacy is "the formulation of a strategy aiming at achieving national interests in the international field,and carrying out of this strategy by diplomats.[4]

The various definitions above reveal the different ways in which the authors have regarded the problem: some of them base their definitions on diplomatic functions and then they generally emphasize the idea of negotiation; others restrict themselves to making it a matter of diplomatic or international law; and further, as in Morton Kaplan's case, the definition covers not only diplomacy proper but policy as well.

Although the basic idea of diplomacy is a permanent one, it has certainly undergone and continues to undergo development in relation to its subject, methods and aims. Today, in speaking of diplomacy, one has the relations between States in mind. But this was not always so, and there have been periods when the authority to designate envoys was not the exclusive privilege of sovereign States; today international practice is already beginning to take note of cases of diplomatic action on the part of the great international organizations. In dealing with the history of diplomacy we shall have also to examine the development of diplomatic methods and here we shall see an important change in the matter of good faith and honesty.

We must also mention the new kinds of diplomacy. In this respect, side by side with what is known as traditional diplomacy, there is multilateral diplomacy and parliamentary diplomacy, each having its own characteristics, and each considerably broadening the field of diplomatic activity.

Multilateral diplomacy

In the beginning, diplomatic relations were conducted on a bilateral basis, but examples can be found even then of the field of activity extending beyond bilateral limits, and today multilaterality has become one of the characteristic of modern diplomacy.

Improvements in means of transport and communications demand more and more multilateral solutions, for today there are few problems which only affect the relations between two single countries. Even certain strictly bilateral questions may lose this restricted bilaterality when their importance and

3. "Traité de Droit International Public", vol. I, n. 654, p. 28.
4. "Introduction to Diplomatic Strategy", in *World Politics*, July 1952, p. 548.

the repercussion they evoke are such as to affect relations with other countries.

In the past, multilateral diplomacy came to the fore above all in post-war years, when the belligerents were forced to have recourse to peace conferences. Diplomacy, at such moments, then took on a collective aspect, but exceptionally and only temporarily. The treaties of Westphalia in 1648 and the Congress of Vienna in 1815 are ready examples of this.

In the nineteenth century States began to feel the necessity of settling common legal, economic and technical problems through discussions with one another, and in many cases realized the convenience of setting up permanent organs to deal with them. In this way there sprang up the first organizations in the field of posts and telegraphs, railways, the protection of trade marks and patent rights, and so on.

Although the idea of multilateral diplomacy evokes political connotations, it is really in the technical and scientific fields that the interests of all States are most closely felt.

Questions connected with meteorology, civil aviation, shipping, the fight against diseases, epidemics and plagues, social assistance in all its forms, the guaranteeing of postal and telegraphic communication, the distribution of radio waves, and innumerable other questions can only be solved satisfactorily through collaboration on a multilateral scale.

But it was in the period following the Second World War that high-level multilateral meetings really showed how extremely useful they could be in solving world problems. Much of their success was due to the great advances in air transport which made it possible for Heads of States and governments to leave their countries for short periods, a thing that up to that time had been next to impossible. The meeting at Munich between Hitler, Mussolini, Chamberlain and Daladier does indeed furnish an important pre-war example, while the meetings at Cairo, Teheran, Moscow and Yalta between the Heads of States or governments of the principal Allied nations were to shape the post-war world.

Multilateral diplomacy is affected either through exchanges of information between States which are linked together by political or economic ties or by means of international meetings.

Exchanges of information on the multilateral plane are carried out in every field. In the western hemisphere, the inter-American system of consultation offers an important example in the political sphere. When crises have occurred on the continent and the problem has arisen of the recognition of *de facto* governments that have come into being through civil wars, the American governments have on more than one occasion acted as a co-ordinated collective body with a view to granting recognition at the same time, i.e. acting as a body but through individual decisions.

But where the need for exchanges of information is most felt, and perma-

nently felt, is in matters concerning health conditions in different countries. Data from all over the world are collected and analysed by the World Health Organization. Similarly, countries exchange data with each other on matters concerning the state of their herds, their crops, their forest reserves. In meteorology, too, multilateral collaboration is absolutely essential for accurate weather forecasting.

The exercise of multilateral diplomacy is more closely felt through international meetings, whether they are *ad hoc* meetings held with the aim of solving a specific problem or periodical meetings of international or regional organizations.

Ad hoc meetings may be held at all levels. Examples of high-level ones are those that took place between the American presidents at Panama in 1955 and at Punta del Este in 1967, and the already quoted ones between the Heads of State and governments of the principal Allied nations during the Second World War and after. The Charter of the Organization of American States expressly provides for consultative meetings between the ministers for foreign affairs who are to be summoned to discuss problems which are urgent or of common interest to the America States.

Multilateral diplomacy as it is practised in the big international organizations is substantially different from traditional diplomacy. The debates are held in an atmosphere of publicity and are known to the general public through all available media of mass communication. The debates in the Security Council or in the General Assembly of the United Nations oblige the diplomats taking part in them to use special techniques to achieve results, for the debates are rarely of such a nature as to lead to solution.

The qualities of the orator, at one time held to be indispensable to the good diplomat, are once more considered important in this new form of diplomacy, to such an extent, in fact, that Sir Harold Nicolson observes that with the democratic diplomacy of the twentieth century, "forensic ability again resumed its clumsy place among the arts of negotiation". Traditional diplomacy, however, continues to be the principal factor in solving questions raised in international organizations, in which, alongside the debates, discussion behind the scenes, the so-called *quiet diplomacy*, is carried on, even in the United Nations. In such organizations, one of the manifestations of multilateral action is *bloc voting*, i.e. the multilateral voting of numerous delegations who are tied together by permanent or perhaps only temporary links.

The growing development of multilateral diplomacy is causing bilateral diplomacy in the traditional sense to lose ground, for there can be no doubt that purely bilateral diplomacy can no longer cope with the responsibility of trying to solve the whole vast range of questions which are bound up with international relations today.

The expression "parliamentary diplomacy" is becoming part of international terminology, although it is not always used correctly. It was used by Dean Rusk to describe the negotiations and discussions carried out in international organizations in accordance with its rules of procedure, but with special reference to the General Assembly and the Security Council of the United Nations. Subsequently, Dean Rusk developed the basic idea and defined the term in details: "What might be called parliamentary diplomacy is a type of multilateral negotiation which involves at least four factors: First, a continuing organization with interests and responsibilities which are broader than the specific items that happen to appear upon the agenda at any particular time – in other words, more than a traditional international conference called to cover specific agenda. Second, regular public debate exposed to the media of mass communication and in touch, therefore, with public opinions around the globe. Third, rules of procedure which govern the process of debate and which are themselves subject to tactical manipulation to advance or oppose a point of view. And lastly, formal conclusions, ordinarily expressed in resolution, which are reached by majority votes of some description, on a simple or two-thirds majority or based upon a financial contribution or economic stake–some with and some without a veto. Typically, we are talking about the United Nations and its related organizations, although not exclusively so, because the same type of organization is growing up in other parts of the international scene".[5]

It is perfectly possibly to widen parliamentary diplomacy's field of activity to cover, in addition, all the conferences carried out under the auspices of the United Nations or other great intergovernmental organizations where the debates are carried on according to the basic rules of procedure, and where decisions result from a majority decision reached in almost every case by means of a general vote. But the fundamental point, the point which really characterizes parliamentary diplomacy, is that the aims are attained by the skilful use of the *rules of procedure*, and not according to the usual methods.

As for the first two factors mentioned by Dean Rusk, we have in the first case what is called "multilateral" diplomacy, and in the second case what is known as "public" diplomacy.

In parliamentary diplomacy the aims or motives are similar to those of traditional diplomacy, but they are striven for, in congresses or public conferences, by using completely different methods. It must be borne in mind that, in using the rules of procedure, delegates at international conferences still need the qualities held to be indispensable in traditional diplomacy,

5. Dean Rusk, "Parliamentary Diplomacy. Debate v. Negotiation", in *World Affairs Interpreted*, vol. 26 (1955), p. 121.

though adapted to fit the particular atmosphere of a conference.

Parliamentary diplomacy was strengthened by the advent of the United Nations. The experience of the League of Nations led to the abolition of the rule requiring an unanimous voto so that the questions being debated were now decided, according to their nature, by either a simple or a two-thirds majority, except in the case of a veto. It is true that the veto came into existence, but it constituted an advance in the sense that its use was reduced to five members and to particular cases, whereas in the time of the League of Nations the unanimity rule was a veto right that could be used by any of the members.

The fact that the United States had played a preponderant part in the early stages of the United Nations and also the fact that the headquarters of the organization were set up in New York, explain the influence of the Anglo-American parliamentary system in the existing rules of procedure. It is symptomatic that the *point of order*, unknown or else acknowledged in different guise in other systems should have been accepted by every delegation, including the French, who are so jealous of the prestige of their language.

In parliamentary diplomacy the central problem is the vote, and in this respect there has been an important development since the beginning of the century. The equality of States, defended so jealously by Ruy Barbosa at the Second Hague Conference, is today regarded as one of the basic points in procedure and in any question decided in an international conference each State shall have the right to a vote, and the vote of the weakest shall be equal in value to that of the strongest.

The abolition of the unanimity rule and the adoption of the rule of the majority vote marked an important step in the development of international organizations. The Charter of the United Nations, after establishing the basic principle that "the Organization is based on the principle of the sovereign equality of all its Members" (Article 2, sub-paragraph 1), recognizes that "Decisions of the General Assembly on important questions shall be made by a two-thirds majority of the Members present and voting". After listing what these important questions are, Article 18 adds that "decisions on other questions, including the determination of additional categories of questions to be decided by a two-thirds majority, shall be made by a majority of Members present and voting".

Fundamentally, the problem is one of knowing whether the item is important for which country or countries, and why. Parliamentary diplomacy comes into play in this respect, for if a question is held to be important the decision must be taken by a two-thirds majority, whereas if it is not, half the votes plus one will be enough. And the decision as to whether the question is important or not is taken by simple majority vote.

The entry of the People's Republic of China into the United Nations in October 1971, with the consequent expulsion of Nationalist China, demon-

strated the importance of the problem. In 1970 the Albanian motion on the entry of the Peking Government received a simple majority, but it was not approved because the qualified majority had been made a requirement. The next year, the General Assembly rejected the United States' proposal that each proposal to expel Formosa should be considered an important question and thus opened the way for the subsequent approval of the Albanian proposal.

The election of the president of an organization may be decisive in parliamentary diplomacy, since he has the power to interpret the rules of procedure. The last word, however, resides with the Plenary Assembly, who may revoke an interpretation given by their president. It is for the president to sense the prevailing atmosphere and avoid entering into never-ending procedural quarrels.

The use of the *veto*, as instituted by the United Nations Charter is another delicate field, since the present tendency is for the permanent Members of the Security Council to do everything to avoid using it.

It is still too early to fix the limits of parliamentary diplomacy and, although a number of works on the *rules of procedure* of certain international organizations can be quoted, doctrine has hardly begun to evaluate their influence in the field of diplomacy. Rules of procedure of international organizations such as the assemblies and councils of the United Nations or the Organization of American States have been termed legal rules "forming part of modern international law".

But there is no doubt that diplomatic aims can be attained through the parliamentary diplomacy, i.e. by the skilful use of rules of procedure and, *contrariu sensu*, an action may fail through ignorance of the rules or through unskilful use of them.

Despite its importance, however, parliamentary diplomacy cannot be dissociated from traditional diplomacy, which has a much wider field of activity. Both these forms of diplomacy have identical aims, parliamentary diplomacy needing to be complemented by traditional diplomacy, which can, behind the scenes, exercise much greater influence away from the public eye. This is an advantage, for publicity is usually harmful to understanding and, in this sense, the quiet diplomacy that Dag Hammarskjold loved to employ is the other complement of parliamentary diplomacy.

Public Diplomacy

The growing public interest in problems relating to international politics has alerted governments to the need, alongside their traditional diplomatic activity, to keep public opinion abroad properly informed about the main lines guiding of their foreign policies, and present them in an attractive manner.

Nowadays governments are perfectly aware of this need and they usually

possess a special service, generally attached to the Ministry for Foreign Affairs itself, whose function is to supply all kinds of information through all possible channels. This kind of diplomatic penetration, which has been termed *public diplomacy*, has always been used, though sporadically and unmethodically. In ancient Greece, diplomatic missions were composed of a number of ambassadors who were supposed, each one, to present the point of view of his own city in a speech before the sovereign or the assembly, which did not prevent the real negotiations being carried on with less publicity, just as happens nowadays. Richelieu was of the opinion that no policy could succeed without the support of the opinion of the whole country and that it was absolutely necessary not only to inform the public but also to guide their opinions as a group. He adopted a system of home propaganda by distributing small leaflets he called "mes petits écrits", the object being to create an atmosphere favourable to his policy. Ideas of this kind became stronger after the French Revolution, and Palmerston preached that "opinions are stronger than armies. Opinions, if they are founded in truth and justice, will in the end prevail against the bayonets of infantry, the fire of artillery and the charges of cavalry".

Strictly speaking, it was only after 1918 that public opinion began to be interested in world problems and really understand what was going on. Wilson's condemnation of secret diplomacy and his defence of open diplomacy does not however correspond to public diplomacy as it is thought of today.

Public diplomacy allows a State to make its foreign policy known, i.e. the guiding lines which will orientate its international conduct, while diplomacy, in the sense of negotiation, goes on normally and in secrecy when circumstances demand.

After the First World War the importance of public diplomacy was perfectly well understood by Nazi Germany, whose information service was a model not only for the other totalitarian countries, but for the democracies as well.

The Fletcher School of Law and Diplomacy teaches that the expression "public diplomacy" is used "to indicate a dimension of international relations beyond traditional diplomacy, and includes the cultivation by government of public opinion in the other countries; the inter-action, outside the frame work of Government, of groups and interests in one country, with those in another; communication between those whose job is communication, as between diplomatists and foreign correspondents; and the result of these processes for the formation of policy and the conduct of foreign affairs". According to this definition, the term public diplomacy does not include information about foreign policy supplied by a government to the public opinion of its country, but only when it is aimed at public opinion in other countries; nor does it necessarily have to have organs of State as its sources, but can also be given out by private bodies, such as pressure groups, by

religious or race minorities, by commercial organizations, or even by private individuals.

It is also the task of public diplomacy to analyse the similar activity of foreign governments and gauge its influence on public opinion and on the formulation and carrying out of foreign policy.

Publicy diplomacy uses every available means of communication, including cultural and educational exchanges, distribution of publications, the press, radio and television, lectures and concerts and the setting up of national libraries.

Public diplomacy must not be despised; on the other hand, it must not be over-estimated, as publicity organs tend to do. Public opinion, especially in a democracy, needs to be guided because in the last resort a country's future lies in the vote of the electorate. The question is to what extent can the government give guidance without affecting the freedom of the press, which in many cases is almost forced to endorse government policy even if the people are known to be unwilling to accept it. At the same time, however, we must not lose sight of the fact that in international matters public opinion is easily influenced, and usually only shows interest in the problems in moments of crisis, when deliberate and calm thought is more than ever necessary.

Chapter II

OLD AND NEW DIPLOMACY

The study of the historical development of diplomacy as an institution shows that through the ages diplomatic motivations and methods have, at least apparently, changed.

Though one can defend the old diplomacy as it was regarded during the eighteenth and nineteenth centuries, this does not mean that we should return to the technique of those times, for modern diplomacy is the product of the changes which, for better or worse, have since taken place on the international scene.

Despite the emphasis given to the idea of the new diplomacy—and every politician is undoubtedly keen to innovate in this sector—we see that most definitions of it apply equally well to the old diplomacy. In other words, the aims or objectives of diplomacy have not changed at all, and the essential qualities required of diplomats to achieve them are the same as they always were. By "aims" and "objectives" is to be understood the art of States negotiating or being represented in each other's countries, not the selection of national objectives or the general outline of activity which one State will pursue in relation to another.

Putting aside semantic arguments as to what we should understand by aims or objectives in diplomacy, we see that diplomatic action is no longer, in fact, restricted to national interests but also embraces problems whose solutions can only be arrived at collectively in most cases, by means of decisions taken in the big international organizations. The very maintenance of peace and international security given as the principal aim of the United Nations, is an obligation laid on all States even when they themselves are not directly affected by events that are taking place. But the greatest advance in the field of multilateral diplomacy is to be seen in the programmes of social and humanitarian assistance, carried out individually or collectively.

The field of diplomatic action has widened considerably, and today most stress is laid on economic and commercial problems. But the importance of international trade is no novelty, as we an see from a glance at Venetian diplomacy, or at the diplomatic activity of the other Italian maritime states, aimed as it was at conquering new markets. English diplomacy has instinctively been motivated by the need to develop international maritime trade and,

in the past, its activity almost always had new markets in view, or aimed at keeping the seaways open to its overseas colonies.

Since the War, international problems have begun to demand even more specific knowledge, and the work of economists has been outstanding, giving the wrong impression that there is an economic diplomacy distinct from the traditional kind. The truth is that diplomatic action is essentially political in nature, and none of the changes witnessed have modified this fundamental consideration.

The Commission organized in Great Britain under the chairmanship of Lord Plowden stressed that the main objective of diplomacy should be economic and commercial and very appropriately emphasized the fact that "all the work of the overseas representational services at home and abroad is directed to political ends. From this point of view there is nothing to be gained from attempting to make an antithesis between *political* work and economic work".

Another preponderant factor in the transition from the old to the new diplomacy has been the enormous improvement in means of transport and in means of communication. The speed with which an instruction can be transmitted and the speed with which a Head of State, his Foreign Minister, a high official or even simply an expert in some field can leave the sending State for the headquarters of a diplomatic mission in order to decide *in loco* some problem that has arisen have deprived the diplomatic agent of the responsibility of having to take decisions at the highest level without having at his disposal precise instructions from his government on the matter. A result of this has been that laymen, unaware of the essence of diplomatic action, have proclaimed that diplomacy is dying and that it will shortly be reduced to an unimportant status with ambassadors merely obliged to carry out instructions received. Nothing could be more untrue. Precisely because of the improvements in transport and communications, the duties of diplomatic missions have increased and continue to increase daily, owing to the greater interdependence that now exists among nations and the expansion of inter-State political, economic, commercial, cultural and social interests. What is happening today in Southeast Asia and in the Middle East affects all or nearly all countries because of the political and also of the economic and commercial repercussions involved.

But diplomatic activity is not just a question of receiving and carrying out instructions. It is much more complex than that. First of all, in most cases instructions are sent on the request of a diplomatic agent who knows how to formulate his inquiry in such a way as to receive in reply precise instructions for the particular case in question. Besides, correct timing may be decisive in presenting the point of view of one's government, and the ambassador, who knows the local conditions and the most influential authorities may be able to find a quick solution for a case under review. Merely dispatching a request

to the Ministry for Foreign Affairs, without the ambassador or any other official belonging to the mission being able to give any explanation of the case to the person entrusted to find a solution for it, may thwart *ab initio* a claim on the part of the sending State.

We see, then, that through the centuries diplomacy has not undergone such a profound change as we might suppose at first sight: the immediate aim of diplomacy has not changed, though the motives for it may seem to have done so; and as for the methods employed, though at time less, and at other times more refined, depending on the historical phase concerned, they are the same, only adapted to contemporary tastes and practices.

Jules Cambon has gone so far as to contend that the alleged differences between the old and the new diplomacy are a popular illusion: "To talk–he writes–about new and old diplomacy is to make a distinction without a difference. It is the outward appearance, or, if you like, the make-up of diplomacy which is gradually changing. The substance will remain–firstly because human nature was never changes; secondly, because there is only one way of settling international differences; and lastly because the most persuasive method at the disposal of a government is the work of an honest man".[1]

1. *apud* Sir Harold Nicolson, "Diplomacy", p. 57.

Chapter III

HISTORICAL DEVELOPMENT OF DIPLOMACY

In Redslob's opinion, "diplomacy is as old as nations themselves".[1] R. Maulde la Clavière was equally categorical when he wrote that diplomacy is as old as the earth and will only disappear when the world comes to an end. We see from these examples that studies trying to prove that diplomacy arose in so-called Classical times have been superseded, and that we must look for the origins of the institution much farther back in history. It is safe to say that "the art of representation and negotiation is as old as social relations and began, in fact, as soon as families, clans, tribes and peoples came into contact with one another and sought to regulate marriage customs and contracts, hunting, trade, navigation, communications, disagreements and wars".[2]

There are two distinct stages in the development of diplomacy, the dividing line coming at the point where permanent embassies arose, but one cannot disregard the practices and customs that had been growing up and changing over the centuries before this happened and which have come down to the present time.

The beginning of the history of diplomacy must be the moment when diplomacy began to be a State activity, to continue uninterruptedly right up to our days.

Any attempt to establish a rigid set of phases in diplomatic history is fated to be criticized, especially if we start from the premise that diplomacy is a continuous and not a discontinuous process. But even if we accept the idea of continuity, we can lay some stress on particular stages that occurred before and after the establishment of permanent missions.

Diplomacy in antiquity

The ancients did not leave us any specific work on diplomacy, but Greek and Roman literature contain many references to it, and archaeological research and the interpretations of historians enable us to go back even farther in time and reveal new and important cases of negotiations, alliances and coalitions of

1. R. Redslob, "Histoire des Grands Principes du Droit des Gens", p. 79.
2. Edmund A. Walsh, "L'évolution de la diplomatie aux Etats Unis", p. 159.

various peoples at a very remote period.

Ragnar Numelin, after studying the intercourse among peoples that took place in the Mediterranean, concluded that it was then for the first time that contacts at international level began to take place in a regular manner, especially in the Nile region. He also concluded that there was a regular exchange of correspondence between kings and Heads of States and that diplomatic envoys travelled from one country to another under precise rules governing their reception and treatment. Finally, questions concerning passports and safeconducts for envoys and diplomatic mails began to be decided by a department specially set up to deal with foreign affairs.[3]

The Jewish contribution we know about from the Old Testament, which at one time was one of the principal sources of the development of international law, but its teachings were not such as to encourage intercourse between peoples, owing to the disdain for foreigners shown by the Mosaic Law.

The wealth of the Nile made Egypt a focal point of commerce and hence brought it into contact with other peoples, so that it became necessary to adopt standards for international intercourse. The most important piece of evidence we have from Egypt is the treaty between Ramses II, King of Egypt, and Hattushilish III, Prince of the Hittites, which dates from approximately 1280 B.C. and deals with the extradition of deserters to their country of origin, with the pledge that neither the guilty, nor their wives, mothers or children will be put to death.

As for Babylonia, archaeological research is gradually making new discoveries which tend to show the existence of peaceful relations with neighbouring countries, while the remarkable code of Hammurabi, drawn up somewhere about 1700 B.C., breathes justice and equity, reflecting a multinational and multilingual community and showing that the elements for the existence of such understanding were already in being.

In ancient China exchange of envoys seems to have been common and protocol was governed by strict rules. Questions of precedence were solved according to accepted principles and envoys were given instructions on how to act so as to maintain peaceful relations with other heads of States.

In the holy book of the Vedas and in the laws of Manu, we find humane principles which suggest the existence of relations with the other Indian States. The laws of Manu contain a veritable code of diplomacy. In ancient India, envoys were sent to foreign courts either with the object of making alliances, most of which had an aggressive intent, or with the aim of obtaining military information that would be of use to their States..

The most interesting and pertinent examples of diplomacy in ancient times come from Greece. The existence of numerous small city-states, their relative nearness to one another, and the high intellectual level of their inhabitants

3. "The beginning of diplomacy", p. 293.

were factors that encouraged the rise and development of an intense flow of activity between these cities.

The data that have come down to us from the fourth and fifth centuries B.C. are already sufficiently precise to show that exchanging envoys had become a general practice by that time and was based on rules already hallowed by usage. The expressive richness of Greek gives us an idea of the development of their diplomacy, for there were a dozen terms to denote the different types of treaties that could be negotiated and another dozen to refer to the various kinds of ambassadors and envoys, depending on the nature and objectives of the missions concerned, which could be to guarantee friendship or neutrality or be connected with religion or even sport.

In ancient Greece there came into being a class of permanent representatives, known as *proxenes*, designated by one city to look after the interests of its nationals in another State. At first, their function was simply to offer voluntary protection to these foreign citizens, but later on the good results of this practice led the city-states themselves to appoint them. They had many different functions to perform, and a list of these would show that these were not exclusively consular functions but diplomatic ones as well. As diplomatic representatives they received embassies from sending States in order to present them to the authorities and the assemblies at the courts and in the temples, and also to facilitate their missions. They also helped in drawing up treaties and agreements, and could be summoned as arbiters or mediators in question which happened to arise between their native cities and the cities they represented.

The attitudes of the Greek to other peoples, whom they considered barbarians and unworthy to have any rights at all, began to change with time, and the cities strengthened their contacts with barbarian countries more and more.

Harold Nicolson, however, is of the opinion that the Greeks made a mess of their diplomacy. "In the first place, they were afflicted with what Herodian called "that ancient malady of the Greeks, the love of discord". Their jealousy was so poisonous that it stung and paralysed their instinct for self-preservation. In the second place the Greeks were not by temperament good diplomatists, but bad diplomatists. Being an amazingly clever people, they ascribed a wrong value to ingenuity and stratagem, thereby destroying the basis of all sound negotiations, which is confidence. They were moreover tactless and garrulous; they lacked all sense of occasion; they were woefully indiscreet. In the third place they failed, in their external as in their internal affairs, to establish a correct distribution of responsability between the Legislature and the Executive . . . It was this final faults that brought them to ruin".[4]

4. Harold Nicolson, "The Evolution of Diplomacy", pp. 20–21.

Rome at the height of its power was the very negation of diplomacy. Imbued with the conviction that its destiny was to dominate the world by imposing the *pax romana*, it started out from the principle that all other nations had to be subjugated, if necessary by force, or even eliminated, as happened in the case of Carthago. Disagreements were solved preferably by resort to arms and Rome was not so much in favour of sending embassies as of receiving them, generally, in submission or vassalage.

But if Rome left little to posterity concerning the art of diplomacy, it did hand down, thanks to its attachment to precise formulas and its love of method, a valuable legacy in the field of law. Up to the eighteenth century the perfect terminology of Roman law was invariable accepted by writers on international law, together with the concepts it enshrined, and which were understood and used by all countries.

If we tend, however, to think of Rome as it was at the height of its fame, we must not and cannot ignore its beginnings and its decline, when it was forced to have recourse to diplomacy. In its decline, formalism and the legal concepts it had sovereignly created came to its aid as the last weapon of a Rome threatened by the barbarians.

With the collapse of the Empire and the barbarian occupation of Italy, the Empire of the East, with its seat at Constantinople, carried on the Roman traditions. The diplomatic embryo developed and the codification of Roman law under Justinian reconciled the old Roman law with Christian teachings and thus established some of the foundations of international law, which was to appear several centuries later.

Diplomacy in the Middle Ages

With the weakening of the Roman Empire of the West and its unhappy fall in 476, the *pax romana* came to an end, thereby obliging the many different nations to settle their claims by negotiation in an attempt to strengthen or to protect themselves against the more ambitious and powerful nations.

But while Europe generally entered on a phase of instability and decadence, in the East, at Byzantium, Roman civilization, now strongly tinged with Greek characteristics, lasted for almost another thousand years.

Even in the early Middle Ages the usual method of regulating relations between countries was through ambassadors, whose principal function was to convey letters or messages to foreign princes and await the replies. The reluctance of certain princes to receive embassies might mean a long stay outside the country until the audience requested was granted. The negotiations between the Byzantines and the Franks which ended in Charlemagne's assumption of the title of Emperor being recognized, went on for no less than ten years, from 804 to 814.

With the barbarian invasions, the Popes also felt the need to send nuncios

to places where the Faith was in danger, but it is not always possible to tell when a Papal mission was of a purely religious character or had political ends in view.

It is easier to study diplomatic relations in the tenth, eleventh and twelfth centuries, for many documents have come down to us which enable us to have a more precise idea of the situation of the Western, Byzantine and Moslem worlds of that period.

The Church was more active and was making determined efforts to eliminate disagreements among the Christian sovereigns who had in the Pope the obvious arbiter or mediator for a solution to their quarrels.

But Byzantium continued to be the great school of diplomacy, even after the sack of Constantinople by the Crusaders in 1204, and its influence spread to Italy via Venice. In the wake of the Crusaders trading posts were set up in the Middle East and in Byzantium by the great Italian maritime cities such as Venice, Amalfi, Genoa and Pisa, which in 1154 signed a commercial treaty with the Caliph of Egypt authorizing the establishment of trading centres at Alexandria and Cairo.

For at least six centuries, from the reign of Justinian to the sack of Constantinople during the Fourth Crusade in 1204, Byzantium dominated the political, cultural and religious life of the Western World and its importance lasted until 1453 when it finally succumbed to pressure from the Turks. The preponderant part played by Byzantium is still neglected by historians, owing presumably to the reluctance of Western Europe to admit that, while barbarism and ignorance held sway there, a new world, the result of the combination of the two classical civilizations, was developing and making progress.

Even at the height of its power Byzantium always refused to resort to using its army and navy, preferring diplomatic methods which would allow it to maintain sovereignty over its less powerful neighbours and play the more powerful ones against the others with the object of keeping them away from imperial territory. But Byzantine diplomacy did not restrict itself to political activities, and the protection of trade was already one of the main concerns of its ambassadors. In this respect, its example was followed and improved upon by Venice and the other Italian maritime cities. Byzantium concluded commercial treaties with numerous nations, particularly with the Moslems and the Russian princes, and it may be said that "the foreign affairs service of Constantinople was, as it were, the school for all the diplomacies of Europe: that of the Holy See has its beginning in the *apocrisiarii* of the Popes at the Court of Byzantium; the famous *Relazioni* of the envoys of the Venetian Republic were only an echo of similar reports required by the Byzantine government from its ministers in foreign countries".[5]

5. Baron Michel de Taube, "L'apport de Byzance au développement du droit international occidental", p. 255.

Thanks to its diplomacy, Byzantium succeeded in enjoying a privileged position when the rest of Europe was in darkness, and even after the sack of Constantinople by the Crusaders it still managed, despite its steadily growing weakness, to resist threats from all sides.

Diplomacy as it is understood today is the fruit of the Italian Renaissance, where it was brought to an unusual pitch of development with the creation of the city-states that were so characteristic of Italian life from the twelfth to the sixteenth century.

Numerous factors contributed to the development of diplomacy in Italy between 1300 and 1450, and among them the outstanding one was the nature of the various States themselves. Another important factor in the development of diplomacy was the change that took place in connection with war in which fighting gradually began to be left to mercenaries, the *condottieri*, who were more concerned about their professional reputation than with exposing their soldiers and weapons to armed clashes which might end in irreparable loss for them. They did not inspire much confidence in those who contracted them and thus the balancing influence of diplomacy began to be necessary. Moreover, the qualities looked for in a diplomat were more admired than the brute valour of the *condottieri*.

The great diplomatic centre was Venice which needed information about the other commercial centres so that it could decide on its policy and carry it out—generally with the aim of placing the chief ports and commercial centres on the Adriatic and the Dalmatian coast under its suzerainty. Besides its *ad hoc* ambassadors it had a network of consuls and the *balio* at Constantinople, who was in charge of eastern affairs and with jurisdiction over the other consuls in the region. Precise laws concerning diplomacy were issued in Venice from the beginning of the thirteenth century. From 1288 dates the obligation of envoys to send in reports on the countries to which they were accredited. These *Relazioni* of the Venetian envoys are famous and have helped to give us today a picture of the political atmosphere of that period.

Florence, in its turn, was a veritable breeding ground of diplomats whose services were used by almost all the countries of Europe. In 1300, on the occasion of the first jubilee of the Holy Year organized by Pope Boniface VIII, there were twelve Florentines among the envoys sent to Rome to attend the solemnity, and they represented not only Florence but France, England, Bohemia and other countries as well. A number of the Florentine diplomats deserve to be remembered: Machiavelli, Dante, Petrarch, Boccaccio and Guicciardini, to mention only the most notable ones who flourished during the golden age of Florentine diplomacy.

Milan was probably the first State to develop continuous diplomatic activity: the Duke of Giangaleazzo who managed, thanks to his mercenaries, to keep Italy in a state of alarm, did not hesitate to use the resources of his treasury to adopt and maintain a long-term foreign policy. Perhaps he under-

stood the dangers of trying to solve all quarrels with troops and preferred diplomatic solutions, and he must have realized that his greatest victories were won this way and at much less cost.

Diplomacy owes much to the Roman Catholic Church. From an early period the Popes adopted the practice of sending representatives to parts of the world where Christianity was becoming consolidated, and also to councils or other important meetings where questions of interest to the Church were debated.

From the eleventh century on, Papal envoys began to assume greater importance, since frequently Cardinals were chosen for this office. When this happened, the envoys were granted the title of *legati de Latere*; if they were not members of the Consistorial Congregation they were merely *legati missi* or *nuntii*.

The importance of Italian diplomacy is undeniable and we must regard it as the true beginning of the development of diplomacy, despite precedents inherited from other countries and civilizations which, in any case, the Italians absorbed into their own.

Permanent embassies

With the passing of time, intercourse between the Italian States constantly increased and soon necessitated the presence of diplomatic envoys for longer periods. By degrees the diplomatic mission developed from an *ad hoc* into a permanent institution. The fact is that in 1440 diplomatic missions were the exception, and by 1460 they were in general use all over Italy. Writers on diplomatic history have attempted to identify the first permanent ambassador, this honour being generally attributed to Nicodemus dei Pontremoli, representative of Duke Francesco Sforza to Cosimo de Medici at Florence. But though it may be possible to raise doubts as to whether Nicodemus dei Pontremoli, "sweet Nicodemus", as he was called, was really the first permanent ambassador, the fact is that he arrived at Florence in 1446 as Sforza's representative and only gave up the assignment twenty years later. In 1450, when Sforza was proclaimed Duke, Nicodemus became a diplomatic agent in the strict sense of the world and he only left Florence on two occasions, to play a decisive part in settling relations between Milan and Florence.

It should be stressed that permanent embassies did not come into being *ex abrupto*, but represented the consolidation of a tendency to prolong the stay of envoys more and more. Before the appearance of permanent diplomatic agents, the Italian States already possessed other types of permanent representatives, and a reference may be made to the consuls, particularly the Venetian ones, who possessed political and diplomatic powers that went beyond mere consular ones: as for Florence, the representatives of its banks all over Europe kept it fully informed, for the political and banking activities of

the Medici went hand in hand.

Up to this time ambassadors could be abroad for long periods, but once the mission was over they had to return with all their suite. With the creation of permanent missions, the arrival or departure of ambassadors did not affect the continuity of negotiations, for in their absence the embassy or legation was left in charge of the highest-ranking official.

The treaty of Château-Cambrésis in 1559 marked the beginning of foreign ascendancy in Italy and the few independent States that still remained, like Venice, the Duchy of Savoy, the Duchy of Parma and Piacenza and the Papal States, were slowly relegated to a secondary position in the concert of nations. The principal rôle in European politics shifted to France, the outstanding figures there being Louis XIV and Cardinal Richelieu. French began to come into use as the *lingua franca* of diplomacy, replacing Latin, which gradually became a dead language.

With the appearance of permanent embassies, diplomacy began to be taught as a science and practised as an art and the first works on diplomacy were written, mostly in Latin, French and Spanish. In them the authors explained the art of diplomacy, the functions of an ambassador, the qualities required, the steps to be taken or avoided, the methods of communication, privileges and immunities, the style to be used in correspondence, and usages at courts.

"L'Ambassadeur et ses fonctions", (1676) by Abraham de Wicquefort, and "De la manière de négocier avec les Souverains" (1716) by François de Callières became the two standard works on the subject. With the parallel development of international law, the chief writers began to study diplomacy from a purely legal angle and the work of Grotius is still considered of fundamental importance in this field.

In 1648 the Treaty of Westphalia was signed which, by encouraging political and commercial relations among the European Powers, and by basing international politics on the idea of the balance of power, came to demand from diplomacy even greater vigilance than before.

The Congress of Vienna, 1815

With the Congress of Vienna in 1815 a new phase opened in the development of diplomacy. Assembled under the double impact of the French Revolution and the Napoleonic Wars, the European monarchs, despite their attachment to traditional diplomacy, felt that they were on the eve of a radical change.

The Regulation on the classification of diplomatic agents had the great distinction of putting an end to the eternal wrangles over precedence which were one of the chief worries of the diplomatic agent. It also cut out another point of friction by adopting the *alternat* system when treaties are signed. It is symptomatic that at Vienna, when the moment came to sign the Final Act,

it was necessary to open an extra door in the hall in order to enable the plenipotentiaries to enter and withdraw simultaneously.

The Regulation, giving a ruling on the precedence of diplomatic agents, was welcomed as a last resort by the Congress of Vienna after other solutions more in line with the thought of the period to determine precedence had been put aside. After two months' deliberation, a committee put forward a proposal to group diplomatic agents into three classes in accordance with a similar grouping of all the States themselves. The proposal fell through, however, mainly because of doubts raised as to how the big republics should be placed. Finding it impossible to adopt a classification of sovereigns and Heads of State, the negotiators finally fell back on a proposal presented in 1760 by the Marquis of Pombal on the occasion of the wedding of Dom Pedro and the Princess of Brazil, which said that thenceforth ambassadors would be received in accordance with the data of their credentials. At the time, the rule was bitterly criticized, but at Vienna it was realized it was the only acceptable solution, and Article 4 was adopted as follows: "Diplomatic employees will take precedence over each other, in each class, according to the date of the official notification of their arrival".

Diplomacy came out of Vienna much strengthened. The creation of real diplomatic services soon followed, and diplomacy, freed from disputes over precedence and the burdensome cost of representative diplomacy, could now develop and make progress. And finally the work of some of the greatest statesmen of the time such as Castlereagh, Metternich, Talleyrand, Nesselrode and the Duke of Palmela, gave diplomacy a prestige it had never had before.

From the ruins of war Europe rose again and diplomacy began to assume greater importance *pari passu* with the progress achieved in the technological field and with the opening up of important new markets.

The invention of the steam engine shortening land and sea travel, and the invention of the telegraph, creating greater interdependence between States and attaching diplomatic missions more closely to their respective governments, considerably enlarged the range of matters which required orientation at the international policy level.

The progress of the United States was another factor which began to make its weight felt on the international scene despite the isolationist policy proclaimed by George Washington in his Farewell Address on 17 September 1796. This policy explains the secondary rôle played by the State Department, which George Washington himself had created in 1789.

The period of the Congress of Vienna coincides with the emancipation of the South American nations, and it is worth noting that the Legal Charter raising Brazil to the category of a Kingdom was due to a suggestion made by the Congress itself and had the result of putting Brazil on an equal footing with Portugal.

The material progress that took place in Europe during the nineteenth

century brought in its train a veritable race for empires, with the great European Powers seeking to extend their dominion all over the world in their anxiety to open up new markets. And all this had diplomatic repercussions.

The ideals of the American and French revolutions and the consequent creation of representative governments now demanded that diplomatic agents, who up to that time had been able to limit their activities to courts, where all decisions were taken, should widen their circles of contacts so as to include members of parliament, journalists, bankers and businessmen, and thus keep their governments properly informed on the national and international situation. Parliamentary debates and their repercussions in the press began to demand that international politics should, at least apparently, be guided by legal, democratic and humane principles, and that governments should be obliged to justify to the satisfaction of their electorates the measures that they had adopted.

International law relating to diplomacy began to be studied more deeply and alongside the teachings of the general treatises on the subject there appeared important specific works such as those by Baron de Charles de Martens in 1832 and by Baron de Garden in 1833, and the still excellent "Cours de Droit Diplomatique" by P. Pradier-Fodéré, first published in 1881.

Once the basic rules in precedence and the classification of diplomatic agents had been fixed by the Vienna Regulation of 1815, it was seen that international law contained quite a harmonious set of rules on diplomacy, to be found in time-hallowed customs and usages that were pretty uniformly accepted internationally. Consequently, it is not surprising that several eminent authorities should have tried to integrate all these principles in codes of international law. In this respect, the outstanding attempts at a code have been those of Bluntschli, David Dudley Field, Fiore and Epitácio Pessoa.

The two Peace Conferences at the Hague, in 1899 and 1907, deserve special mention, for it was with them that multilateral diplomacy, strictly speaking, was born, and that the Foreign Ministeries realized that the great international objectives could in some cases be more easily and rapidly attained when they were studied on a multilateral basis.

The assassination at Sarajevo of Archduke Franz Ferdinand of the Austro-Hungarian Empire, on 28 June 1914, set in motion a series of factors which were lead Europe to a disastrous war destined to end by bringing in the whole world and placing face to face roughly a hundred and twenty million people on one side and two hundred and thirty-eight millions on the other. The war which Moltke had prophesied would be over in six weeks dragged on for more than four years, ruining Europe and marking the beginning of the decadence of some European States.

The consequences of the First World War on diplomacy were heavy indeed. The incredible slaughter that took place, the trail of misery it brought with it, the collapse of the empires of the vanquished and the beginning of the collapse of the empires of the victors, the sheer size of the conflict which ended up by bringing in not only Europe but also countries in America, Asia and Africa,—all this had a very strong impact on the mass of the people in all the countries which on the eve of war had accepted the idea and even welcomed it enthusiastically, fascinated as they were by the vision of a quick and glorious victory.

When the results were added up, the scapegoats had to be identified, for by this time the general opinion was that people everywhere wished only to live in peace, and so the responsibility could only belong to the rulers and was the result of the secret confabulations of their envoys.

This conviction gained even more strength when Woodrow Wilson in the first of the Fourteen Points, on January 8, 1918, proposed that in future there should be nothing but "open convenants of peace openly arrived at", and that "diplomacy should proceed always openly and in the public view". The Fourteen Points were followed by the Four Principles, the Four Ends and the Five Particulars, all of which was most confusing. Woodrow Wilson's high ideals could not be ignored, but between the ideal and practical reality there was a wide gap, as events soon proved. At Versailles, faced by irreconcilable interests and extreme positions, many of which he had listed in his Fourteen Points, Wilson reverted to secret diplomacy and together with Clemenceau, Lloyd George and Orlando held more than a hundred and fifty meetings behind closed doors, with marines outside and only a secretary and an interpreter present. In fact, Wilson introduced an idea that was disastrous for diplomacy, and the Senate of his country enshrined another yet more harmful one, namely, that international treaties signed in good faith could be rejected by national parliaments.

The post-war period, however, brought in some less malign innovations, most of them connected with the League of Nations. It was realized that the existence of an international *forum* in which all countries could ventilate their just grievances was an advantage and that many evils could be avoided and solutions found when these grievances were debated by all together. Finally, the peoples of the world, which were daily showing more interest in international problems, began to follow the foreign policies of their own countries with truer understanding of what was involved, and either gave or refused their support for their governments when the time came for elections.

Despite the importance of the League of Nations in the development of diplomacy, it proved to be short-lived and its last years were spent in an atmosphere of frustration and failure. Germany's aggressive foreign policy

under the leadership of the National Socialists (Nazism) and the occupation of the Rhineland, the invasion of Manchuria by Japan, the invasion of Abyssinia by Italy and the futility of all the sanctions advocated by the League of Nations, the Spanish Civil War and United States isolationism were determining factors in the worsening of the international political situation which culminated in the Munich Agreement of 30 September 1938 between Hitler, Mussolini, Chamberlain and Daladier. Multilateral understandings at high level were now recognized as a way of solving big international problems, for with them the League of Nations had been born and with them the last attempt to avert the danger of an imminent war was made.

The Second World War and the United Nations

The Second World War ended under the impact of the same ideals as in 1914-18, but strengthened by the notion that more positive measures would have to be thought of to prevent mankind from being once more defrauded of what it had a right to expect. The failure of the League of Nations had not shaken the faith of peoples and their rulers in the necessity of having the main responsibility for the maintenance of peace centralized in an international organization.

The United Nations Conference on International Organization held its first session at San Francisco on April 25, 1945, with forty-five States represented.

It is not our purpose here to analyse the results of the San Francisco discussions and we shall only point out that the Charter of the United Nations was signed on June 26, 1945. What is important to remember is that the structure of the organization very soon proved unsatisfactory. Created before the first atomic bomb and at a time when the war still bound the three Great Powers together, the United Nations, whose keystone was the system of collective security, saw itself facing problems it had not foreseen, including the cold war which started soon afterwards.

The structure worked out at San Francisco depended on harmony between the two super-powers in the post-war period. But among the victors, Great Britain and France emerged from the war completely exhausted, and the break-up of their colonial empires was only a matter of a few years.

As for Germany and Italy, they were only longing for an opportunity to attempt a reconstruction which would release them from the painful situation in which they found themselves. In other words, the great traditional European diplomacies now carried little weight in the international set-up, in which the two new great powers, the United States and the Soviet Union, were prominent. The former were traditionally indifferent to diplomacy and did not possess a foreign service capable of facing the responsibilities that now confronted them; the latter were to introduce new diplomatic methods.

Multilateral and parliamentary diplomacy suffered a violent metamorphosis

with the entry into the United Nations of numerous countries that had only recently been created and which did not have even the slightest diplomatic tradition. Such States, which in the past would normally have followed the lead of more powerful delegations, began to form regional blocs whose weight in the voting sessions of the General Assembly was frequently decisive.

The ease and speed with which Heads of State or government and Ministers for Foreign Affairs and other departments could now travel from one country to another was another factor which profoundly modified diplomatic activity. The last year of the war had demonstrated the great advantages of such direct contacts at high level and *Summit diplomacy* became an intergral part of international life.

The preponderance of the United States, its immense wealth and its undeniable spirit of philanthropy also came to modify diplomatic objectives with the creation of missions for technical, social, financial, military and similar kinds of assistance. Before the war the assistance could have been called indirect intervention, but now it began to be asked for. States less prominent internationally, which before 1939 had been jealously fighting for the recognition of a *status* of equality with the great Powers, now reversed their position and, publicly proclaiming in the various international organizations that they were in an underdeveloped condition, began to demand from more favoured States the necessary assistance to help them towards development.

Diplomacy began to embrace professional activities of every kind and require from the diplomatic officer a more than superficial knowledge of the problems debated in the numerous specialized agencies set up under the auspices of the United Nations, such as organs or conferences with economic, financial, social, cultural, legal, military, administrative and technological ends in view.

The so-called underdeveloped States were no longer content just to have achieved political emancipation; they now demanded economic and technological emancipation in addition. The provision of technical assistance in the medical, scientific, social and industrial fields, to promote national progress, had until a short time before been granted *ex gratia* by the more powerful countries; but now it began to be demanded from them as an obligation.

Technical progress and the assistance necessary to achieve it began to be a new factor in international rivalry and a new characteristic of the diplomacy of the Great Powers.

The impact of nuclear energy soon made itself felt in international relations and, consequently, in diplomacy, and it is sufficient to remember, as has been said, that the whole of the system thought out at Dumbarton Oaks for the benefit of the post-war world has now become completely outdated. Diplomatic action today with regard to nuclear matters is concerned chiefly with two main questions: the proliferation of nuclear weapons and the peaceful use of nuclear energy, with the important reservation that in practice it is

not always possible to dissociate one point from the other.

The negotiations that ended in the 1967 Treaty banning nuclear weapons in Latin America and the negotiations around the 1968 Non-Proliferation Treaty demonstrate the high degree of specialization in nuclear matters required by a diplomat called on to defend his country's point of view in one of these international debates.

The fantastic increase in the military strength of the Super-Powers has not been translated into a corresponding increase in their security, but rather on the contrary, into a decrease, as a result of the obvious superiority of means of attack over means of defence.

In view of the ability to *overkill*, war has ceased to be, at Super-Power level, a way of attaining political objectives by other means or, to use the formula of Clausewitz: "war is not only a political act but also a political instrument, a continuation of political relations".

But nuclear energy is only one example of how technology has widened diplomacy's field of action. Greater technical knowledge is daily expected of diplomats, and it is no longer enough for them to be mentally agile and alert; a basic specific knowledge is also required, considering the objectives of foreign policy in the field of science and technology. In these circumstances the diplomacy of a developing country cannot restrict itself to projecting abroad national aspirations to progress; it must also carry into domestic debate the great themes of international concern today and so try to keep the country alerted to such problems and their possible effects on their nation's progress.

The Vienna Convention on Diplomatic Relations

The first multilateral treaty of international law dealt with diplomatic intercourse and was signed at the Congress of Vienna in 1815. Almost a century and a half was to pass before the nations, in the same city of Vienna, adopted in 1961 a Convention on Diplomatic Relations which codified the subject definitively.

The work of codifying international law was handed over by the United Nations to the International Law Commission, which began its activities in 1949. The problem of diplomatic intercourse and immunities was included among the topics which it was considered desirable and feasible to codify and in 1953 it was given priority by the Commission.

In 1953 the International Law Commission appointed Professor A.E.F. Sandström as special rapporteur, and in the following year he put forward an outline of a convention accompanied by an explanatory commentary. A draft convention concluded by the International Law Commission in 1958 served as a basis for the work of the Vienna Conference in 1961. A comparison of the Convention on Diplomatic Relations with the draft put forward by the

International Law Commission shows us that many of the amendments approved have not substantially altered the 1958 text and that the changes agreed on are not always an improvement on the previous work. Among the substantial modifications we should mentions the reaction of the Conference to the liberal guidance accepted by the Commission as to persons entitled to privileges and immunities, and to the wide sense given to the notion of free communication in connection with the use of radio transmitters by diplomatic missions.

The United Nations Conference on Diplomatic Intercourse and Immunities met at the Neue Hofburg from 2 March to 14 April 1961, with delegates from eighty-one States represented. The Conference was held in Vienna at the invitation of the Austrian Government, who wished to establish a link between the Conference and the Congress of Vienna in 1815.

At the Vienna Conference it was realized that owing to frequent and rapid changes in the relations of States, international law could transform any practice that is disputed up to the time of signing the treaty into a rule of law. The two most interesting examples of this adaptability of international law are to be found in Article 11, which deals with the size of diplomatic missions, and Article 26, in which the right of the receiving State to prohibit the entry of members of a mission to a particular zones is upheld. Both articles deal with problems that arose after the Second World War, and which were being disputed right up to the moment when the Convention was signed.

The Vienna Convention on Diplomatic Relations is undoubtedly the most important document on the subject that exists, besides being a landmark of the highest significance in the codification of international law. It can be criticized, and diplomacy may develop in other directions in the future, but there can be no doubt that the approved text is highly satisfactory and lays down standards that are very relevant to present-day conditions.

Part II

The Diplomatic Mission

Chapter IV

THE DIPLOMATIC MISSION AND DIPLOMATIC RELATION

The influence of the Second World War in the field of diplomacy was similar to that felt in all fields of social science. Diplomacy after the First World War had to adapt itself to the new world order in which public opinion could no longer be ignored. The post-war period, which began with the signing of the United Nations Charter in 1945, witnessed new and radical developments in the field of diplomacy where an almost imperceptible change finally made itself felt, that of making the diplomatic mission as an organic whole the centre of all diplomatic activity, and relegating the ambassador or minister to a secondary role. In other words, before the First World War, all the emphasis was on the ambassador or minister, who had under him the diplomatic and non-official personnel; after 1945 the emphasis passes to the diplomatic mission. The ambassador, however, still maintains an important position, in his capacity as head of the mission.

When the International Law Commission began to examine diplomatic intercourse and immunities its members kept this important change in mind and the Vienna Convention on Diplomatic Relations also reflected it.

The expression *diplomatic mission* can be used in more than one sense, all of them legally valid and most of them linked *inter se*.

In the first place, it is used to designate the mission, the incumbency, which the sending State assigns to its diplomatic agent in particular and to the embassy as a whole, *vis-à-vis* the receiving State or in an international conference. In this sense, we can also speak of the period of time spent by the diplomatic agent in the fulfilment of the said assignment.

It is equally correct to use the expression diplomatic mission to designate the ambassador, the diplomatic personnel and the other members of the staff of a mission in a given State. In this sense, it corresponds to the expression *members of the mission* which we find in sub-paragraph *b* of Article 1 of the Vienna Convention, i.e. "Members of the mission are the head of the mission and the members of the staff of the mission".

In its third and most important meaning diplomatic mission is the permanent administrative organ established in a foreign country, on a hierarchical basis, for the purpose of maintaining friendly relations between States and protecting the rights and interests of the country and its nationals. In a still

broader sense, this third meaning also includes the permanent missions and delegations to inter-governmental organizations as well as the embassies and legations.

Chapter V

THE RIGHT OF LEGATION

As soon as a State becomes an international person, it begins to enjoy certain fundamental or essential rights which, in the words of the Charter of the Organization of American States, depend "upon the mere fact of its existence as a person under international law" (Article 6). Among such rights is that of establishing diplomatic relations and missions, which has traditionally been known as the *right of legation*.

The right of legation is divided into two separate rights: the active right of legation (*jus activum*), which is the authority to establish diplomatic missions in foreign countries; and the passive right of legation (*jus passivum*), which refers to the correlative right to receive foreign diplomatic missions. This distinction is, however, almost academic, for it is difficult to admit the division in respect of a truly sovereign State, the few examples that can be quoted being of little theoretical value.

Even those authors who accept the existence of a right of legation are unanimous in stressing the fact that no State has the obligation either to accept the diplomatic agents of another or to open diplomatic missions in foreign countries. If we accept the fact that rights may be perfect or imperfect, then the right of legation is an example of imperfect right. However that may be, Italian writers, on re-examining the question, have shown how flimsy a concept the right of legation is. Anzilotti, who uses the expression, is of the opinion that it does not seem possible to demonstrate its existence; according to Angelo Sereni, international usage does not confirm the existence of such a norm, which cannot be justified in general international law.[1] Putting aside the case when there is a specific treaty between the two parties, where the existence of the right is beyond question, it cannot be denied that if one can theoretically speak of a right of legation, in practice a State is not obliged to establish or even to continue relations with another; the inexistence of a corresponding obligation on the part of other States offers little basis for a right of legation.

1. Anzilotti, "Cours de Droit International", vol. I, p. 265; Sereni, "Diritto Internazzionale", vol. II, p. 494.

The Vienna Convention of 1961, accepting the guidance of the International Law Commission, does not mention the right of legation. It is true that Professor Sandström's draft did recognize such a right when it said, "if two States possessing the right of legation agree to establishment permanent diplomatic relations with each other, each of them may set up a diplomatic mission in the other". But in the debates various members of the Commission stressed the impropriety of making any reference to an imperfect right, and consequently an amendment of Sir Gerald Fitzmaurice's was finally accepted, finding its way with slight modifications into the Vienna text.

The Vienna Conference was wise to endorse such an opinion, for it was inadvisable to include such a right in a Convention on Diplomatic Relations. The 1961 debates, show, however, that it is still too early to eliminate the expression from legal terminology, which is accepted in international practice and by doctrine.

The Right of legation of dependent States

The authority to send and receive diplomatic missions has traditionally been regarded as a right of sovereign States, the exercise of the right of legation being conceded to dependent States only in a few special cases. Although this norm may be acceptable in theory, it is not always possible to know if a particular State possesses the necessary requisites of independence that would justify its claims to be represented in its own name and not through some more powerful State. In practice the problem of determining if a State has full sovereignity or is a partially sovereign State has never been solved satisfactorily.

This question is solved by States pragmatically and Article 2 of the Vienna Convention reflects, as it were, the solution adopted: the establishment of diplomatic relations between States takes place by mutual consent. In other words, relations arise from an agreement in which each party tacitly admits, so to speak, the ability of the other to maintain such relations without taking into consideration the degree of sovereignty or the existence of basic elements, such as population or territory. In studying the *status* of States whose right of legation is in doubt, reference should first be made to those States whose territorial extent has been regarded as insufficient to justify their international personality. Before the Second World War, Monaco, Liechtenstein, San Marino and Andorra were cases in point. All of these, for various reasons, are attached to more powerful States in whose territory they form enclaves or on which they border, and which take it upon themselves to protect their interests in most countries. There is, however, nothing to prevent these small States from exercising their right of legation directly, and they only prefer not to do so for reasons of economy.

The sovereignty of San Marino has not been contested, despite its close

links with Italy, in whose territory it is situated. It has diplomatic Missions in Rome, Paris and the Vatican.

The sovereignty of Liechtenstein was recognized by the Congress of Vienna in 1815 and confirmed after the First World War by the Treaty of Saint-Germain. In 1949 it applied to be a party to the Statute of the International Court of Justice and, in answer to the objections raised, it was observed that "the majority of writers and jurists consider Liechtenstein a sovereign State". Its application was agreed to by a large majority and, as a party to the Statute of the International Court of Justice, it has been invited to participate in the international conferences held under the auspices of the United Nations, such as those in Vienna in 1961, 1963 and 1969.

Despite its links of dependence with France, the proof of the independence and sovereignty of Monaco is the existence of its diplomatic and consular representatives and its participation in international treaties and organizations. It has diplomatic missions in Paris and Rome and is represented at the Vatican.

The situation of Andorra, however, is quite different, for, by virtue of a treaty of 1278 which is still in force, and by another of 1806, it is placed under the joint protectorate of France and the Bishop of Urgel, paying symbolic monetary tribute annually to both. Andorra does not maintain diplomatic relations with foreign countries, for France has assumed them since the nineteenth century .

As for the several small States that have arisen since the Second World War, their right of legation has not been contested. There have, however, been objections to the participation of these micro-States in international organizations, especially the United Nations, for, unlike the small European States, they have not got a long tradition of history and independence behind them.

Member-States of the British Commonwealth of Nations are true States and as such enjoy all the rights of other States, such as the right of legation. In the past, much was written on the status of the Dominions, but since the Second World War the problem has become a mere historical reminiscence. The members of the Commonwealth exchange High Commissioners with each other and with the British Government. These High Commissioners are included in the diplomatic lists on an equal footing—save for one small difference—with other ambassadors.

In principle, only fully sovereign States enjoy the right of legation, and thus those whose sovereignty is restricted, those that are dependent on another State, cannot send or receive diplomatic missions. This is the situation of States under protectorate, vassal States and the trust territories.

As for protectorates, it may be presumed that the treaty of protection might recognize the exercise of the active and passive right of legation, but in practice this is not generally the case. It is true that the Bey of Tunisia could

receive foreign diplomatic agents (but could not send his own), but their relations with the Bey were through the Résident Général appointed by the French Government. The same occurred in Morroco, whose Sultan in 1912 signed with France a treaty modelled on the Tunisian protectorate.

During the Second World War eight Governments whose territories had been occupied by Nazi Germany set themselves up in Great Britain. They were entitled Governments in exile, an expression which, however, does not give a correct idea of their status, which was *de facto* that of the only sovereign power of countries whose territory was under enemy domination. During the First World War, the Belgian Government moved to Sainte-Adresse in France and the Serbian Government established itself in the island of Corfu in Greece.

From the point of view of international law the question is one of recognition of a government or of an authority and of the non-recognition of the territorial occupation.

With the aim of giving prestige to the exiled Governments in London, Great Britain put them all on an equal footing, recognizing the diplomatic privileges and immunities appartaining to the members of the allied governments set up in Great Britain, to their staffs and to the diplomatic agents accredited to them. The Diplomatic Privileges (Extension) Act of 1941 does not include Heads of State, since they normally enjoy such privileges and immunities when abroad.

The right of legation of the Vatican and of the Order of Malta

In discussing entities which may send and receive diplomatic missions, special reference must be made to the Vatican and to the Order of Malta. In both cases, the right of legation was, up to a particular moment in history, exercised normally, for although these entities were not identical with other States, they did possess the material elements which characterize them, namely, territory and population.

The right of the Supreme Pontiff to send legates and nuncios and to receive ambassadors or ministers was never called in question until October 1870, when the Popes were deprived of their temporal power. Once the Papal States had become extinct, it was held, at first, that right of legation had also, *ipso facto*, come to an end. Strongly influenced by the doctrine of nationalities, Italian jurists endorsed this opinion, which soon won some support from other countries.

But it was not upheld by history, for many States continued to send envoys to the Supreme Pontiff and on 13 May 1871 the Italian Government itself promulgated the Law of Guarantees.

Although the doctrine of international law at the time only recognized the international personality of States, and denied it to other entities, the truth is

that the temporal power of the Popes was a mere accessory: the importance and category of nuncios did not depend on the maintenance of that power.

All the difficulties that arose sprang from a short-sighted view of the situation and from a desire to force certain political and social facts into pre-established moulds that were not made for them. Indeed, the statesmen and diplomats, precisely because they went about the problem pragmatically, showed themselves more practical than certain theoretical jurists who, hypnotized by the idea of territorial sovereignty, would not admit that the Pope, after 1870, could be regarded as a sovereign entity.

The Lateran agreements of 1929 complicated the problem even more by adding a third element: the Vatican City. While some analysts saw in the Vatican City a true State, though a tiny one, others denied that it was a State at all.

In any discussion on these doctrinal opinions, we are bound to bear in mind the era in which they were expressed: between 1870 and 1929, between 1929 and the Second World War, or since then. We perceived that time seems to have undertaken to clarify the matter and that there has been an natural development, so much so that conclusions expressed at the end of the last century, and which were the correct ones at the time, are no longer valid for the situation as it is. As far as the Vatican City is concerned, we perceive that there is a tendency not to talk of a *State* any more. The Vatican may be regarded as a State, but excessive emphasis on its territorial characteristics has the disadvantage of relegating to the background the very factors which make the Vatican an entity distinct from that other Italian enclave, the Republic of San Marino, which, unlike the Vatican, is of little international significance. The international status of the Vatican, as defined by the Lateran Treaties, cannot be dismissed, but it obviously is not a sovereign State and any analysis which fails to take into consideration its complete attachment to the Holy See will only lead to false conclusions. This was one of the disadvantages of the excessive importance attached, after the Lateran Treaty, to the fact that the Vatican possessed territory and population. We can sum up by saying that the Vatican City is a partially sovereign State, entirely dependent on the Holy See.

After the Papal States had been annexed and it was seen that other States continued to maintain diplomatic missions accredited to His Holiness, doctrine was in general agreement in identifying the Pope as the entity which possessed the international personality and which had the right of legation. Today, the tendency seems to be to regard the Pope as the Head of the Church, while the international personality is felt to reside in the Holy See. A study of the Vienna Convention will show us that its right of legation can no longer be questioned, for not only did it take part in the Conference in 1961, but there are also specific references to the Holy See, nuncios and inter-nuncios. In addition, Article 16 expressly recognizes the diplomatic pre-

cedence of the representative of the Holy See.

The *Sovereign and Military Order of Malta* is another example of a non-State entity which enjoys and exercises the right of legation. The Order was originally one of the two great military orders of chivalry of Jerusalem, where it was founded in the eleventh century. On the loss of the Holy Land, the Order first set up headquarters on the island of Rhodes. Expelled in 1522 when the island was occupied by the Turks, it then established itself on the island of Malta.

Napoleon occupied Malta on his way to Egypt at the end of the eighteenth century, but the Order failed to get it back during the negotiations following the battle of Waterloo; instead, it passed into British hands. Some years later, the Order reappeared in Rome, where it became established during the second half of the nineteenth century and added to its title the word *sovereign*. It then tried to reopen diplomatic relations not only with the Holy See but also with various foreign States.

In the report to the Pope on the situation of the Order, published in April 1953, it is stated that "the Order is truly sovereign and is an international person with the right to exchange diplomatic agents".

Today the number of Embassies or Legations accredited to the Order of Malta is sufficient to endorse the opinion of those who defended its right to exchange diplomatic missions. Indeed, if any agreement takes place between any sovereign State and the Order of Malta with reference to the establishment of relations or diplomatic missions, then it is individually recognized to be an international person.

Once an Embassy or Legation of the Order of Malta has been established, its juridical situation is analogous to that of other diplomatic Missions. The Representative of the Order also stands on a footing of equality with other diplomatic agents unless he is a national of the receiving State, in which case he may be subject to certain restrictions, particularly in fiscal matters.

International Organizations and diplomatic representation

The received view today, based on actual international practice, is that certain international organizations may be included among entities possessing the right of legation.

The question is a relatively recent one, for it only began to arise when the Brazilian Government informed the Secretary-General of the League of Nations that it had decided to set up a permanent delegation in Geneva and that its representatives, bearing the rank and having the prerogatives of an Ambassador, would be accompanied by a Minister counsellor, a first secretary and a second secretary. Brazil's example was followed by Poland, Chile and Argentina, and the practice gradually became general.

With the growing number of delegations at Geneva, the League of Nations'

right of legation was recognized in both respects: the passive right of legation as the result of the appointment of permanent representatives, and the active right because the League's own representatives now enjoyed diplomatic privileges and immunities in member-countries.

The doubts that existed in the early years of the League of Nations were not repeated with the United Nations, and all members-States are represented in New York by permanent *missions*. The United Nations Charter (Article 105, paragraph 2) provides that representatives of the Members of the United Nations and officials of the Organization shall enjoy all the privileges and immunities that are necessary for the independent exercise of their functions in connection with the Organization.

In the list of the entities that have the right to receive and send diplomatic representatives we must include the great regional organizations like the Organization of American States, the Arab League and the European Communities. The right is not, however, extended to specialized intergovernmental organizations like the International Labour Organization, UNESCO, FAO, IMCO, ICAO, and others.

It is true that a great many States do appoint permanent representatives to such organizations, but although they enjoy prerogatives and immunities, they cannot be regarded as holding their positions by virtue of the right of legation.

In connection with the Organization of American States, we note that when the Governing Board of the Pan-American Union was set up in 1928, it was laid down that Latin-American ambassadors at Washington could represent their respective countries in it. Later at Chapultepec, in 1945, it was decided that the States would appoint *ad hoc* delegates to the Governing Board bearing the rank, the privileges and immunities of ambassadors, but these delegates could not be the permanent representatives accredited to the Government of the United States. Three years later, at Bogota, this restriction was abolished, in view of the difficulties felt by some Spanish-American countries in maintaining two representatives in Washington. In 1967, the Protocal of Buenos Ayres, in modifying the OAS Charter, once more prohibited the accumulation of representative functions by members of the new Permanent Council.

The Organization of the Arab League is very similar to the Interamerican one in this respect, and the Arab countries have permanent representatives attached to the League in Cairo.

Members of the European Communities maintain very active relations among themselves and with other States, although the Treaty of Rome only lays down the passive right of legation. As Jean Raux comments: "If practice has given very clear sanction to the Community's passive right of legation, it has not, on the other hand, been able to make up for the lack of provisions referring to the Community's active right of legation. The active right of

legation does not, therefore, exist in the positive law of the Community".[2] It is, however, true that the Resolution adopted by the European Parliament on 19 November 1960 states that "the European Communities, in view of their international legal personality, enjoy active and passive rights of legation".

The appointment of representatives or delegates to the United Nations and to the Organization of American States does not depend on previous consultation. But with the European Economic Community the position is different, for that organization possesses certain supra-State rights, and the members of non-member countries ("pays tiers") are accredited as "Heads of mission".

Although international organizations play a preponderantly passive part in international relations, their *paradiplomatic* relations must not be overlooked, i.e. relations between one international organization and another. These are undertaken by one organization sending observers or liaison agents to another, in order to harmonize their activities and facilitate communication. The observers are, in principle, high-ranking international officials who, when circumstances require it, are given the task of actively representing their particular organization on the deliberative body of another. In carrying out their duties, they may take part in debate, but unlike the delegates of member-States, they have no voting rights. Liaison agents are generally technical experts assigned to represent their organizations on an administrative or technical board of another in order to collaborate in working out and discussing studies and proposals where no right of vote is involved. *Paradiplomatic* relations may exist between regional organizations, between regional and functional organizations or between functional organizations alone.

2. Jean Raux, "Les relations exterieures de la Communauté Economique Européenne" (Paris, 1966), p. 227.

Chapter VI

ESTABLISHMENT OF DIPLOMATIC RELATIONS AND MISSIONS

Article 2 of the Vienna Convention on Diplomatic Relations states that "The establishment of diplomatic relations between States, and of permanent diplomatic missions, takes place by mutual consent". This Article, therefore, draws a distinction between two different legal situations: the establishment of diplomatic relations and the establishment of permanent diplomatic missions.

It is also necessary, if confusion is to be avoided, to draw a sharp distinction between the according of recognition and the establishment of diplomatic relations.

When from a sociological point of view a State comes into existence, the so-called right of legations appears simultaneously, but its exercise depends on the international recognition of the new State. States can be recognized expressly, but recognition can also be implied. In the first case it results from a formal declaration which can be consubstantiated in a treaty, in a diplomatic note or by a governmental decree; in the latter case recognition occurs if the government of a State performs an act, such as establishing diplomatic relations, from which it can be inferred that the new State is considered to be an international entity.

Just as States can grant recognition if they wish to do so, they have, conversely, the right to refuse to recognize any situation they consider the result of a violation of international law.

The doctrine of non-recognition, or the Stimson doctrine, resulted from identical notes addressed to the Chinese and the Japanese Governments on January 7, 1932, by the Secretary of State Henry. L. Stimson, in which he said that the United States Government did not intend "to recognize any situation, treaty, or agreement which may be brought about by means contrary to the convenants and obligations of the Pact of Paris of August 27, 1928, to which both China and Japan, as well as the United States, are parties".

Although criticized, the doctrine of non-recognition is frequently invoked and is the basis of the non-recognition by the United States of the annexation of the Baltic States by the Soviet Union during the Second World War. The

Vatican also continues to recognize the aforementioned States and the name of the Lithuanian chargé des affairs continues to appear on the diplomatic list printed by the Vatican.

This idea was also behind the Hallstein doctrine, officially proclaimed by Adenauer on December 9, 1955, and according to which acts implying the recognition of the German Democratic Republic as a sovereign State would bring in their wake the severance of diplomatic relations with the State that had so proceeded. As a result of the Hallstein doctrine, the Government of Bonn broke off relations with Yugoslavia because the latter had established diplomatic relations with the Government of Pankow. But on January 31, 1968, relations between the two countries were re-established.

In 1971, the recognition of the German Democratic Republic by the Chilean Government did not cause a severance of relations. The Government of Bonn merely declared that it would respect its previous commitments but that it did not intend to grant new benefits to that country.

The establishment of diplomatic relations usually takes place after the act of recognition. Although the establishment of diplomatic relations is convenient, no State is obliged to establish relations with another state against its will.

The non-obligation is tacitly recognized by Article 2 of the Vienna Convention when it says that the establishment of diplomatic relations with other States takes place by mutual consent.

In Vienna, the Delegation of Czechoslovakia proposed the adoption of a rule prescribing that differences in constitutional, legal and social systems should not prevent the establishment and maintenance of diplomatic relations between States. This idea was accepted and we find it in the Preamble of the Convention, in the following terms: "Believing that an international convention on diplomatic intercourse, privileges and immunities would contribute to the development of friendly relations among nations, irrespective of their differing constitutional and social systems". Resolution 2625 (XXV) adopted by the General Assembly of the United Nations on 24 October 1970, and which was called "Declaration on Principles of International Law, concerning friendly relations and co-operation among States in accordance with the Charter of the United States", welcomes the same idea: "States have the duty to co-operate with one another, irrespective of the difference in their political, economic and social systems in the various spheres of international relations, in order to maintain international peace and security and to promote international economic stability and progress, the general welfare of nations and international co-operation free from discrimination based on such differences".

Diplomatic relations between States become perfect and effective when there is an exchange, by mutual consent and on a reciprocal basis, of diplomatic missions, with the resulting exchange of ambassadors or ministers.

The rule is that States exchange diplomatic missions of the same rank, but this rule is subject to exceptions: one of the States may establish a mission even if aware of the fact that the other will not proceed likewise.

Chapter VII

CLASSES OF DIPLOMATIC MISSION

When States, by mutual consent, decide to exchange diplomatic missions it is usual for them to determine whether they will be embassies or legations, or in exceptional cases, whether some different term should not be applied to them.

Hierarchically, embassies, nunciatures and high commissions figure in the first class, according to the classification we find in Article 14 of the Vienna Convention on Diplomatic Relations. Nowadays, however, the only difference between an embassy and a legation is that the former is headed by an ambassador and the latter by a minister. Both missions are placed on an equal footing in international law, although in matters of precedence and etiquette certain distinctions are made between ambassadors and ministers.

In the past, up to the First World War, States that had the right to receive and appoint ambassadors were loath to extend such a privilege to minor States. The custom that only empires and the principal monarchies could exchange ambassadors began to change with the emergence of the United States and other important republics on the international scene. The end of the Second World War brought about a radical change in this sense and witnessed the opening of embassies in countries which, considering their secondary role, would normally have been represented by legations.

The practice of appointing ambassadors or ministers according to the political or economic importance of States was, however, contrary to the principle of the legal equality of States and was open to criticism.

The *high commissions* correspond to Embassies and are exchanged between members of the British Commonwealth of Nations.

The *nunciatures* are the most important permanent diplomatic missions of the Holy See. They are headed by nuncios or pro-nuncios and in their absence by chargés d'affaires *ad interim*. The status of the nunciatures differs from that of the other diplomatic missions: besides representing one State in another, they are also in charge of the relations with the local Catholic authorities.

Certain nunciatures, due to their importance or to historical tradition, are considered cardinalate, i.e. once the nuncio's term of office is over he becomes a cardinal.

Nunciatures exercise diplomatic and ecclesiastical functions. In the former we have the official relations with the receiving State governed by international law; in the latter we have the relations with the national Catholic hierarchy and the body of Roman Catholics in the receiving State, governed by canon law.

The second class of diplomatic missions comprises legations and internunciatures. The *legations* are headed by envoys or ministers plenipotenciary or by chargés d'affaires *en pied*. Although differences exist between ambassadors and ministers in questions of protocol, embassies and legations receive the same treatment in international law and therefore have the right to the same privileges and immunities. From a domestic point of view, both embassies and legations have the same functions and are run on the same lines. In principle, embassies are the more important missions, but nothing prevents a given legation from having a larger staff and a larger share of responsibility than certain other legations of the same country; in certain cases, for exclusively political reasons, a diplomatic mission that would normally be elevated to ambassadorial level is kept as a legation.

It is precisely due to this essential identity between embassies and legations that the tendency is gradually to abolish the remaining legations.

According to the Vienna Convention, the *internunciatures* are placed in the same class as the legations. The internunciatures are headed by internuncios. In 1947, the Holy See had internunciatures in the Netherlands and Luxembourg, since in those two countries the papal representatives were not *de jure* doyens of the diplomatic corps. Subsequently, however, the Holy See opened up a number of diplomatic missions in new States where a similar position existed, i.e. where a nuncio was not automatically the doyen of the diplomatic corps. By 1965, the number of internuncios had increased to a point at which the Holy See deemed it advisable to reconsider its position and, consequently, in those countries in which the representatives of the Holy See did not enjoy a privileged position, it began to appoint pro-nuncios, who figure on the same level as ambassadors and may become doyens of the diplomatic corps, even though they do not become doyens automatically, as occurs in Catholic countries.

Neither the Vienna Regulation of 1815 nor the Vienna Convention of 1961 mention *diplomatic representations*, which could correspond to a third class of diplomatic missions. The names given to these representations vary accordingly to their aims and the title of the head of mission.

After the Second World War and before the signature of the peace treaties the States which had been defeated began to appoint members of their diplomatic and foreign services to the Capitals of the allied countries. Prior to the coming into force of the peace treaties, the ex-enemy States, Italy, Austria, Finland, Hungary and Roumania had been represented in London by diplomats who, although enjoying private diplomatic privileges, were considered

mere *Political Representatives*.

In those countries where it does not maintain diplomatic relations the Holy See sends apostolic delegations. The apostolic delegate is a priest with a non-diplomatic function sent by the Pope as his representative to work in a given ecclesiastical region with the Catholic hierarchy, the priesthood and members of the Catholic church. His jurisdiction generally includes various bishoprics, dioceses and apostolic prefectures which may be located in different States.

In 1916, Pope Benedict XV determined that the title was to be used exclusively by papal envoys without diplomatic status. In spite of the categorical terms of the "Acta Apostolica Sedis", apostolic delegates do maintain a certain diplomatic status, so much so that they are usually appointed from among the diplomatic personnel of the Vatican and have on their staff precisely the same personnel as is to be found in the nunciatures, but without official diplomatic titles.

In the list of diplomatic missions special reference must be made to the permanent delegations and missions accredited to international organizations.

In this respect, Brazil was the first country to inform the Secretary General of the League of Nations, in 1925, that it had decided to organize in Geneva a permanent delegation headed by an ambassador. This step met with a negative reaction among jurists, but the objections raised were due to the discussion on the right of legation of the League of Nations. Nowadays, it is no longer a moot question and every member State of the United Nations has in New York a permanent mission.

In the Interamerican system, the creation of permanent representations to the Pan-American Union goes back to 1928 when a governing body of the organization was created and in which each of the member States had a representative who could be the ambassador or minister in Washington. The Charter of the Organization of American States of 1948 maintained the permanent delegates who could also be simultaneously accredited to the Government of the United States. The Buenos Aires Protocol, of 1967; reversed this policy forbidding an ambassador of an American State in Washington from being accredited at the same time as the permanent representative of the aforementioned State in the Organization of American States.

The functions of a permanent mission or delegation to an inter-governmental organization are identical to those enumerated in Article 3 of the Vienna Convention, namely representations, negotiation, observation and information. The exercise and importance of these functions vary according to the different characteristics of multilateral and parliamentary diplomacy.

A permanent mission or delegation may be accredited simultaneously to two or more inter-governmental organizations.

Chapter VIII

PREMISES OF THE MISSION

According to the Vienna Convention on Diplomatic Relations the premises of the mission "are buildings or parts of buildings and the land ancillary thereto, irrespective of ownership, used for the purposes of the mission including the residence of the head of the mission" (Article 1, sub-paragraph *i*). The draft of the International Law Commission did not include this expression in its Article 1, but considering the recurrence of the term it was thought advisable to use the definition which was to be found in the commentary to Article 20, dealing with the inviolability of the premises of the mission. This goes on to say that "the premises comprise, if they consist of a building, the surrounding land and other appurtenances, including the garden and car park".

The Vienna Convention was an innovator in this field since some of the rules adopted had been considered up to 1961 more of a domestic nature than pertaining to international law. But the difficulties encountered in some countries in purchasing or even renting a building for the use of the embassy and also the tendency of certain countries to install the mission itself or subsidiary offices away from the seat of the government of the receiving State showed the necessity of having certain rules adopted on an international level.

The whole diplomatic mission can be installed in one building but in most cases the tendency is to separate the residence of the head of mission from the offices in which all the sections of the embassy will be centralized.

States have the right to fly their national flag and use their emblem on the premises of the mission and on the residence and means of transport of their ambassadors or ministers. This is a minor point but the adoption of a rule was considered desirable in view of the existence in certain countries of restrictions concerning the use of flags of foreign States. In the case of the embassies accredited to the Holy See the custom has developed of placing next to the emblem of the sending State the coat-of-arms of the reigning Pope, in order to show that the mission is accredited to the Holy See and not to the Italian Government. A similar practice is adopted in the case of those diplomatic missions which are also accredited to the Order of Malta.

The premises of the mission should be established at the seat of the government, but frequently the residence of the head of the mission may be installed in a new residential quarter on the outskirts, which may, from an

administrative point of view, be outside the limits of the Capital of the State. Such a practice, however, does not create difficulties. But it must not be confused with that in which the diplomatic mission is established in a city which is not the Capital of the receiving State. In Saudi Arabia, for example, the Government itself is against the establishment of foreign diplomatic missions in Riyadh and, therefore, they have had to install themselves in Jidda.

A similar situation occurs in the case of the Holy See, since the various embassies and legations cannot be established in the small area of the Vatican City, with its 108,7 acres. In consequence, they are established in Rome—therefore in a foreign State—where they enjoy diplomatic privileges and immunities under the terms of the Lateran Treaty. During the Second World War, however, the Vatican received the diplomatic agents of those countries that were at war with Italy or had broken off diplomatic relations with her.

The case of Jerusalem is unique. When the State of Israel was created by the United Nations resolution of 1947, Jerusalem was considered a *corpus separatum*, to be administered by the Trusteeship Council on behalf of the United Nations. Tel-Aviv therefore became the Capital, and the Ministry for Foreign Affairs and the foreign diplomatic missions were established there. When the Parliament of Israel proclaimed Jerusalem as the nation's Capital, a delicate international situation arose since most of the States which maintained diplomatic relations with Israel were morally bound by the 1947 resolution, which had been restated on more than one occasion. Hence, most of these countries still maintain their embassies in Tel-Aviv, in spite of the attempts of the Government of Israel to have them moved to Jerusalem.

Article 12 of the Vienna Convention states that "The sending State may not, without the prior express consent of the receiving State, establish offices forming part of the mission in localities other than those in which the mission itself is established". This proviso was adopted at the suggestion of the Government of the Netherlands, which objected to the tendency of some foreign governments to transfer part of their diplomatic missions away from The Hague to Amsterdam or Rotterdam. This suggestion was adopted by the Rapporteur and met with the approval of the Commission. Mr. Bartos said that his practical experience of the problem made him favour the proposal. One mission in Yugoslavia had suddenly announced that the office of the military attaché would in future be in Split, while another had established its commercial attaché at Zagreb, because most of its commercial contacts were there. Ambassadors with little diplomatic business to transact in Yugoslavia had even been known to establish themselves in watering places. He went on to add that a practical objection to the establishment of a mission away from the receiving State's Capital was that it would make it difficult for the receiving State to ensure full enjoyment of privileges and immunities by diplomatic missions. Some other examples were mentioned, such as Germany with resi-

dences and offices in Bonn, Cologne and Frankfurt, Switzerland (Berne and Geneva), and the United States (Washington and New York). This rule turned out to be extremely important to Brazil when it transferred its Capital from Rio de Janeiro to Brasilia. Due to the reluctance of most of the diplomatic missions to leave Rio de Janeiro and face the hardships of a new Capital, located far away from the principal cities of the country, it was legally permissible for the Brazilian Government to fix a time-limit according to which the diplomatic list would only name, as from September 7, 1972, the members of diplomatic missions who resided in the new Capital and that diplomatic privileges and immunities would no longer be granted to those who did not qualify accordingly.

When the draft article of the International Law Commission was brought up in Vienna, the Swiss Delegation tabled an amendment reading: "The sending State may not, without the consent of the State of residence, establish the seat of its mission or subsidiary offices in town other than those containing the seat of the government". It was subsequently withdrawn after Mr. Dejany of Saudi Arabia pointed out that this amendment, as well as another similar one by Mexico, would have unfortunate political implications of great importance and consequences for certain countries, including his own, because of the situation of Jerusalem. He went on to say that as a result of the resolution of the General Assembly many States having diplomatic relations with Israel had been unwilling to transfer their missions to Jerusalem: acceptance of the amendments would deny to such States the right to establish their missions elsewhere else than in Jerusalem without the consent of Israel and concluded that "that in effect would encourage violation of the General Assembly resolution".

The premises of the diplomatic mission can belong to the sending State, but the question of ownership is irrelevant from the point of view of international law, as can be seen in sub-paragraph *i* of the Article. It is obvious that from the sending State's point of view the best solution is to own the premises or, better still, to be able to build premises specially designed to serve as an embassy. But many States cannot afford to incur such an expense.

The Harvard Draft contained the following rule: "A receiving State shall permit a sending State to acquire land and buildings adequate to the discharge of the functions of the latter's mission, and to hold and dispose of such land and buildings in accordance with the law of the receiving State". In its comment on the Article it said that "so far as is known, no State has, since the establishment of permanent diplomatic missions refused to permit a sending State to acquire property for the purposes of the mission". Since then, however, the situation has changed and in 1958 Sir Gerald Fitzmaurice deemed it necessary to suggest the adoption of a similar article, since the Special Rapporteur had refrained from including any provision on the lines of the Harvard draft "because he was aware of the difficulties with respect to countries

where the acquisition of real property by aliens was prohibited."

Introducing his proposal, Sir Gerald said that its purpose was to establish the right of the sending State to obtain suitable premises for its mission in the receiving State, in view of certain difficulties that had arisen in that connexion in the past. In some countries missions had had to acquire premises by roundabout methods, such as purchasing them in the name of the head of the mission or of the sending State's central bank. He concluded that "there were other countries in which it was doubtful whether a foreign Government as such was entitled to acquire property at all". The suggestion met with some opposition, such as that of Mr. Bartos who stressed that it was based on obsolete *bourgeois* legal concepts. Professor Tunkin said that the proposed paragraph brought difficulties in its wake since in a number of countries, including his own, all land was the property of the State and could be bought neither by the citizens of the country, nor by alien persons or organizations.

The resulting article, couched in carefully chosen language, is the result of the subtle modifications it suffered in the International Law Commission and subsequently in Vienna in 1961, even though Professor Tunkin said he had no objection to the draft article and Ambassador Joaquim de Souza-Leão, from Brazil, pointed that the provision did not in any way compel the sending State to acquire the premises necessary for its mission since it was open to the receiving State to ensure adequate accomodation for the mission "in some other way". The resulting article was weakened, but, at the same time, widened, since the receiving State instead of being required to *permit* the acquisition of premises must either *facilitate* their acquisition "in accordance with its laws" or *assist* the sending State in obtaining accomodation in some other way.

Paragraph 2 of Article 21 rules that the receiving State shall "where necessary, assist missions in obtaining suitable accomodation for its members". This provision was proposed by the Delegation of Venezuela and can only be regarded as a mere suggestion to the receiving State since it does not create an obligation. The International Law Commission in its commentary stressed that the obligation contained in its Article 20 did not apply to the residences of the members of the staff of the mission "because it would impose too heavy a burden on the receiving State".

Chapter IX

DIPLOMATIC COMMUNICATION

One of the most important functions of the diplomatic mission is to collect and relay information and to receive dispatches from its Ministry for Foreign Affairs, as well as from other offices and other diplomatic missions of the sending State. Unless the mission enjoys complete security in the prompt sending and receiving of official communications, it will not be in a position to send frank and often unfavourable reports on local conditions.

The opening words of Article 27 of the Vienna Convention prescribe the general principle involved: "The receiving State shall permit and protect free communication on the part of the mission for all official purposes". The Article goes on to describe the means which can be employed and the various persons or entities with which to whom such communications can be held: "In communicating with the Government and the missions and consulates of the sending State, wherever situated, the mission may employ all appropriate means, including diplomatic couriers and messages in code or cipher. However, the mission may install and use a wireless transmitter only with the consent of the receiving State".

Paragraph 2 of the draft article of the International Law Commission said simply and clearly that "the official correspondence of the mission shall be inviolable". This is the basic rule from which all the other provisions we find in Article 27 derive. The inclusion of the word *official* avoids the possibility of a diplomatic mission claiming that private mail addressed to it be granted this special protection. Private mail only enjoys diplomatic protection after it has been duly incorporated into the archives of the mission.

The second sentence of paragraph 2 of Article 27 was proposed by the United States and barely passed in the Plenary owing to the reluctance of certain delegations in having a definition of "official correspondence" included in the article, on the ground that it would be liable to interpretations which might result in weakening the basic rule.

The official correspondence of the mission can be sent by ordinary mail in envelopes, with visible external marks in order to avoid possible violations, or else in diplomatic bags or pouches. The diplomatic bag is inviolable and paragraph 4 of Article 27 says that it must bear visible external marks of its character and "may contain only diplomatic documents or articles intended

for official use". This final part is of doubtful legal value since it does not explain what measures can be taken in the case of abuse. At Vienna some delegations suggested the adoption of an additional sentence mentioning the very exceptional cases in which a diplomatic bag may be opened. An amendment by France reads as follows: "Where, however, there exist especially serious reasons to suspect that the diplomatic bag is being used for purposes other than those to which this article applies, the Ministry for Foreign Affairs of the receiving State may authorize the competent authorities of that State to open the bag in the presence of a representative of the mission". Neither this amendment nor another similar one of the United States was carried.

In the case of highly confidential or secret dispatches States usually employ diplomatic couriers. Couriers appeared with the first diplomatic missions and in spite of the amazing improvements in means of communication they are still widely employed and are considered the safest means of communication. The difficulty lies in giving a clear definition of a diplomatic courier since the inviolability of the diplomatic bag extends to his person. The Vienna Convention provides that he must be provided with an official document indicating his status and the number of packages constituting the diplomatic bag.

In Vienna two extra paragraphs were added to Article 27. The first, which became paragraph 6, provides that "the sending State or the mission may designate diplomatic couriers *ad hoc*. In such cases the provisions of paragraph 5 of this Article shall also apply, except that the immunities therein mentioned shall cease to apply when such a courier has delivered to the consignee the diplomatic bag in his charge". In introducing the amendment the Chilean delegate said it reflected a practice that was well established in his country and which had caused no difficulty. He added that the proposed provision was a restriction rather than an extension of the right to appoint diplomatic couriers.

From a practical point of view this addition was superfluous since the only apparent difference between a diplomatic courier and a courier *ad hoc* is that the immunities of these couriers will cease to apply when they have delivered the diplomatic bag in their charge. If we consider that under paragraph 5 the diplomatic courier shall only be protected by the receiving State "in the performance of his functions", even the existence of this difference is doubtful.

Paragraph 7 also transforms into a rule of international law a practice of certain governments that entrust their diplomatic bags to the captains of commercial aircraft. The new paragraph reads as follows: "A diplomatic bag may be entrusted to the captain of a commercial aircraft scheduled to land at an authorized port of entry. He shall be provided with an official document indicating the number of packages constituting the bag but he shall not be considered to be a diplomatic courier. The mission may send one of its

members to take possession of the diplomatic bag directly and freely from the captain of the aircraft". Since the captain of the aircraft is not considered to be a diplomatic courier, the proviso is superfluous since the inviolability of the diplomatic bags is fully guaranteed by paragraph 3.

The invention of wireless completely changed the horizons of diplomacy, since a diplomatic mission was now in a position to receive instantly its instructions from the Ministry for Foreign Affairs, thus reducing the responsibility of the head of mission. The draft of the International Law Commission recognized the right of diplomatic missions to "employ all appropriate means", without mentioning any limitations, thus permitting the use of wireless transmitters. The commentary to the article pointed out that if a mission wishes to make use of its own wireless transmitter it must, in accordance with the international conventions on telecommunications, apply to the receiving State for special permission. "Provided that the regulations applicable to all users of such communications are observed, such permission must not be refused".

At Vienna the employment of wireless transmitters as a matter of right met with profound opposition from the majority of States, which at present cannot afford the installation of such means. The various amendments to the end of paragraph 1 were withdrawn in favour of a joint amendment which read: "However, the mission may install and use a wireless transmitter only with the consent of the receiving State and after making proper arrangements for its use in accordance with the laws of the receiving State and international regulations". Introducing the joint amendment Mr. Krishna Rao, of India, explained in detail why so many delegations considered the draft of the International Law Commission unacceptable on this point. Answering those delegates who were against a reference to domestic laws and regulations, he pointed out that the Vienna Convention itself says expressly in Article 41 that the "it is the duty of all persons enjoying such privileges and immunities to respect the laws and regulations of the receiving State", and that "the premises of the mission must not be used in any manner incompatible with the functions of the mission". In case of abuse, the receiving State had the right to declare the head of mission or the responsible member of the mission *persona non grata*. The sponsors of the amendment, he added, were not saying that the mission could not use wireless transmitters, but only that the consent of the receiving State should be obtained and that international rules and regulations should be observed. He went on to mention the obligations of the States parties to the International Telecommunications Convention under which the Contracting Parties were obliged to take the necessary steps to ensure the establishment of the channels and the installations necessary to carry on the rapid and uninterrupted exchange of international telecommunications. The international telecommunications regulations allotted frequencies to countries and a transmitter had to work on the frequency allotted to

the country in which it was installed, irrespective of ownership. Furthermore, the system of radio communication could not possibly function if some forty or fifty embassies in the same Capital broadcast on any channel they wished. He concluded that it could not be said thet the right to install a transmitter without permission was recognized by international law and the joint amendment was, therefore, based on existing practice.

The joint amendment was opposed by the delegates from the major powers, namely those from the United States, the U.S.S.R. the United Kingdom and France. Sir Francis Vallat pointed out that in the United Kingdom the Government did not require a diplomatic mission to seek authorization before operating a wireless transmitter, nor did it insist on licences and that, in its experience, the diplomatic missions in London recognized their moral obligation to co-operate with the authorities in order to avoid any possibility of harmful interference, just as United Kingdom missions abroad co-operated with the authorities of the receiving State.

After a prolongued discussion, in which the debate was adjourned in order to work out a generally acceptable provision concerning the use of radio transmitters, the joint amendment was put to the vote and was adopted by 41 votes to 20, with 9 abstentions. Later, the authors of the joint amendment agreed to withdraw the reference to the laws of the receiving State and to international regulations, but the essence of the rule remains the same: a diplomatic mission may only install and use a radio transmitter with the consent of receiving State.

In order to safeguard the secrecy of their communications States have since ancient times used codes and ciphers. The Vienna Conference recognizes the right of States to use such methods, but only in official communications between the government, diplomatic missions and consulates.

Professor Sandström's original draft also mentioned, in the opening paragraph of the article, communications with the nationals of the sending State in the receiving State, but this suggestion was abandoned and neither the draft of the International Law Commission nor the Vienna Convention on Diplomatic Relations contain a proviso on the subject.

Since the relations with nationals is primarily a consular function, it is in the Vienna Convention on Consular Relations that we find the pertinent rules. Article 36 of the 1963 Convention, which was the result of a very long debate, gives us the guide-lines, stating that consular officers shall be free to communicate with nationals of the sending State and to have access to them and that the nationals shall have the same freedom with respect to communications with and access to consular officers of the sending State.

Finally there is the question of communications between diplomatic missions and the authorities of the receiving State. The Vienna Convention of 1961 says that all official business with the receiving State must be conducted with or through the Ministry for Foreign Affairs of the receiving State (Ar-

ticle 41). In 1957 Professor Sandström consulted the International Law Commission on whether it was its wish to include a provision on the lines of Article 13 of the Havana Convention stipulating that diplomatic officers should address themselves only to the Minister for Foreign Affairs and approach other authorities only through that channel. He added that in his opinion international law was not infringed when a diplomatic agent approached authorities without passing though the Minister for Foreign Affairs. Professor Tunkin was also of the opinion that it was unnecessary to include such a provision in the draft and Professor Spiropoulos said that it was not an important legal problem but rather a matter of protocol in the broadest sense. Although the initial reaction of the Commission was unfavourable it ended up by including a proviso in the draft which was finally adopted in Vienna.

In this context we feel that Sir Gerald Fitzmaurice gives us the correct approach to this delicate problem: although it was still the rule for the strictly diplomatic members of a mission to deal only with the Minister for Foreign Affairs, it was fairly settled practice for the numerous specialists who had been added to missions to have direct contact with the departments dealing with their speciality. Indeed, he concluded, unless such direct contacts were permitted, it would be extremely difficult for the various attachés to discharge their functions and most countries actually preferred them to address themselves to the competent departments.

Chapter X

FUNCTIONS OF A DIPLOMATIC MISSION

Diplomatic missions have the task of maintaining friendly relations between the sending and the receiving States as well as that of protecting the interests of the country represented and its nationals. This very wide definition goes to show that the primary tasks of a diplomatic mission have not changed over the years or over the centuries. But if the functions of a diplomatic mission have remained unchanged in one respect, we are forced to recognize that since the Second World War a significant change has taken place with regard to the volume and the context of such functions. Nowadays the Ministry for Foreign Affairs must receive constant information from all parts of the globe and on a very wide range of subject. The *Plowden Report*, submitted to the British Parliament by the Prime Minister in February 1964, and which had a decisive impact on the foreign service of the United Kingdom, analyses this phenomenon in a masterly manner: "In no circumstances must work be stinted which can be expected to have a significant bearing on issues affecting war or peace or is in support of trade. Subject to this, there will always be scope for changes in direction and emphasis. Priorities will constantly change, both geographically and functionally. Countries previously regarded as political backwaters can become almost overnight areas of critical importance. Countries which were closed to our trade can again become promising markets, whilst existing markets can be closed by financial, economic or political changes. At some posts there will be a need to devote the main effort to commercial work at the expense of political, information or consular work. At other posts a quite different order of priorities will be justified. The imperative need is for a high degree of flexibility and adaptability. Our recommendations are therefore directed at securing a high degree of alertness to changing circumstances and of administractive flexibility in meeting them".

Another point which has been raised is that in this changing world diplomatic missions nowadays are charged with certain functions which would have been considered until quite recently as uncalled-for interference in the domestic problems of the receiving State. These functions especially in the field of international co-operation, are more often than not welcomed by the receiving State which some years ago would have reacted testly if such an offer had been made. In the United States, which has generously offered its

co-operation to many developing and even to developed nations in a wide field of activities, the Senate Foreign Relations Committee was warned by one of its consultant institutions that "the involvement of our government in the essentially domestic affairs of another nation entails grave risks of friction and enmity" .

In spite of all the changes, the enumeration of diplomatic functions remains unchanged; the basic functions may still be grouped under the heading of *representation, negotiation, observation, and protection*. This enumeration, which can be found in most books on the subject, was adopted by the Vienna Convention, which simply added the necessary legal framework in paragraph 1 of Article 3:

The functions of a diplomatic mission consist *inter alia* in:

a) representing the sending State in the receiving State;

b) protecting in the receiving State the interests of the sending State and of its nationals, within the limits permitted by international law;

c) negotiating with the Government of the receiving State;

d) ascertaining by all lawful means conditions and developments in the receiving State, and reporting thereon to the Government of the sending State;

e) promoting friendly relations between the sending State and the receiving State, and developing their economic, cultural and scientific relations.

The Vienna Convention avoided a detailed enumeration of all the functions of the diplomatic missions, for this would have ended by being very lengthy and probably incomplete. By including the main categories usually mentioned by textwriters and by adding the expression *inter alia* it was able to cover a very wide field.

Representation is the principal function of a diplomatic mission and the exercise of it is entrusted above all to the head of mission, in whose credentials it is always mentioned. The Plowden Report gives the highest priority to *representational* work and points out that "We are conscious that, to many people, *representation* suggest, though wrongly, little more than a round of cocktail parties and attendances at formal gatherings of little practical consequence. We want to make it clear that by a representational service we mean a civilian service whose duty it is to make known and to defend Britsh interests by diplomatic as opposed to military or other means. The interests which have to be represented, promoted or defended are substantial and vital. No one can doubt the prime importance of safeguarding peace throughout the world. The promotion of British trade is equally essential to us. In both of these our representational Services have an indispensable part to play". (§ 26). The Plowden Report also insists on what it calls *representational entertainment*, about which it fears "there is no small degree of public uncertainty and misunderstanding". It goes on to add that "in our view, representational entertainment remain indispensable as a means of acquiring and maintaining the contacts necessary to advance Britsh policies and protect

British interests. It has a part to play in making policies informed, effective and persuasive. Members of the Government and Parliament of the country to which a Head of Mission is accredited as well as leaders in all walks of life ought to come to look on the British Embassy or High Commission as the house of a friend. There is no substitute for this kind of personal relationship; this applies even in countries where official relationships are easy. In countries where there are difficulties, it is the task of the Head of Mission and his staff to make these difficulties less. Representational entertainment may be among the best means open to them". (§ 170).

Even though representation is pre-eminently a function of the ambassador, the other members of the mission must equally take on a part of this function, especially the higher members of the mission and the service attachés. It must also be borne in mind that in most countries the governments are of a representative nature and that the ultimate decision no longer rests exclusively with the Head of State; therefore the diplomatic agent has been forced to widen the range of his representational functions in order to have access to all the decision makers of the receiving State.

Article 3 of the Vienna Convention mentions in the fifth place the promotion of "friendly relations between the sending State and the receiving State, and developing their economic, cultural and scientific relations" (subparagraph *e*). This fifth function, however, is an aspect of the representational function, but the emphasis can be justified in view of the steadily increasing importance given to these functions in consequence of the establishment of the United Nations.

In practice it is difficult no distinguish between *negotiations* and representation, although one can say that the latter is a generic description which can be used to cover each of the other tasks mentioned. In spite of the representational function being the more important one, the idea of negotiation is more closely linked to the idea of diplomacy, so much so that a good many definitions of diplomacy are based on the notion of negotiation.

Negotiation may concern an international treaty, but usually the diplomatic agent is called upon to negotiate or discuss a minor question. In the negotiation of treaties, the present trend is to hand over the technical details to specialists, leaving it to the diplomatic agent to fill in the formal part of the treaty, that is, those articles which refer to the final clauses. The large number of essentially technical treaties signed nowadays goes to show that a diplomatic mission would have immense difficulties in negotiating these treaties without the assistance of the specialized branches of the administration.

Negotiation is an art and to reach a satisfactory solution the diplomatic agent must be endowed with certain qualities, such as tact, sense of opportunity, patience and persistence, as well as a complete knowledge of the subject under discussion.

Jules Cambon writes that "the art of diplomacy stems from the art of governing, for every diplomatic action ends in negotiation, and whoever says negotiation means, at least in part, compromise".[1] In a real compromise both States are satisfied with the final result of the negotiation. But a good diplomat must realize where the real compromise lies and thus avoid making unnecessary concessions. It has been pointed out that one of the reasons why ministers of State and other high ranking government officials, as well as parliamentary politicians, make such poor negotiators is that they usually have to return on a given day and are obliged to settle the negotiation at once without getting to the root of the matter.

The function of *observation* is linked to that of informing the sending State and is to be found in sub-paragraph *d* of Article 3: "ascertaining by all lawful means conditions and developments in the receiving State, and reporting thereon to the Government of the sending State". The range of subjects on which the diplomatic mission must keep its government informed about is limitless and increases every day. The problem consists in determining the limit which must be set to the range of activities, otherwise expansion will go on indefinitely and consequently the Ministry will be unable to cope with all the information received. Nowadays, in spite of the interest of governments in being fully informed on all matters, most of them are also seriously concerned about the necessity of reducing the volume of reports received.

In the past the obtaining of the necessary information was no easy task; today, in most States, work is facilitated by the interest of the local governments in keeping the public well informed and by the practice of publishing most of the pertinent data.

The Vienna Convention, however, makes it quite clear that the liberty of the diplomatic mission in this respect suffers an important limitation, namely that the information must be obtained by "lawful means". The difficulty consists precisely in determining what means are lawful and when a diplomatic mission oversteps the limits of such lawfulness and its conduct becomes incompatible with friendly international relations.

This problem is closely linked with that of espionage, considered in the past as only being practised in time of war. Nowadays, however, one can say that the question of espionage, or that of obtaining all sorts of information by every conceivable means, is more important in time of peace than in time of war. The silence of textwriters and of governments on this matter can be explained: espionage during a war is justified since it is practised against an enemy; but nations are loath to admit such a practice in peace-time since "spying implies enmity when enmity is not officially admitted; it is aimed at breaching the target nation's security which is itself a hostile act".[2]

1. Jules Cambon, "Le Diplomate", pp. 14-15.
2. Frederick Hartmann, "The Relations of Nations", p. 169.

In a certain sense, the aim of espionage is to obtain data or information, the disclosure of which is considered harmful to national security, in order to supplement other data or information obtained by normal and lawful means.

Since ancient times, embassies have been used to cover the practice of espionage, but nowadays the big powers all maintain special services entrusted with the delicate task of obtaining precisely that information which the receiving State does not wish it to have.

The members of the staff of a diplomatic mission whose functions may be considered illicit may have their names included in the diplomatic list. In this case, the receiving State will have its hands tied since such a person enjoys personal inviolability (he cannot be arrested) and immunity from jurisdiction. The solution is to declare him *persona non grata* and demand his immediate recall.

The question is more delicate when the person involved does not enjoy diplomatic privileges and immunities or if he has the right to certain privileges and immunities such as occurs with career consuls, members of the staff of intergovernamental organizations or members of commercial missions without diplomatic status.

The Gubitchev case can be cited in this respect. Valentin A. Gubitchev a Soviet national, was employed by the United Nations Secretariat and was indicted for violations of the United States espionage laws. His motion to dismiss on the ground of diplomatic immunity, since he entered the United States on a diplomatic passport and with a diplomatic visa, was rejected. The court held that "such status does not *per se* confer diplomatic immunity under generally accepted principles of international law". The judge added that "even if we assume that he is a foreign emissary and that he entered as such, it is clear that he was not so received". After Gubitchev retained consel of his own choice re-argument was granted and the motion to dismiss the indictment again rejected. In the re-argument a member of the Soviet Embassy appeared and submitted a communication to the court from the Soviet ambassador drawing the attention of the court to the fact that Gubitchev was an officer of the soviet diplomatic service and that the Soviet Government had not revoked his diplomatic status. Denying the immunity, the court said, among many other things, that "the Department of State has in the past had occasion to remind foreign governments that even if they have the right to interpose the defense of diplomatic immunity, they should not, under international law, so interfere with the course of justice or permit such privileges, if they exist, to shield from just punishment a perpetrator of crimes such as the one here charged".

We also have the case of Igor Gouzenko, who worked in the Soviet Embassy in Ottawa as a cryptographer, and who, in 1945, handed over to the Canadian authorities documents proving the existence of a highly developed espionage network involving persons who had access to secret information. As

a result of the investigations carried out the Canadian Government demanded the recall of all the members of the Soviet Embassy incriminated.

The third classic function of a diplomatic mission is that of *protection* in the interests of the sending State and its nationals. But in legal terminology *diplomatic protection* is used to designate the right of a State to protect its nationals or the rights of its nationals in the receiving State.

It is a fundamental principle of international law that every State has the right to protect its nationals, both individuals and bodies corporate, from any violation on the part of the authorities of the receiving State or of its nationals.

A foreigner, from a legal point of view, is under the jurisdiction of two States: that of the receiving State and that of the sending State. Diplomatic protection must be exercised in such a way as to avoid clashes between these two jurisdictions. Diplomatic protection is a right and a duty: it is a right *vis-à-vis* the receiving State; it is a duty towards the nationals of the sending State.

The protection of nationals used to be primarily a consular function, but with the amalgamation in most countries of the diplomatic service with the consular service the distinction between diplomatic and consular protection no longer stands. Both the Vienna Conventions (on Diplomatic Relations and on Consular Relations) mention the protection of nationals.

The Vienna Convention of 1961 lays down that the diplomatic mission must protect the interests of its nationals "within the limits permited by international law". This clause did not exist in the draft of the International Law Commission and one can reasonable ask if this addition has any special legal significance or if it is superfluous. Strictly speaking every provision we find in the Vienna Convention, as in every other multilateral treaty, must be performed within the limits laid down by international law. However, at Vienna in 1961 some Latin-American delegations, with a still vivid recollection of past abuses of the right of diplomatic protection, deemed it necessary to stress the existence of such limits, *ex abundante cautela*.

Diplomatic protection can only be given if three conditions are fulfilled: first, the person must have the nationality of the sending State; secondly, the victim must have exhausted all the means available to him in the foreign jurisdiction for redressing his injuries; thirdly, the sending State must be willing to defend the interest of its national.

The first and most important condition is that the claimant must have the nationality of the protector State and this point has been stressed by various decisions of the International Court of Justice and by the Permanent Court of International Justice. Difficulties can arise when the claimant has double nationality, but international law at present is quite clear that a diplomatic mission cannot protect the interests of one of its nationals if he also has the nationality of the receiving State.

The second condition was embodied in Article 4 of the draft convention adopted at The Hague Conference for the Codification of International Law, held in 1930: "The State's responsibility may not be invoked as regards reparation for demages sustained by a foreigner until after exhaustion of the remedies available to the injured person under the municipal law of the State". Judge Córdova in the *Interhandel* case, judged by the International Court of Justice in 1959, said that "A State may not even exercise its diplomatic protection, and much less resort to any kind of international procedure of redress unless its subject has previously exhausted the legal remedies offered him by the State of whose action he complains".

If no remedy is available through the machinery of the offending State, or where it has been exhausted, the injury is complete and the State incurs responsibility in international law. It is, therefore, necessary that the local remedy should exist not only legally but also *de facto*. In other words, it is not possible to demand the exhaustion of remedies that do not exist.

Thirdly, as was pointed out earlier, diplomatic protection can only occur if the sending State endorses the claims of its nationals. There seem to be two schools of thought with regard to the question of whether the nationals of the sending State may demand the necessary protection from the diplomatic mission. The laws and regulations of some countries give the impression that the diplomatic mission is bound to afford such protection; while in other countries the protection cannot be demanded as a right.

The International Court of Justice in its judgement of February 5, 1970, on the case of the *Barcelona Traction*, *Light* and *Power Company Limited* pointed out quite correctly that "the promoters of a company whose operations will be international must take into account the fact that States have, with regard to their nationals, a discretionary power to grant diplomatic protection or to refuse it" (§ 99).

The decision of the International Court of Justice in this case cleared a problem that was beginning to become too complex, namely the right of a State to protect the rights of its shareholders in a foreign company. In its judgement the Court held that "the adoption of the theory of diplomatic protection of shareholders as such, by opening the door to competing diplomatic claims, could create an atmosphere of confusion and insecurity in international economic relations. The danger would be all the greater inasmuch as the shares of companies whose activity is international are widely scattered and frequently change hands. It must first of all be observed that it would be difficult on an equitable basis to make distinctions according to any quantitative test: it would seem that the owner of 1 per cent, and the owner of 90 per cent, of the share-capital should have the same possibility of enjoying the benefit of diplomatic protection. The protector State may of course, be disinclined to take up the case of the single small shareholder, but it could scarcely be denied the right to do so in the name of equitable considerations.

In that field, protection by the national State of the shareholders can hardly be graduated according to the absolute or relative size of the shareholding involved".

Negotiation, observation and protection and the overall representational function are common to every diplomatic mission, but the sending State may also order its missions to perform other tasks. The expression *inter alia* we find in Article 3 covers these miscellaneous functions, such as the registration of births, deaths or marriages, the issue of passaports or of visas and the exercise of consular functions.

The exercise of such functions, however, depends on favourable legislation or the practice of the receiving State. In certain countries, for example, diplomatic missions may not celebrate marriages between its nationals.

The Vienna Convention only mentions specifically the performance of consular functions. The International Law Commission was of the opinion that the Convention on Diplomatic Relations should not mention such functions, but in 1961 the Conference, after a lengthy discussion, adopted paragraph 2 of Article 3, in spite of the strong objections raised by some delegations. In 1963 with the signature of the Vienna Convention on Consular Relations it was amply proved that the inclusion of the aforementioned paragraph had been premature, so much so that Article 70 of the 1963 Convention goes into the subject in a more complete and precise manner.

Part III

The Diplomatic Agent

Chapter XI

THE HEAD OF THE DIPLOMATIC MISSION

The expression *head of mission*, in currect terminology, applies to ambassadors, high commissioners, ministers and envoys and to the representatives of the Holy See, such as nuncios, pro-nuncio and internuncios. As for the acting heads of mission, the expression used is *chargé d'affaires*, except in the case of the substitute of a high commissioner who is called the acting high commissioner.

Formerly other denominations were used to designate the heads of mission, such as *apocrisarii, responsales, legati, ambaxadeur, ablegatus* and *bailo*.

However, regardless of any specific denomination, one realizes that the expression *diplomatic agent* used in the 1815 Regulation of Vienna was not very precise; the expression "*head of mission*", adopted in 1961, is more appropriate and leaves no doubt as to its meaning.

Classification of heads of mission

Around the middle of the seventeenth century, heads of mission could be classified in two categories. The first one was composed of ambassadors and *legati*, representing either a sovereign or the Holy See. The second one comprised agents, residents, envoys and the *ablegati*, many of those titles being used synonymously.

The question of denomination and classification of the various heads of mission was decided on March 19, 1815, by the Vienna Regulation of 1815, which aimed at ending the eternal disputes over precedence and also settled the problem of the categories of diplomatic agents. It established three classes of heads of mission: that of ambassadors, legates or nuncios; that of envoys, whether styled ministers or otherwise, accredited to sovereigns; and that of *chargés d'affaires*, accredited to the Ministers for Foreign Affairs.

The Vienna Regulation suffered its first modification three years later at Aix-la-Chapelle, when a new category was inserted between the second and third class, namely that of *minister resident*.

When the British Dominions began exchanging among themselves and with the United Kingdom diplomatic missions, a new category of heads of missions

was created, that of high commissioners.

After the First World War, with the birth of new States and the disappearance or weakening of some of the former great powers, doubts were raised as to the practice of reserving the title of ambassador only for the agents of certain States.

The existence of two classes of heads of mission based on the power of the State was considered contrary to the principle of the legal equality of States. The fact that those two classes enjoyed the same privileges and immunities and that the only difference between them concerned questions of ceremonial provided another reason in favour of revising the Vienna classification of 1815.

Furthermore, some countries, such as Switzerland, which traditionally only exchanged ministers, and not ambassadors, reversed their policy.

Thus, when the International Law Commission began its works on diplomatic intercourse and immunity, it had to take into account not only the Regulation of 1815 but also some new terms for heads of mission, and the tendency to place all heads of mission on the same footing.

Professor Sandström's report reflected this tendency, but his views were not accepted. The International Law Commission in its 1957 draft maintained the two classes, besides the *chargés d'affaires*, on the assumption that it was premature to include such a change in the Vienna Convention.

Article 14 of the Vienna Convention is very similar to the Regulation that was signed almost a hundred and fifty years before in the same capital. Heads of mission are classified into three classes, namely: a) that of ambassadors or nuncios accredited to Heads of State and other heads of mission of equivalent rank; b) that of envoys, ministers and internuncios accredited to Heads of States; c) that of chargés d'affaires accredited to Ministers for Foreign Affairs.

In 1965, that is, four years after the signing of the Vienna Convention, the title of pro-nuncio was created. The Holy See only appoints a representative with the title of Apostolic Nuncio when he is automatically the doyen of the diplomatic corps. In those countries where such precedence was not attributed *de jure* to the papal representative, the Holy See was represented by an Internuncio, who was not entitled to any of the privileges accorded by protocol. As the number of internuncios was on the increase, and considering that most States were exchanging representatives at ambassadorial level, the papal representative began to be placed after all the other heads of mission.

International law is indifferent as to the head of mission's position in his country's internal hierarchy: if the receiving State accedes to his appointment he will enjoy all the privileges and immunities that the other heads of mission are recognized as having.

The envoys, ministers or internuncios accredited to Heads of State form the second class of heads of mission. The denominations *envoys* and *ministers*, recognized in Article 14 of the 1961 Convention as well as in the

1815 Regulation, are used interchangeably today and both have the same meaning, although that of minister is more often used. The origin of the term extraordinary which is given to some heads of mission, even though these missions are really permanent, goes back to the old custom of giving ambassadors extraordinary precedence over the ordinary ones. The qualifying adjective *plenipotentiary* is also a historical reminiscence: the ministers are not plenipotentiary and if they sign a treaty they must produce appropriate full powers.

Paragraph 2 of Article 14 states that the only differences between ambassadors and ministers concern precedence and etiquette: ambassadors enjoy precedence over ministers. Apart from this, they perform the same functions, have the same powers of negotiation and enjoy the same immunities.

The internuncios are also tending to disappear, especially since the creation of pro-nuncios by the Holy See.

The chargé d'affaires

The Vienna Convention, repeating the 1815 Regulation, includes among the heads of mission "the chargées d'affaires accredited to the Minister for Foreign Affairs" (Article 14).

There are two types of chargés d'affaires : permanent chargés d'affaires (*en pied* or *en titre*) and acting chargés d'affaires (*ad interim*).

Curiously enough the English language uses the French expression *chargés d'affaires*, which corresponds to *incaricato d'affari* (Italian), *Encarregado de Negocios* (Portuguese), *Geschäftsträger* (German). In Russian, the title is *Povérrennyi v Dielach.*

The permanent chargés d'affaires rank among the heads of mission. This category is about to disappear and nowadays very few countries maintain permanent chargés d'affaires.

The 1815 Regulation referred only to the permanent chargés d'affaires. However, in spite of the similar terminology, the Convention on Diplomatic Relations comprises both categories. During the 1961 Conference and in the International Law Commission the abolition of the distinction, between permanent and acting chargés d'affaires was proposed on more than one occasion. It was further suggested that the word *ad interim*, in Articles 5 and 19, should be deleted, but the suggestion was not taken up, so that the distinction between the two types of chargés d'affaires subsists.

Although sub-paragraph *c* of Article 14 refers to both types of chargés d'affaires, it is perfectly clear that the chargés d'affaires *ad interim* rank after those accredited in a permanent capacity.

Whereas the acting chargé d'affaires becomes temporarily the head of a diplomatic mission simply through a note sent by the ambassador in a routine way to the Ministry for Foreign Affairs, the chargé d'affaires *en pied* takes

over in a formal way; he receives a note signed by the Minister for Foreign Affairs of the sending State to be solemnly handed over to the Minister for Foreign Affairs of the receiving State.

Article 19 of the Vienna Convention lays down the following rules with regard to the acting chargés d'affaires: "If the post of head of the mission is vacant, or if the head of the mission is unable to perform his functions, a *chargé d'affaires ad interim* shall act provisionally as head of the mission. The name of the *chargé d'affaires ad interim* shall be notified, either by the head of the mission or, in case he is unable to do so, by the Ministry for Foreign Affairs of the sending State to the Ministry for Foreign Affairs of the receiving State or such other ministry as may be agreed".

The appointment of an acting chargés d'affaires can be made in two different ways, both of them tacitly admitted by the Vienna Convention: first, in the case of a vacancy, when there is no ambassador or minister, such as occurs with a new mission in which the permanent head of mission has not been appointed, or when the head of mission left before the appointment of his substitute, and, secondly, in the temporary absence of the ambassador or minister.

The name of the chargé d'affaires *ad interim* is notified to the Ministry for Foreign Affairs by the ambassador or minister when he leaves the receiving State temporarily or for good. If the diplomatic mission is already headed by an acting chargé d'affaires, practice requires that the name of the new chargé d'affaires be submitted by the Minister for Foreign Affairs of the sending State. This can be done by telegram.

Nowadays notification of the name of acting chargés d'affaires is obligatory, except in the case of the death of a head of mission, when his substitute will automatically take over.

In the absence of the nuncios or internuncios, the senior counsellor or auditor takes charge of the mission with the title of chargé d'affaires. When the head of a diplomatic mission is a high commissioner, his substitute will be the Acting High Commissioner.

The chargés des affaires

The *chargés des affaires* are subordinate personnel, with no diplomatic qualifications, who are in charge of the archives of a diplomatic mission. They are appointed when there is no diplomatic officer capable of taking over in the absence or death of the head of mission.

The draft of the International Law Commission did not mention the chargés des affaires. In Vienna, however the Danish delegation tabled an amendment on the basis that countries with a relatively small diplomatic staff should be permitted to appoint as chargés des affaires staff members not of diplomatic rank. The rule finally adopted reads: "In cases where no member

of the diplomatic staff of the mission is present in the receiving State, a member of the administrative and technical staff may, with the consent of the receiving State, be designated by the sending State to be in charge of the current administrative affairs of the mission".

The Vienna Convention avoided using the expression *chargé des affaires* since it is almost identical to *chargé d'affaires*.

Chapter XII

ACCEPTABILITY OF THE HEAD OF MISSION

Although every State is free to choose its ambassadors or ministers, the receiving State has the right to refuse to accept the heads of mission chosen by another State. Textwriters quote several instances of non-acceptance of ambassadors and ministers in the past. In order to avoid such a situation, which invariably brings about a cooling or even a breaking off of diplomatic relations, States have developed the practice of previously consulting the receiving State. The practice of inquiring beforehand whether the nominee has or not the approval of the receiving state aims, therefore, at conciliating those two absolute rights: the right to appoint and the right to refuse. Although a State should receive the envoys of a friendly nation, this does not mean that it is obliged to accept anyone. It would even be self-defeating for a State to have as its representative a person disliked in the other State, and who might have taken a hostile attitude towards the receiving State in the past.

Once the head of mission has been chosen, the sending State must confidentially obtain the consent of the receiving State, i.e., the sending State must seek to know if its candidate is considerred *persona grata*. In diplomatic terms, the act of accepting a head of mission is called *agrément*.

In the beginning some States, were unwilling to accept this practice. The United States Government was reluctant to ascertain the opinion of a foreign Government towards an individual accredited to it as an ambassador. In 1885, the Austro-Hungarian Government called the attention of the United States "to the generally existing diplomatic practice of asking previously to any nomination of a foreign minister the *agrément* of the Government to which he is accredited". The Secretary of State replied that "no case be found in the records of the Department of State in which the acceptability of an envoy was inquired about or ascertained in advance of his appointment to the mission for which he was chosen, and that there were reasons, growing out of the frequent recurrence of elections and changes of administration in the United States, why the practice should not be adopted".

A well-known instance of refusal is that of the Emperor Nicholas of Russia to receive Sir Stratford Canning as British Ambassador in 1832, on the ground that the appointement was made without previous consultation. Pal-

merston maintained that a Government was perfectly free to choose its heads of missions and that if the Czar insisted on his refusal, he would consider that attitude as an insult to the King of England. He then announced that Canning should go immediately to his post. To prevent that from happening, Nesselrode, Russian Minister for Foreign Relations, instructed his Ambassador in London, the Prince of Lieven, to inform the British Government that Canning would not be received by Czar Nicholas and that if Palmerston insisted, the Russian Ambassador would be recalled and the Embassy would be handed over to a *Chargé d'Affaires*. In 1835, Lord Dunham, who was to be replaced by Canning, returned to Saint-Petersburg as British Ambassador.

Nowadays, no Government would think of appointing a head of mission without requesting the *agrément* previously and no sovereign State would accept a head of mission whose name had not been previously submitted for its approval. According to paragraph 1 of Article 4 of the Vienna Convention "the sending State must make certain that the *agrément* of the receiving State has been given for the person it proposes to accredit as head of the mission of that State".

Some examples of cases in which the receiving State suggested the name of the head of mission can be cited. Napoleon asked the Italian Government and the Sultan of Turkey to appoint Knight Nigra and Mehemet-Djemil Pasha to the French Court. In 1912, the Department of State pointed out that "it is contrary to the custom of nations in their international relations for one government to intimate in any way to another that the appointment of a particular person as ambassador or minister from the latter would be agreable to it". Today, such a request would be self-defeating and would not be welcome.

Once the choice has been made, it is up to the sending State to consult the other on the name of the head of mission it intends to appoint. If there is an embassy or legation in the receiving State, the head of mission, who may be either the envoy to be replaced or a chargé d'affaires, will submit to the receiving State the name of the person to be accredited. The request must be made to the competent authority, verbally or in writing, according to local tradition. This authority may be the Minister for Foreign Relations himself, the Secretary General or the head of Protocol. If the sending State does not have a diplomatic mission in the receiving State, the request may be made directly by the Minister for Foreign Relations to the other Minister, but, in this case, the confidential nature of the request may suffer; therefore, the best solution is to make the consultation through the embassy of a friendly nation in the receiving State.

The present tendency is to deliver a note or a note verbale, with the *curriculum vitae* of the nominee. The receiving State, generally through its Protocol, will then examine whether the *agrément* should be granted or not.

By the way a State grants an *agrément*, it can demonstrate its pleasure or

displeasure with the name submitted. When its wants to stress its high regard for the person of the nominee, it will grant the *agrément* immediately; if the State has no such intention it simply lets the case follow the normal procedure and, according to the information obtained, answers within a month; if by any chance a State objects to the person proposed, but does not want to refuse the *agrément* in order not to offend the sending State, it puts off the answer.

In Vienna, some delegations tried to fix a period within which the *agrément* should be granted, since a delay may bring about a certain degree of ill-feeling. But the adoption of such a period for the concession of the *agrément* may, in some cases, be self-defeating, since, for political or bureaucratic reasons, the answer may be delayed in spite of the good-will of the receiving State. In other words, a time limit may create difficulties more serious than those it is trying to avoid.

The *agrément* usually takes the form of a note or a *note verbale*. Whereas in the consultation the note is confidential, in the answer it need not be so.

Should the *agrément* be refused, the answer should not be written. In practice, a long delayed answer may be interpreted as a tacit refusal; if an answer is demanded, it should, in such a case, be given verbally.

A question raised before the International Law Commission was that of knowing whether an *agrément* should be asked for Chargé d'Affaires. The Government of Chile, commenting on the 1957 draft article, stated that the article might lead to the mistaken assumption that the *agrément* of the receiving State is necessary for all heads of mission, when it is only required for ambassadors and ministers, since, in practice, it is not the rule for *chargés d'affaires*.

Article 4 states that the heads of mission must obtain an *agrément* and since under Articles 14 and 19 of the Convention *chargés d'affaires* are considered as such, doubts might be raised as to whether an *agrément* must be obtained in every case. In Vienna it was clarified that international practice had not changed; an *agrément* is only necessary in the case of *chargés d'affaires en pied*.

There are a number of reasons why a head of mission may be declared *persona non-grata*. Since requests for an *agrément* are rarely revealed, there are very few examples of refusal to be quoted and those we find are generally older cases.

The main reason for a refusal is a previous record of hostile acts against the receiving State. In 1885, the United States Government appointed Mr. A.M. Keiley as Minister at Rome. As soon as it was informed of the appointment, the Italian Government asked that another choice might be made without assigning any reason, but it was evident that it was due to a speech made fourteen years before Mr. Keiley at a Catholic meeting in which he critized the annexation of the Papal States to Italy. Secretary of State Bayard recog-

nized the full and independent right of the King of Italy to decide the question of personal acceptability to him of an envoy. Mr. Keiley, on being made acquainted with the refusal, did not hesitate to resign his commission.

The appointment of Mr. Henry W. Blair as United States Minister to China gave rise to a similar example. Before he had taken up his post, the Chinese Minister for Foreign Relations and the Viceroy protested by wire against the appointment, on the ground that Mr. Blair had bitterly abused China and the Chinese workers in the Senate from 1882 to 1889, during the debates on the *Exclusion Act*. Blair did not deny that he had criticized the entry of Chinese workers in the United States affirming that Chinatown in San Francisco was "a seething, roaring, bloodcurdling curse". He explained, however, that a politician obliged to express his viewpoints should not be confused with a representative of his country abroad and presented his resignation.

The fact that a head of mission has been considered *persona non grata* by one State may prevent another Government from accepting that diplomat. In 1926 the Brazilian Government refused to give an *agrément* to Mgr. Beda Cardinale as Apostolic Nuncio in Rio de Janeiro, because the Government of Argentina had declared him *persona non grata*, owing to a dispute with the Archbishop of Buenos Aires. The Holy See considered the refusal unacceptable and hinted at sending an Apostolic Delegate to Rio, which could virtually imply a break in its diplomatic relations with Brazil. Thanks to a demarche of the Brazilian Ambassador to the Vatican, the incident was averted: the Holy See appointed Mgr. Benedetto Aloisio Masella, and Brazil, anxious to put an end to the dispute, immediately gave its *agrément*.

Attitudes taken during a war may later prevent the acceptance of a head of mission. After the First World War, Germany indicated Von Lucius and Solf as its representatives to Japan and Italy, but both were refused owing to incidents in which they had been involved and which made them undesirable.

The case of Ambassador Aunós is somewhat similar to the previous examples. The Spanish diplomat was considered *persona non grata* after the Brazilian Government had given its *agrément* in view of the fact that certain documents published subsequently placed him in a delicate position. In this case, however, there was not a refusal, but a declaration that he was *persona non grata*.

Some past examples, however, would hardly recur nowadays. The King of Sardinia refused to accept Baron Charles de Martens, in 1820, because his wife was the daughter of a regicide. France declined to receive the Duke of Buckingham as ambassador extraordinary from Charles I of England, because on a previous visit to the French Court he had posed as an ardent lover of the Queen.

In some countries the head of mission has his name included in the diplomatic list once the *agrément* has been granted. In this case, it is usually pointed out that the new ambassador has still to present his credentials.

Should there be a change of government or a new Head of State, is a new *agrément* necessary? Theoretically, the answer is no: the *agrément* is in some respects a kind of agreement and in such a case changes of regime or dynasty or constitutional changes do not affect obligations assumed by the former Government.

In the case of a *de facto* State or Government, the concession of the *agrément* to a head of mission means that such a State or government is tacitly recognized.

As soon as a favourable answer has been received, the sending State will appoint its ambassador. In several republics, the appointment also depends upon another formality, i.e. the approval of the head of mission by parliament.

A delicate issue raised in the past consisted in knowing whether, in the case of refusal of the *agrément*, the receiving State was or was not obliged to justify its attitude. It would seem that an explanation could only favour the good relations between the two States. In practice, however, this does not happen; the sending State may consider the explanation unsatisfactory, giving rise, by its attitude, to an possible misunderstanding between the two States. Since the request for the *agrément* is of a confidential nature the refusal does not affect the nominee. Moreover, the reasons for the refusal may refer to his private life or to that of a member of his family and in such a case the explanation might be very embarrassing.

To end doubts on the subject, the Havana Convention of 1928 adopted a provision saying that States could freely refuse to accept a head of mission "without being obliged to state the reasons for such a decision" (Article 8). In Vienna paragraph 2 of Article 4, adopts a similar rule: "the receiving State is not obliged to give reasons to the sending State for a refusal of *agrément*".

These two conventions put an end in inter-American and international relations to the discussions on the subject.

It may happen that after having received a favourable *agrément* the sending State decides to indicate another head of mission. In those countries where the appointment of an ambassador or minister also depends upon the approval of the Senate, such a situation may well occur. A new *agrément* may also be requested in the case of serious illness of the former ambassador, for political reasons, or if the diplomat previously indicated is seriously involved in a scandal.

In April, 1947, the British Government informed the Brazilian Government that Mr. Victor Frederick William Cavendish-Bentinck, whose *agrément* had been granted, would not assume his post. This decision of the British Government was the result of a petition for divorce by Mr. Cavendish-Bentick against his wife in which the judgement turned out very unfavourably to him. In such a case the appointment of another head of mission only shows the regard the sending State wishes to demonstrate to the receiving State.

Chapter XIII

THE MEMBERS OF THE DIPLOMATIC MISSION

The composition of the diplomatic mission has changed greatly since the establishment of the first permanent embassies. Although a diplomatic mission is an impersonal entity, it is composed of a number of members organized on a hierarchical basis under the direction of an ambassador or minister.

The first missions essentially consisted of the person of the ambassador, who took with him his personal suite which enjoyed, by extension, the privileges and immunities reserved for the head of mission. It was up to the ambassador to decide whether or not he would take his personal secretary, who, legally, was on an equal footing with the other members of the ambassadorial suite.

Diplomatic missions, although composed of the head of mission and of the secretaries and attachés, were characterized in the nineteenth century by the small number of officials assigned to them. It was only after the Second World War that a radical transformation came about and together with officials of diplomatic status others were appointed with specific technical functions who at times came to be included among the top-ranking officials of the mission.

Diplomatic missions were considered as composed of official and non-official personnel, the latter comprising the members of the families of the diplomates as well as their private secretaries and private servants. This classification of the members of the mission was unsatisfactory and one of the principal merits of the Vienna Convention was precisely that of establishing the various categories of the members of the mission with greater precision. Although the identification of those who would benefit from diplomatic privileges and immunities was the most delicate problem that the Vienna Conference had to face, the solution finally arrived at has proven to be most satisfactory.

It is in Article 1 that we are presented with the *definitions* of the expressions used in the Convention, which gave greater clarity to some classic expressions of whose meaning there had not been agreement such as "members of the mission", "members of the service staff" and "private servant". Under sub-paragraph *b*, *members of the mission*" are the head of mission and the

members of the staff of the mission", while the *members of the staff of the mission* "are the members of the diplomatic staff, the administrative and technical staff and the service staff of the mission".

The diplomatic staff

The Vienna Convention defines *the members of the diplomatic staff* as being the "members of the mission having a diplomatic rank". Evidently we have here a barely satisfactory definition, which is, moreover, tautological. At the Vienna Conference such faults were brought out and the Delegation of Ireland proposed that the sub-paragraph should read as follows: "The 'diplomatic staff' consists of the members of the staff of the mission having diplomatic rank and comprises the following classes: ministers, ministers-counsellors, counsellors, first secretaries, second secretaries, third secretaries, attachés".

The meaning given to the expression "diplomatic agent" in Vienna in 1961 differs from that which was presented in the Regulation signed in the same city in 1815. Then the diplomatic agent was understood to be solely the Head of Mission, while nowadays the term refers to the other members of the diplomatic staff as well. In the last analysis the determination of the status of the members of the diplomatic staff depends primarily upon the sending State, which may freely appoint whom it deems expedient whether dealing or not with a regular member of its diplomatic service; and, secondly, upon the receiving State by the inclusion of the person in the diplomatic list. In short, members of the diplomatic staff are Ministers-counsellors, counsellors, first secretaries, second secretaries and third secretaries of embassy or legation as well as the naval, military and air attachés and the civilian attachés dealing with special matters such as commercial, financial, cultural and press affairs, etc.

Article 7, while recognizing the liberty of the sending State to appoint the members of its staff, refers in the first sentence to a series of limitations laid down in other articles with respect to the exercise of diplomatic functions in two or more States (article 5), to the nationality of diplomats (article 8) and to the size of the mission. Besides these general limitations, the article also refers to Article 9 which deals with members of the mission who are *non-grata* or unacceptable. The article also provides that the receiving State has the right to demand that the names of military, naval and air attachés be submitted beforehand for its approval. Consequently, one can conclude that no such formality exists with regard to the other members of staff of the mission.

Ample powers have been given to the receiving State by Article 9, which recognizes its right to declare at any time and without having to explain its decision that a member of the mission is *persona non grata* or unacceptable.

In Vienna, with the intention of establishing the moment at which a diplo-

mat is considered accepted by the receiving State, amendments were submitted stipulating that inclusion in the diplomatic list constituted recognition of diplomatic status by the receiving State. In many countries the diplomatic list is published only once or twice a year and, thus, the diplomat would remain dependent upon such action, but the inconvenience would be by-passed by the adoption of a clause by which the benefit of the privileges would be recognized as a courtesy.

The Vienna Convention made no differentiation between members of the diplomatic staff who belong to the diplomatic career and others.

Among the members of the diplomatic staff of the mission there do, however, exist differences. Thus, strictly speaking, in the absence of the Head of Mission, the status of chargé d'affaires can only be attributed to a diplomat, that is a Minister Counsellor, Consellor, First, Second or Third Secretary or a Diplomatic Attaché.

With the development of the diplomatic service, the natural tendency of governments is to structure its members within a body organized on a professional basis. The diplomatic service is composed of persons who generally enter it through a system of selection, and rise gradually by merit or seniority, once having complied with certain conditions, until they attain the highest positions, being automatically retired upon reaching a certain age.

Within such a system, the officer should progress, *grosso modo*, through three distinct phases of his professional training: the first being initial or probationary; the second the intermediate or preparatory phase, and the third that of head of mission. The existence of such phases can be seen in the principal diplomatic organizations, although they do not always correspond precisely to each other, depending upon the number of grades which exist in a given service.

Embassy Attachés

The promotion of friendly relations and the development of economic, cultural, and scientific relations between States constitutes one of the characteristics of modern diplomacy. This extension of diplomatic activity has caused the appointment of technicians to represent the sending State in inter-governmental organizations or to collaborate with the receiving State in the area of their speciality.

Such experts receive the title of attaché with the mention of their speciality and are usually included in the diplomatic list. There also exist the diplomatic attachés, although only a few countries still maintain the title of attaché to designate the diplomatic officers on the first level of the career.

Although the number of different kind of attachés goes on growing and the service which they give may be advantageous, the amount of available work does not always justify their appointment. Frequently their functions can be

satisfactorily fulfilled by a diplomat who may have specialized in the subject. In other words, it is necessary to distinguish the functions that could be fulfilled by a diplomat who may have special preparation from those which demand the presence of an expert, in the strict sense of the word.

Currently, there are a great many kinds of attachés. The diplomatic list of the diplomatic corps in Brazil assigns the following specializations: commercial, economic, financial, political, cultural, legal, labour, information, press, emigration, immigrations, technical cooperation, scientific, mineralogical and consular. To this list could be added, *inter alia*, tourism, exhibitions, public relations, medical, recruitment, atomic energy, civil aviation, fisheries, navigation, petroleum, supply, veterinary, colonial and customs.

Governments are free to give to their attachés the qualifications they judge appropriate; *contrariu sensu*, a receiving State can refuse to accept officers of a particular category or to refuse to recognize the diplomatic status of the officers. The Argentine Government of General Peron created, within the labour organization it followed, the *agregados obreros* by a decree of March 1949, which constituted a corps with hierarchies equivalent to the foreign service up to the class of Counsellor First Class. When the Argentine Government nominated its first *agregado obrero* to Rio de Janeiro, Brazil had no hesitation in recognizing his status as a member of the Embassy but he was included in the diplomatic list only as an attaché, without any reference being made to his function.

By virtue of an act of the Congress of the United States in 1925, officers of the Treasury were nominated to serve in its diplomatic Missions with the title of Customs Attaché. The requests for recognition of such attachés were refused by almost all countries and, as a consequence, the State Department sent instructions to its diplomatic Missions and Consular offices stating that "it was obviously not advisable for the government to exert greater efforts concerning the recognition of the diplomatic status of these customs Attachés".

In the listing of the non-military attachés special reference should be made to the commercial attachés that exist in almost all countries, and whose functions and responsibility tend to increase parallel to the increase of responsibilities of the diplomatic missions in securing markets for national products and the multiplication of inter-governmental organizations with economic and commercial objectives.

Before the First World War, from 1815 to 1914, economic and commercial problems were held as being outside the jurisdiction of the Ministry for Foreign Affairs, although an ever-increasing number of examples during the past centuries would tend to show an interrelation of the foreign policy of great nations and their commercial interests. After 1918, the panorama began to change substantially and came to demand of the foreign service an increase of responsibilities and the training of specialized officers.

Upon the even of the Second World War the use of commercial attachés

had already become generalized, further developing after 1945, and the increase in number of organs and conferences of a commercial, economic or financial nature came to demand the training of an even larger number of specialists. The developments in Great Britain in this respect were characteristic: the Plowden Report of 1964 was based upon the principle that economic and commercial affairs should be considered as those of most importance within the British Diplomatic Service and that diplomatic personnel should receive specialized training, if not exclusively, in this field.

The development of cultural and scientific relations between States today represents one of the important tasks of the foreign service, and is usually the responsibility of the cultural section of the embassy. The appointment of cultural attachés—and the same applies to most of the other specialized attachés—must take into account which cultural activities are liable to be acceptable abroad as well as the usefulness of publicity of this or that activity in the receiving State where local conditions may affect its acceptance. Today the cultural activities of an embassy manifest themselves in various ways. First, we have the classic activity of publicizing national culture and language, principally carried out through the creation of special courses or professorships in local universities. The distribution of informative material, books, magazines, and pamphlets is another highly utilized method, but only publications of high quality are acceptable, and this is a very costly matter.

Service attachés appeared on the diplomatic scene, with the functions and status they still retain, in the middle of the nineteenth century. Austria, Prussia and Russia inaugurated the custom of appointing officers attached to their High Commands to their diplomatic missions so as to accompany the development of the armed forces of the receiving State. France followed their example in 1860.

Today certain countries also send abroad military missions as well, to instruct the local armed forces or to purchase specialized equipment. Sometimes by virtue of treaty, the members of these missions enjoy diplomatic privileges and immunities and may have their names included in the diplomatic list, although they are not service attachés in the strict sense of the word.

Service attachés are usually designated according to the branch of the armed forces to which they belong, but the abolition of these titles has been recommended; the creation of attachés who represent the armed forces as a whole being preferable. The Plowden Report points out that there is room for improvement in the procedure by which the need for service attachés at particular posts is assessed, and that present difficulties seem to stem largely from the fact that the service attachés and advisers have hitherto been borne on the votes of individual departments and not on the vote of the Ministry of Defense.

Service attachés are included on the diplomatic list in conformity with the

general rule of precedence of the sending State, and enjoy the same privileges and immunities granted to the members of the diplomatic staff of the mission.

Service attachés can represent more than one of the three armed forces and be accredited to several countries, as long as the receiving States do not express objection to such a procedure.

The primary function of the service attaché is to observe and inform, but in carrying this out he must pay strict attention to Article 3 of the Vienna Convention that provides for "ascertaining by all lawful means conditions and developments in the receiving State, and reporting thereon to the Government of the sending State". In other words, the exercise of this function is subject to limitations which cannot be ignored. In this sense, the mission of a service attaché is more delicate than that of a diplomatic agent, since there is always the added possibility of any initiative being considered espionage and the limits between the licit and the illicit can be very tenuous. It might be added that frequently service attachés, taking advantage of the privileged situation granted to members of the diplomatic staff of the mission, have acted as spies or stimulated such activities. The numerous examples of service attachés being considered *persona non grata* and invited to leave the receiving State at short notice represent a step backwards in this sense.

Another important task of the service attachés is to maintain links with the armed forces of the receiving State and to act as a channel for the exchange of military information. In many countries they also help to promote the sale of military equipment and the Plowden Report points out the help which they can give to companies selling aircraft or other military and civil products to foreign governments and recommends that "more should be done to make this function of service attachés more widely known". Conversely, service attachés of non-industrialized countries should advise their government with regard to the latest improvements, purchasing and paying for the military equipment that is ordered.

The representational functions of the service attachés can be as important as those of the members of the diplomatic staff of the mission. They must represent the sending State in military functions and maintain constant social contact with all branches of the armed forces of the receiving State and with the other service attachés, who will be in a position to pass on very useful military information. In certain countries service attachés enjoy an added privilege not granted to the members of the diplomatic staff, namely that of being received by the Head of State. In 1906, Secretary of State Root sent instructions to the diplomatic missions of the United States that had naval or military attachés. After referring to this practice he went on to stress that "the peculiar and delicate functions of military and naval attachés, combining membership of the official diplomatic representation of their own government with the added privilege of direct intercourse with other than the diplo-

matic branches of the foreign administraction and even of official association, on some occasions with the Head of the State and with the highest officers of its military establishment, make it desirable that American officers serving in those capacities shall enjoy no less privileges than their colleagues of other nationalities".

Among the functions of the service attachés special mention must be made of his position as technical adviser to the head of the mission. The complexity of foreign policy and its ever growing interrelation with military power makes it necessary in certain circumstances for the ambassador to be able to receive instant and appropriate advice on military matter. Perfect understanding between the sections of an embassy is also important so as to prevent the various governmental departments with international responsabilities from receiving conflicting information on a given subject.

The various specialists in a diplomatic mission, including the service attachés, must be fully integrated into the team of the head of mission under whom they serve. In the United States relations between ambassadors and the military have frequently been a source of misunderstanding. President John Kennedy in a letter dated May 29, 1961, sent to all the ambassadors of the United States, went into this problem in detail. The letter reads: "You are in charge on the entire U.S. Diplomatic Mission, and I shall expect you to supervise all of its operations. The Missions includes not only the personnel of the Departament of State and the Foreign Service, but also the representatives of all other U.S. agencies. ... As you know, the U.S. Diplomatic Mission includes service attachés, military assistance advisory groups, and other military components attached to the Mission. It does not, however, include U.S. military forces operating in the field where such forces are under the command of a U.S. area military commander. The line of authority to these forces runs from me, to the Secretary of Defense, to the Joint Chiefs of Staff in Washington and to the area commander in the field. Although this means that the Chief of the American Diplomatic Mission is not in the line of military command, nevertheless, as Chief of Mission, you should work closely with the appropriate area military commander to assure the full exchange of information".

Part IV

Diplomatic Privileges and Immunities

Chapter XIV

DIPLOMATIC PRIVILEGES AND IMMUNITIES

The principle of the inviolability of emissaries goes back to the very origins of diplomacy, since it was understood that no agreement could be reached if the envoys were murdered on arrival or during the negotiations.

This inviolability of the envoy was the basis from which all other privileges and immunities derived: since his person was inviolable, his residence was to enjoy a similar privilege and local courts could have no power to judge him.

These privileges and immunities have developed over the centuries and the Vienna Convention on Diplomatic Relations is the result of this long evolution. The Convention, following the guidelines of the International Law Commission, separates the privileges and immunities of the diplomatic mission proper from the privileges and immunities of the diplomatic agent and other members of the mission.

In some countries the privileges and immunities became law, as occurred in Great Britain in 1708 with the Act of Anne. In Great Britain "it is well established that it is the common law of this country that not only ambassadors but members of their suites are exempt from judicial process. The Statute of Anne is declaratory in the first, second and third section, and it really does not achieve any change in the law by the subsequent sections. It is not a change in the law, but an addition to the law . . ." (The Amazone case).

The title of the pertinent section of the draft of the International Law Commission was "Diplomatic Privileges and Immunities". This phrase was also adopted by Professor Sandström in his original draft and when the Commission began to study it Professor Verdross said that in his opinion it would be preferable to speak of "diplomatic privileges" only, since immunities were included in those privileges. Personally we feel that the suggestion should have been accepted, giving the word *privileges* an over-all meaning embracing all the inviolabilities, immunities and exemptions. The majority of the Commission, however, preferred the traditional phrase. Professor Bartos recalled that there had been a prolonged discussion of the difference between privileges and immunities during the drafting of the Convention on the Privileges and Immunities of the United Nations and it had been decided to maintain a distinction between them, on the ground that immunities generally had a legal basis, whereas only certain privileges were based on law, the others being

matters of courtesy. Professor Zourek also justified the expression on the grounds that immunity had been associated since the Middle Ages with the idea of exemption from local jurisdiction; privileges, or prerogatives, were based on international law, customary or written, and gave the diplomatic agent positive rights which other inhabitants of the receiving State did not possess.

This phrase was previously adopted by the League of Nations' Committee of Experts for the Progressive Development of International Law. In the introductory comment of the Harvard draft we read that "no attempt has been made to distinguish sharply between privilege and immunity". In the Havana Convention on Diplomatic Officers, the expression used is "immunities and prerogatives of diplomatic officers".

The Vienna Convention on Diplomatic Relations includes under the general heading *privileges and immunities* the inviolabilities, immunities and exemptions of the diplomatic missions and of the diplomatic agents, giving each a precise and specific meaning and it is to be hoped that textwriters will adopt its terminology.

Chapter XV

PERSONAL INVIOLABILITY

Personal inviolability is the fundamental principle from which all diplomatic privileges and immunities have been derived. The International Law Commission in its commentary on article 20 of the 1958 draft, however, points out that the inviolability of the mission premises is not the consequence of the inviolability of the head of the mission, but is an attribute of the sending State by reason of the fact that the premises are used as the headquarters of the mission. Such an affirmative corresponds to present international law under which the diplomatic mission is the principle subject and its personality must not be linked to that of the head of mission as in the past.

The receiving State is under the obligation to afford special protection as regards the safety of the person of the diplomatic agent. It must prevent its agents from exercising measures which might represent direct coercion against a diplomatic agent and must take the necessary steps for the prevention of offences. Article 29 of the Vienna Convention embodies these rules in the following way: "The person of the diplomatic agent is inviolable. He shall not be liable to any form of arrest or detention. The receiving State shall treat him with due respect and shall take all appropriate steps to prevent any attack on his person, freedom or dignity".

Even though the principle of inviolability is universally recognized the term has been used with a variety of meanings. The Harvard draft, for example, avoided using the expression and its article 17 reads "A receiving State shall protect a member of a mission and the members of his family from any interference with their security, peace, or dignity". The Vienna Convention adopts the sense which is most generally found in textwriters.

In the case of an attack against the person of an ambassador the receiving State is under the obligation to take every step to ensure that the author of the attack be captured, tried and punished, otherwise it will incur international responsibility for its omission. This principle was duly recognized by the Committee of Jurists appointed by the League of Nations to answer a number of legal questions arising out of the controversy between Italy and Greece as a result of the murder of General Tellini in 1922. In one of its answers the Committee said: " The responsibility of a State is only involved by the commission in its territory of a political crime against the persons of

foreigners if the State has neglected to take all reasonable measures for the prevention of the crime and the pursuit, arrest and bringing to justice of the criminal".

In order to guarantee increased protection to diplomatic agents the criminal laws of some countries contain special articles on the subject. It seems that the earliest legislation in this sense was enacted by the Netherlands in 1651, which forbade "offending, damaging, injuring by word, act or manner, the ambassadors, residents, agents, or other ministers of the kings, princes, republics or others having the quality of public ministers; or to do them injury or insult directly or indirectly, in any fashion or manner whatever, in their own persons, gentlemen of their suite, their domestic servants, dwellings, carriages, etc. under penalty of being corporeally punished as violators of the law of nations and disturbers of the public peace".

According to English Criminal Law, everyone is guilty of a misdemeanour who, by force, or personal restraint, violates any privilege conferred upon the diplomatic representatives of foreign countries, or who sues forth or prosecutes or executes any writ or process whereby the persons of any diplomatic representative of a foreign country, or the person of a servant of any such representative, is arrested or imprisoned.

The Law of the United States is as follows: "Every person who assaults, strikes, wounds, imprisons, or in any other manner offers violence to the person of an ambassador or a public minister, in violation of the law of nations, shall be imprisoned for not more than three years and fined, at the discretion of the court" (Section 255 of title 22).

The Italian Criminal code punishes with at least twenty years imprisonment an attempt against the life of a head of mission and life imprisonment in case of death.

Henrique C.R. Lisboa, writing in 1908, was of the opinion that in the relations between civilized States reference to inviolability as a special diplomatic privilege was useless and an offence to the sovereignty of States. "Every civilized legislation proclaims the inviolability of the inhabitants of the country, nationals or foreigners, as long as they obey the laws; since the only laws that diplomatic agents obey in the receiving State are those which are based on international law and which civilized States accept expressly or implicitly". Unfortunately, recent examples show us that it is absolutely necessary to afford diplomatic agents special protection and to mete out severe punishment to those who commit attempts against their persons. The cold-blooded murder of the Ambassadors of the United States and of Germany in Guatemala in 1968 and 1970, and the kidnapping of ambassadors and other members of diplomatic missions in Brazil, Uruguay, Canada and Turkey are proof of the necessity of such legislation.

The Convention to Prevent and Punish the Acts of Terrorism Taking the Form of Crimes Against Persons and Related Extorsion That Are of Inter-

national Significance, signed under the auspices of the Organization of American States, in Washington, on February 2, 1971, establishes that the contracting States "undertake to co-operate among themselves by taking all measures that they may consider effective, under their own laws, and especially those established in this convention, to prevent and punish acts of terrorism, especially kidnapping, murder, and other assaults against the life or physical integrity of those persons to whom the state has the duty according to international law to give special protection, as well as extortion in connection with those crimes".

The Vienna Convention considers the personal inviolability of the diplomatic agent as being absolute, since no exceptions were made to the basic rule. Some of the members of the International Law Commission while accepting the principle of absolute inviolability tried to formulate the rule in such a way as to recognize the right of the receiving State to adopt *vis-à-vis* diplomatic agents measures of coercion in some very restricted cases. In this sense they were merely trying to put into the text certain situations which have been accepted by the principal writers. The International Law Institute's 1895 resolution includes in article 6 the three exceptions most generally mentioned. The article provides that: "Inviolability may not be invoked: 1. In case of lawful defence on the part of individuals against acts committed by persons who enjoy the privilege; 2. In case of risks run by the said persons, voluntarily or unnecessarily; 3. In case of reprehensible acts committed by them, compelling the State to which the minister is accredited to take defensive or precautionary measures; but, except in case of extreme necessity, this State must confine itself to making the facts known to the government of said ministers, requesting the punishment or recall of the guilty official, and if necessary, to surround his house to prevent illegal communications or public expressions of opinion".

Professor Sandström's draft contained a provision under which inviolability could not be invoked if a party acted in self-defence. This paragraph was not considered necessary and was included in the commentary where we read that inviolability does not "exclude in respect of the diplomatic agent either measures of self-defence or in exceptional circumstances, measures to prevent him from committing crimes or offences".

If a diplomatic agent commit acts of violence liable to disturb the internal order of the receiving State the necessity might arise of putting him under restraint for the purpose of preventing similar acts. Should the diplomat suffer from a fit of madness or be under the effect of alcohol or of drugs, local authorities are entitled to use coercion until he returns to normal. The protest lodged by the Brazilian Government in 1947 against measures taken against a Secretary at its Embassy in Moscow, who had to be tied in order to prevent him from damaging the property of an hotel, was, therefore, unjustified.

If the diplomatic agent should behave in a manner considered incompatible with normal diplomatic relations, the receiving State may demand his immediate recall. It may take extreme measures in very exceptional cases, but such measures of coercion should cease as soon as possible.

Chapter XVI

INVIOLABILITY OF THE DIPLOMATIC MISSION

Originally the inviolability of the diplomatic mission was a consequence of the personal inviolability of the head of mission. Under the Act of 7 Anne and under the law of the United States, which is modelled on that of Great Britain, the inviolability of the mission is a consequence of the privileged situation of the ambassador. The Havana Convention on Diplomatic Officers of 1928 also adopts this theory in Article 14 which deals with inviolability in the following terms: "Diplomatic officers shall be inviolate as to their persons, their residence, private or official, and their property".

The Vienna Convention, however, broke with this theory, and in the commentary on Article 20 of the International Law Commission it is clearly stated that "the inviolability of the mission premises is not the consequence of the inviolability of the head of mission, but is an attribute of the sending State by reason of the fact that the premises are used as the headquarters of the mission".

As a result of the policy adopted by the Commission all the provisions regarding the mission were included before those relating to the diplomatic agent, emphasizing the growing importance of the mission in comparison with the situation of the diplomatic agent.

The theory of exterritoriality, which is no longer accepted, had a marked influence on the inviolability of the mission since by virtue of that concept the premises of the mission were considered as being within the territory of the sending State and subject to its laws and tribunals.

If we were to admit such a theory the results would in certain cases be illogical: a crime committed by strangers in an embassy would have to be judged and punished accordingly to the law of the sending State; if a criminal should seek refuge in an embassy, he could only be handed over to the local authorities after all the conditions provided by the law of extradition of the sending State had been fulfiled; and, in certain cases the diplomatic agent would be able to perform marriage ceremonies between local inhabitants, even if the laws of the receiving State forbade such ceremonies.

Certain interpretations given in the past to the principle of inviolability or exterritoriality would be inconceivable nowadays. There were cases in which the ambassador not only judged members of his retinue but also meted out

drastic punishment. The Duc de Sully, who was sent in 1603 on a special mission from France to James I, condemned a member of his mission—Combault—to be decapitated for having killed an Englishman and sent a message to the Mayor of London asking for the services of an executioner. The Mayor counselled moderation and Sully handed over Combault asking the Mayor to take charge of him and inflict whatever penalty the law of England might prescribe. Eventually, Combault was pardoned by James I. A Spanish Ambassador in Venice did not hesitate: he condemned one of his servants to death and had him hanged forthwith from a window of the embassy.

The Harvard draft framed Article 3 in such a way as to avoid the implication of exterritoriality. It also proceeded upon the theory that such general terms as inviolability are misleading and that little progress is made by replacing the concept of exterritoriality with that of inviolability. The aforementioned article provides: "1. A receiving State shall prevent its agents or the agents of any of its political subdivisions from entering the premises occupied or used by a mission, or occupied by a member of a mission, without the consent of the chief of the mission; provided that notification of such occupation or use has been previously given to the receiving State. 2. A receiving State shall protect the premises occupied or used by a mission, or occupied by a member of a mission, against any invasion or other act tending to disturb the peace or dignity of the mission or of the member of a mission; provided that notification of such occupation or use has been previously given to the receiving State".

The corresponding article of the Vienna Convention reverts to the word inviolability but otherwise follows the general idea we find in the Harvard draft. It begins by stating that "the premises of the mission shall be inviolable" but subsequently spells out what such inviolability means.

Inviolability of the mission's premises means that the receiving State must forbid its agents from entering an embassy and that it has the special duty to protect the premises against any instrusion or damage and to prevent any disturbance of its peace or dignity.

In given circumstances local agents may, however, enter the premises of a diplomatic mission. The Vienna Convention admits such an eventuality if the consent of the head of mission has been given. In certain cases the prior consent for entry is implied, as when the premises are on fire, in the case of earthquakes or similar cataclysms or where there is imminent danger that a crime of violence is about to be perpetrated upon the premises. In these cases it would be absurd to wait for the consent of the head of mission and the possibility of a refusal would still be more absurd. At Vienna some delegations tried to insert these exceptions into the text, but none were accepted. The amendments were also rejected because they would weaken the principle of the inviolability of the mission, considered by some delegations in the 1961 Conference as the paramount diplomatic privilege.

The deplorable increase in the number of violations of diplomatic missions in recent years, in which frequently local authorities have not lifted a finger to prevent them, justifies the absence of a clause in the Vienna Convention which might have been construed as an exception to the absolute nature of the principle of inviolability.

International law prohibits the serving of writs, summonses, orders or processes within the premises of a diplomatic mission. This rule derives from the principle of inviolability and from the rule we find in Article 22 paragraph 1 which forbids the agents of the receiving State or of any of its political subdivisions from entering the mission. Commenting on the principle of inviolability the International Law Commission says that "a special application of this principle is the rule that no writ may be served within the premises of the mission, and that no summons to appear before a court may be served in the premises by a process server. Even if process servers do not enter the premises but carry out their duty at the door, such an act would constitute an infringement of the respect due to the mission". In Vienna the Japanese delegation submitted an amendment with the idea of incorporating this commentary in the article; it reads: "No writ may be served by a process server within the premises of the embassy". Later on Mr. Takahashi declared that his delegation was prepared to withdraw the amendment, on the understanding that it was the unanimous interpretation of the Committee of the Whole that no writ could be served, even by post, within the premises of the embassy.

The service of writs and similar judicial documents should be through the ministry for foreign affairs. The laws of various countries contain provisions in this sense. The commentary of the International Law Commission also says that "there is nothing to prevent service through the post if it can be effected that way".

In this case the problem is not one of inviolability of the diplomatic mission but immunity of members of the mission from jurisdiction. In the case of diplomats, such writs should be served through the authorities of the sending State. In 1928 the Supreme Court of Japan declared void a writ of summons served through the mail on the ground than such an act is none the less an exercise of the jurisdiction of the court.

Although every judicial or administrative measure which affects the premises of a mission can be considered contrary to the mission's inviolability, the Ambassador must, in certain cases, understand that the serving of summonses or orders cannot be considered as an affront to the embassy. Frequently municipal authorities may demand from the owner or lessee of a building, in this case a diplomatic mission, the payment of dues, taxes or fines from which they are exempt; in most cases, a mere explanation to the municipal authorities that the embassy enjoys exemption from the aforementioned dues or taxes will be enough to clarify the problem; the

lodging of a protest in such a case is uncalled for.

A sending State may, by invoking the inviolability of its diplomatic mission, prevent the receiving State, or municipal authorities, from carrying out vital public works, such as the opening up of new roads or the widening of existing one. The International Law Commission considered it inadvisable to adopt a provision on this problem since it might weaken the principle of inviolability. The Commission, however, went on to say that "the sending State should cooperate in every way in the implementation of the plan which the receiving State is contemplating; and the receiving State, for its part, is obliged to provide adequate compensation or, if necessary, to place other appropriate premises at the disposal of the sending State".

In spite of the judicious remarks of the Commission, the Mexican delegation reintroduced the question in Vienna and suggested the addition of a paragraph reading: "If the receiving State needs the land on which the premises of the mission are situated in order to carry out public works, it shall inform the sending State with a view to agreement on a reasonable period for vacation of the premises. If necessary, the receiving State shall help the sending State to obtain other suitable premises". The proposal was received with misgivings, but the French delegate said he would agree to support it if the representative of Mexico would agree to the introduction of two important ideas: first, that if the premises had to be vacated, the receiving State should negotiate with the sending State on the principle as well as on the time to be allowed; and, secondly, that the receiving State should compensate the sending State as well as providing suitable alternative premises. The Mexican delegation agreed to include a reference to the right of compensation, but later on withdrew its proposal.

Two other privileges enjoyed by diplomatic missions and which are logical consequences of its inviolability are the right of chapel and exemption from billeting.

The right of chapel or the freedom of worship was of great importance in the past when Protestant States considered its Catholic subjects as potential traitors and when Catholic States severely punished any subject that confessed to heresy. Nowadays this privilege has a mere academic importance. Mentioned by some textwriters, the right of chapel is duly covered by the inviolability of the mission's premises.

The Vienna Convention on Diplomatic Relations contains a specific article on the right of billeting, which states: "The receiving State shall exempt diplomatic agents from all personal services, from all public services of any kind whatsoever, and from military obligations such as those connected with requisitioning, military contributions and billeting" (Art. 35). It goes withour saying that this right of billeting is amply justified by the maxim *omnis coactio abesse a legato debet*, since to have soldiers forcibly lodged in a diplomatic premises would be a positive hindrance to the performance of

diplomatic functions not to mention the invasion of privacy.

In a sense, Article 35 is superfluous since the situations envisaged are covered by other articles of the Convention: Articles 22 and 30 guarantee the inviolability of the mission's premises and of the private residence of diplomatic agents, while Articles 23 and 34 refer to the fiscal exemptions of the mission and of diplomatic agents.

Chapter XVII

DIPLOMATIC ASYLUM

The granting of asylum in diplomatic missions is possibly one of the most controversial diplomatic privileges. Recognized and practised to a considerable extent in the past, and quite often abused, its existence in international law has been denied by most non-American countries and the United States. But among the Latin-American countries the right of asylum is considered as part of their international law and those very few cases in which this has been denied by one of them can be regarded as exceptions that confirm the rule.

The granting of asylum, whether in an embassy, in a military camp or aboard a warship, as well as territorial asylum, can be fully justified on humanitarian grounds, and some authors feel that the right of asylum should be numbered among the human rights recognized by international law.

In the opinion of Alona E. Evans, of the United States, "the viability and universality of the institution of political asylum, whether territorial, diplomatic, or some more exotic variety, cannot be questioned today. A casual survey of grants of political asylum during the past ten years suggests the scope of the practice. Diplomatic asylum has been granted by twenty-one States, six of which were not Latin-American States. Some embassies have had from forty-four to seventy-six asylees at a time within their walls".[1]

The granting of asylum is a time-honoured tradition. It was formerly recognized and practised to a considerable extent in Europe and may even be considered a proof of civilization, so much so that it was customary in Greece, but unknown among the barbarians. Owing to its humanitarian basis, it was also adopted by the Church, despite its pagan origin. In the case of the Church, however, we feel that the granting of asylum was a way of counteracting medieval justice. The violation of asylum granted in a church was punished with excommunication. In 1852, Pope Pius IX granted permission for officers of justice to enter churches in order to obtain the testimony of refugees, ordering also that those involved should leave the precints.

In Europe, in the sixteenth and seventeenth centuries, ambassadors strove successfully to extend the inviolability of the mission beyond its original

1. In "Report of the Fifty-Third Conference (Buenos Aires, 1968) of The International Law Association", p. 252.

limits and began to assert their right to protect not only their suite but any one else who took refuge therein. Once this right of asylum was established certain embassies began to expand this privilege in order to place the immediate neighbourhood under their protection. In Madrid and in Rome, the *franchise du quartier*, as this aspect of the right of asylum was known, became firmly established creating veritable havens for all sorts of criminals and smugglers. It was only in the seventeenth century that Pope Innocent XI induced the Emperor, the Kings of Spain, Poland, England and France and the Republic of Venice to agree to the abolition of the privileges claimed.

A radical reaction against these unjustifiable extensions of the inviolability of the diplomatic mission later took place in Europe, where the right of asylum is today no longer admitted. Nevertheless, innumerable examples of diplomatic asylum in Europe can be cited, the most notable being that of Cardinal Mindszenty in the American Legation in Budapest since 1956, which is peculiar in that it occurred in a mission of a country that has repeatedly proclaimed that it does not recognize the doctrine of asylum.

During the Spanish civil war, however, certain diplomatic missions in Madrid granted asylum in 1936 to numerous Spaniards known to be hostile to the regime. In the beginning the Spanish Government deemed it best to disregard this action, in order to maintain cordial relations with the foreign diplomatic missions, especially the Latin-American embassies, where most of the refugees were to be found. The circumstance that the doyen of the diplomatic corps was the Chilean ambassador, in whose Embassy about 150 Spaniards, some of them armed, had taken refuge did not help matters. In October 1936, in a formal communication to the doyen of the diplomatic corps, the Spanish Minister of State declared that the Spanish Government had respected the right of asylum "through a spirit of tolerance and not because it is obligated to do so by agreements which Spain has not accepted in international relations". The note concluded that the Government "sees itself obliged to terminate the attitude of extraordinary tolerance adopted by it up to the present with regard to the practice of the right of asylum, reserving to itself the action against the abuses already committed that may be required in each case by the high interests of the Republic".

In Latin America, however, the right of asylum has been recognized both by custom and by treaty. This may be explained by frequent civil wars and periods of unrest and also by the humanitarian sentiments and the spirit of hospitality which exist in the Latin-American countries. It has been pointed out that thanks to the asylum granted to politicians momentarily in disgrace, the lives of may eminent men who later on were able to serve their countries have been spared.

The necessity of adopting certain positive rules on the right of asylum began to be felt in the middle of the nineteenth century and in 1889 a Treaty on International Penal Law was signed in Montevideo, title II of which has to

do with "Asylum" (Articles XV to XVIII). In 1939 a Treaty on Political Asylum and Refuge was also signed in Montevideo, which elaborated on the 1889 treaty. The basic treaties on the subject, however, are those signed under the aegis of the Interamerican System, namely the Havana Convention on Asylum (1928), the Convention on Political Asylum (Montevideo, 1933) and the Convention on Diplomatic Asylum at Caracas, 1954.[2]

The Havana Convention, which adopted many of the rules laid down in Epitacio Pessoa's draft code (1911), deals in detail with the granting of asylum in legations, military camps or on warships or military aircraft. The Convention respects the asylum of political offenders, but requires the surrender upon the request of the receiving State of persons accused of or condemned for common crimes as well as deserters from the army or navy. The granting of asylum to political offenders is subject to conditions of urgency and limitation of time and also for the sending of asylees out of the country under conditions conducing to their personal safety and public order. In signing this Convention, the United States established as an explicit reservation its "placing on record that it does not recognize or subscribe to as part of international law, the so-called doctrine of asylum".

A series of revolutions which occurred in 1930 required a reappraisal of the 1928 Convention on Asylum and the necessity of an article qualifying the nature of the crime, whether a purely political offence or a relative political offence; as well as the inclusion of a provision safeguarding the inviolability of the asylee and the possibility of his leaving the country.

Five years later, in 1933 at the Montevideo Conference, a new Convention of Political Asylum was adopted in which Article 1 was redrafted and a provision was adopted specifically determining that the decision as to the political nature of the offence rested with the State granting asylum.

In 1950 the Juridical Committee of the Organization of American States was entrusted with the study of the topic "Regimen of Political Exiles, Asylees and Refugees". The Committee prepared two separate draft conventions, namely, on Territorial Asylum and on Diplomatic Asylum. The principal question raised in connection with the draft on Diplomatic Asylum was that of determining who should be competent to decide as to the political character of the offence of the asylee, for the issue had become acute as a result of the prolonged controversy between Peru and Colombia over the asylum given to Haya de la Torre by the Colombian Embassy in Lima, a question which had been submitted to the International Court of Justice. The two drafts, as revised by the Council of Jurists, were submitted to the Tenth Interamerican Conference of Caracas in 1954 and the corres-

2. The full texts in English of these five treaties are reproduced in Marjorie Whiteman's "Digest of International Law", vol. 6 (Washington, D.C., 1968), Chapter XV, § 16.

ponding Conventions were duly signed, subject to ratification. With regard to the decision as to the nature of the offence and the degree of urgency, the Convention laid down that "It shall rest with the State granting asylum to determine the nature of the offense or the motives for the persecution"; "If a case of urgency is involved, it shall rest with the State granting asylum to determine the degree of urgency of the case".

Diplomatic asylum only takes place at moments of political unrest and when the granting of such asylum to a person hostile to the government is liable to provoke ill-feeling towards the diplomatic mission that granted it. Therefore, in the study of the conditions which must surround the granting of asylum in an embassy it is important to bear in mind that the head of mission must, above all, use his common sense. Diplomatic asylum constitutes an exception from the jurisdiction of the local authorities and is therefore a form of interference in the domestic affairs of the receiving State. Owing to the high feelings which are often roused, the granting of asylum is frequently damaging to the good relations between the two States involved and may even result in the rupture of diplomatic relations or the head of mission being declared *persona non grata*. Conversely, the refusal to grant asylum to a given political offender may equally turn out to be unfortunate in the event of the opposition being victorious as a consequence of the political turmoil.

However it may be, and taking into account the foregoing remarks, it is possible to lay down seven basic rules governing the granting of diplomatic asylum.

Diplomatic asylum can only be granted to those whose prosecution is sought for political offences. The determination of the nature of the offence rests exclusively with the State granting asylum. In the case of a relative political offence, i.e. for offences of a mixed character, the diplomatic mission is under the obligation to refuse asylum except if the criminal aspect of the offence was amply justified for political reasons. Traditionally, homicide or an attempt against the life of the Head of a State or of a high ranking member of the government cannot be considerd a political offence and does not therefore, qualify for political asylum. The recent Convention signed in Washington in February 1971 to prevent terrorism also obligates the contracting States to take every measure to prevent and punish acts of terrorism, especially murder, kidnapping and other crimes of this nature against the lives of those persons whom States have the duty to afford special protection. It goes without saying that the author of any of the crimes enumerated in the Convention must be surrendered by a diplomatic mission in which he has sought asylum.

Asylum should only be granted in States that admit it as a right. In the case of the Latin-American States, most of them are linked in one way or another by bilateral or multilateral treaties, and, in the absence of a written commitment, one may say that customary international law can be invoked. In 1968

the Government of Haiti informed the Secretary-General of the Organization of American States that it had decided to denounce all the treaties on asylum; but the jurists were of the opinion that the various diplomatic missions in Port au Prince continued, under customary international law, to have the right to grant asylum to any person whose life or liberty was in peril. Conversely, a State that does not recognize in its territory the right of foreign embassies to grant asylum should not, in theory, grant asylum itself, as in the case of the Government of the United States. In this respect, however, the Convention signed at Caracas in 1954 adopts a very liberal rule in Article XX which reads: "Diplomatic asylum shall not be subject to reciprocity".

Asylum cannot be given to persons accused or condemned for common crimes. This rule, laid down in the Havana Convention of 1928, was open to abuse, since the receiving State frequently began proceedings against asylees on trumped-up charges. In order to remedy this situation the 1954 Convention elaborated on this rule, providing in Article III that "it is not lawful to grant asylum to persons who, at the time of requesting it, are under indictment or on trial for common offences, or have been convicted by competent regular courts and have not served the sentence".

Asylum must only be granted in extreme cases, that is in urgent cases. This rule has raised difficulties in the past, and Article VI of the Caracas Convention contains a satisfactory enumeration of cases in which such urgency exists. Asylum cannot, for instance, be granted to a person who merely feels that he is likely to be threatened. In 1952 the Brazilian Government received a request on these lines from Agostín Rodriguez Araya, an outstanding politician in Argentina, but refused it.

The diplomatic mission that has granted asylum is under the strict obligation to forbid any political activity on the part of the asylee, who is not permitted to maintain any further political contacts. If the receiving State requests that the asylee be withdrawn from the country and grants him the necessary safe-conduct, the State granting the asylum must agree to such a measure.

Asylum is a temporary measure and should be granted for the shortest possible period.

Finally, a diplomatic agent must never on his own initiative offer asylum to a person who in his opinion is in danger.

The two sentences of the International Court of Justice on the asylum granted by the Colombia Embassy in Lima to Haya de la Torre are the outstanding example of diplomatic asylum. The sentences received wide publicity and were the object of various learned papers; those written in Spain and in Latin America were, with rare exceptions, highly critical of the stand taken by the International Court of Justice. The sentence passed in 20 November 1950 was most unsatisfactory and avoided taking a clear stand on

the various points raised. From a Latin American point of view it contains certain affirmations which simply went to prove that the Court was not qualified to pass judgement since it had examined a typical Latin American juridical institution exclusively from a European and biased point of view. Among the arguments put forward by the Court we read the following, which are completely unacceptable: "The facts brought to the knowledge of the Court disclose so much uncertainty and contradiction, so much fluctuation and discrepancy in the exercise of diplomatic asylum and in the official views expressed on various occasions, there has been so much inconsistency on the rapid succession of conventions on asylum, ratified by some States and rejected by others, and the practice has been so much influenced by considerations of political expediency in the various cases, that it is not possible to discern in all this any constant and uniform usage, accepted as law, with regard to the alleged rule of unilateral and definitive qualification of the offence. The Court cannot therefore find that the Colombian Government has proved the existence of such a custom. But even if it could be supposed that such a custom existed between certain Latin-American States only, it could not be invoked against Peru which, far from having by its attitude adhered to it, has, on the contrary, repudiated it by refraining from ratifying the Montevideo Conventions of 1933 which were the first to include a rule concerning the qualification of the offence in matters of diplomatic asylum . . . For these reasons, the Court has arrived at the conclusion that Colombian, as the State granting asylum, is not competent to qualify the offence by a unilateral and definitive decision, binding on Peru."

Colombia and Peru were unable to come to an agreement on the basis of the sentence laid down and the Court was requested to determine the manner in which effect should be given to its judgement and whether Colombia was, or was not, bound to hand over Haya de la Torre. In a judgement delivered 13 June 1951, the International Court of Justice concluded "that the asylum must cease, but that the Government of Colombia is under no obligation to bring this about by surrendering the refugee to the Peruvian authorities". Once again the decision of the Court was completely unsatisfactory, for it still left the question in suspense. Finally, on 22 March 1954, the Governments of Peru and Colombia worked out a solution and signed an agreement which gave scant consideration to the Court's decision: the Colombian Embassy declared the asylum of Haya de la Torre at an end and turned him over to the Government of Peru, which on the same day issued a decree expelling him. He was placed on board a plane bound for Mexico, thus ending an asylum which has lasted five years.

Just as the sentences of the International Court of Justice on the question of the international status of South-West Africa made most Afro-asian States distrust the Court, the Haya de la Torre case alienated most Latin-American States, thus contributing to the atmosphere of ill-will which characterizes the

relations of most States with the principal judicial organ of the United Nations.

At its First Session in 1949, the International Law Commission included "Right of Asylum" in its list of fourteen topics selected for codification, but has avoided considering it on the dubious ground that the topic is of considerable scope and raises a number of political problems.

The Vienna Convention on Diplomatic Relations does not concern itself with the question, following in this aspect the position assumed by the International Law Commission in 1957. Paragraph 3 of Article 41, which aims at preventing the inviolability of the mission being used in a manner incompatible with its functions, was drafted in such a way as to permit, in given circumstances, certain acts normally forbidden by the Convention, in particular, the granting of diplomatic asylum, as the discussions in Vienna and in the International Law Commission attest.

In order to avoid any doubt, the commentary of the Commission to Article 40 of the 1958 draft says that "the question of asylum is not dealt with in the draft but, in order to avoid misunderstanding, it should be pointed out that among the agreements referred to in paragraph 3 there are certain treaties governing the right to grant asylum in mission premises which are valid as between the parties to them". Furthermore, during the discussions in the International Law Commission it became perfectly clear that the right to grant asylum was not dependent upon agreement between States.

Chapter XVIII

INVIOLABILITY OF ARCHIVES AND CORRESPONDENCE

Absolute inviolability of the archives and of official correspondence is indispensable for the normal exercise of diplomatic functions. The lack of guarantees with regard to official correspondence, whether by post or telegraph, would almost reduce the diplomatic functions to those of a representational nature, since it would no longer be worth-while to send confidencial dispatches.

In consequence, as a supplementary protection, diplomatic missions have the right to send their correspondence by code or cipher or in a special valise, which is locked and sealed, called a *diplomatic pouch* in the terminology of the State Department or a *diplomatic bag* in that of the Foreign Office and of the Vienna Convention.

Inviolability of diplomatic correspondence means that the receiving State is under a special duty not to violate or censor mail intended for or sent by the mission and to afford it a superior protection to that given to the correspondence of the other inhabitants of the country.

From the fifteenth to the seventeenth century it was almost universally agreed that an ambassador's couriers and dispatches should not suffer interference. But as E.R. Adair points out "in practice so tempting was the possibility of finding out the real views of the ambassador or of his government that dispatches were intercepted and read whenever it could be done with safety, and couriers were always liable to be arrested so that their dispatches might secretly be opened or some diplomatic advantage might be gained by their delay".[1]

In the 1520s Cardinal Wolsey and Charles V's minister, Cattinara, operated with forthright simplicity: when they suspected that an ambassador was up to something they disapproved of, they stopped his courier and opened his dispatches. In Thomas Cromwell's days things were somewhat more subtly done: dispatches were delayed by accident and opened by mistake. Such measures were rarely justified by the receiving State, which usually put the blame on an over-zealous clerk.

1. E.R. Adair, "The Exterritoriality of Ambassadors in the Sixteenth and Seventeenth Centuries", Longmans, Green amd Co London, New York, Toronto, 1929, p. 170.

During the Second World War there were some cases of interference with diplomatic correspondence. In April 1944, as part of the security precautions preceding the Allied invasion of Europe, it was provided that diplomatic envoys, in the same way as all other foreigners in Great Britain, on being required to do so should declare whether they were carrying letters, written messages, etc., and, if necessary produce them. The transmission and receipt by diplomatic missions of telegrams in code was suspended and the inviolability of diplomatic couriers was also suspended. Commenting on these measures, A. B. Lyons teaches that "the effect of war is to restrict the privilege of freedom of communication. This follows from the paramount right of a State at war to take all steps necessary to ensure the unhindered conduct of the war, including the restriction of individual specific rights".[2] Some governments felt it their duty to point out that the measures taken by the British Government were contrary to those laid down in international law. In its answer the Brazilian Government said that it had some reservations to make about those measures and was surprised that they should have been taken without previous consultation, since Brazil, as an ally, was fighting for the same cause and would, without hesitation, have co-operated with the British Government by instructing its diplomats to comply with its requests and desires.

From April 23 to May 2, 1959, every diplomatic valise which arrived in Cairo was sealed and only handed over after May 2. This measure was taken in order to avoid the reintroduction into Egypt of $ 50 and $ 100 notes which had been taken of circulation and were being sold abroad in the black market for a tenth of their value. The French Government of General Charles de Gaulle had adopted a similar measure in 1945.

In 1946, Judge Bissonnette, of Quebec (Court of King's Bench), in dismissing an appeal against the conviction of a member of the Canadian Parliament for supplying information to Soviet agents in Canada, dealt at length with the defendant's objection that the documents taken from the Soviet Embassy by an embassy employee could not properly be used in evidence against him. The defendant claimed no diplomatic status, and neither the former employee nor the Soviet Embassy claimed immunity with respect to the documents. Judge Bissonnette said in part: "International law created as presumption of law that documents coming from an embassy have a diplomatic character and that every Court of Justice must refuse to acknowledge jurisdiction or competence in regard to them. But can this presumption be avoided, rebutted or destroyed? If the acts committed by the diplomatic corps were contrary to the legislation of the country to which it is accredited and if, *a fortiori*, they had the immediate purpose of putting the safety of the

2. A.B. Lyons, "Personal immunities of diplomatic agents", in *British Yearbook of International Law*, vol. XXXI (1954), p. 337.

State in peril, there is no longer any freedom of the dwelling or of the documents, chattels, effects or armaments which may be found there... Without stressing it unduly, I point out that competence to repress the abuses of a diplomatic agent *reposes exclusively in the executive power*. If immunity is not admitted by the executive, any discussion becomes purely academic. If documents seized are then turned over to a Court of Justice for the prosecution of a crime committed by one of the citizens of the country, the Court cannot give effect to immunity, cannot counteract the decision of the executive of the country, cannot exercise competence in a field, upon a matter exclusively governed by the rule of external sovereignty, that is to say, from the absolute and exclusive authority of the State to condition and determine its own relations with other States".

The Vienna Convention on Diplomatic Relations lays down in Article 24 that "The archives and documents of the mission shall be inviolable at any time and wherever they may be". It might be said that this Article is superfluous since the inviolability of the premises is sufficient guarantee for the archives and that Article 27 also stipulates that the official correspondence of the mission shall be inviolable. But the importance of the problem is such that a specific article was indispensable since the provisions mentioned above do not cover every hypothesis.

The archives of the mission are composed of all the documents which are deposited in them, even though they may no longer be in use. The Government of the United States in its remarks on the 1957 draft suggested that the words "and documents" should be omitted, as the phrase was unnecessary and confusing. At Vienna, in 1961, the United States delegation suggested the addition of an extra paragraph reading: "for the purposes of this convention the words 'archives and documents' mean the official records and reference collections belonging to or in the possession of the mission". The amendment was withdrawn since the definition was considered as a limitation to the inviolability of the archives and the phrase "*reference collections*" would demand an additional definition in the French, Spanish, Russian and Chinese versions of the Convention.

The draft of the International Law Commission stated concisely that "the archives and documents of the mission shall be inviolable". At Vienna the words "at any time and wherever they may be" were added since in the opinion of the French Delegate the inviolability of the archives should be absolute wherever they happened to be, even outside the premises of the mission. The Franco-Italian amendment also provided that outside the premises of the mission "they must be identified by visible official signs", but this part of the amendment was not carried.

With respect to the localization of the archives of the mission, two attitudes can be mentioned. In the first place we have the position which has been defended by the United States Government on more than one occasion.

The Harvard draft, for example, was in favour of granting inviolability to the archives, wherever they may be located within the territory of the receiving State "provided that notification of their location has been previously given to the receiving State" (Article 5). In its observations to the 1957 draft of the International Law Commission the United States Government said that it could not agree with the statement in the commentary that the inviolability applied to "archives and documents, regardless of the premises in which they may be". In its opinion "the inviolability which properly attaches to the archives of the mission presupposes that archival material will be on the premises of the mission, in ordinary transit by courier or sealed pouch, or in the personal custody of duly authorized officers of the mission for use in the performance of their functions".

This position can be justified from a practical point of view: the receiving State must know precisely where the archives are located in order to prevent their violation. On the other hand, the enumeration of details aimed at protecting the archives may be interpreted as conditions for the recognition of inviolability, creating therefore restrictions to a privilege that must be absolute.

The position defended by Italy, and endorsed by Article 24 of the Vienna Convention, is that the inviolability of the archives exists wherever they may be.

Article 24 also says that the archives and documents shall be inviolable "at any time". This phrase was deemed redundant but in the case of a rupture of diplomatic intercourse there is an interval in which the archives and documents do not enjoy satisfactory protection. Article 45, however, seems to cover this point since it lays down that if diplomatic relations are broken off the receiving State must "even in case of armed conflict, respect and protect the premises of the mission, together with the property and archives".

Chapter XIX

LEGAL BASIS OF IMMUNITY FROM JURISDICTION

Diplomatic agents and their families enjoy jurisdictional immunity in the receiving State, whose courts therefore are not competent to pass judgement on them. This privilege, even though contested in certain circumstances, has a long tradition behind it and is generally recognized in every country.

Immunity from jurisdiction is usually considered a personal privilege of the diplomat, but current practice shows that a distinction must always be drawn between situations which refer to the diplomat and those that refer to the diplomatic mission. The Vienna Convention which followed this *rationale* overlooked this point and only mentions the immunity enjoyed by the diplomatic agent, in spite of the fact that a civil case may be submitted to the court involving only the diplomatic mission. It is true that in such a case the judge is in reality faced with a question of the immunity of the foreign State. Even so, reference should be made to those exceptional cases in which immunity is claimed by a diplomatic mission and not by a diplomatic agent.

The word immunity is used in more than one sense but is generally employed, as in the Vienna Convention, in those cases in which the judiciary intervenes and the recognition of exemption from local law and jurisdiction is implied. In international law, immunity usually applies to civil and criminal cases, but can be invoked equally in administrative and labour cases and a reasonable body of jurisprudence exists in this respect. The Vienna Convention, after declaring that "a diplomatic agent shall enjoy immunity from criminal jurisdiction of the receiving State", goes on to mention immunity from civil and administrative jurisdiction, subject to certain exceptions.

In the fifteenth and sixteenth centuries the leading textwriters tried to find an overall theory for the legal position of diplomats and to explain the fundamentals of their privileges and immunities.

Various theories were put forward and we shall deal with them separately according to the basic differences between them.

The International Law Commission in its commentary on Article 18 listed the principal theories that exercised an influence on the development of diplomatic privileges and immunities, namely the *exterritoriality* theory, the *representative character* theory and the *functional necessity* theory. The Commission went on to declare that it was guided by the third theory in

solving problems on which practice gave no clear pointers, while also bearing in mind the representative character of the head of mission and of the mission itself.

Determining the juridical bases of diplomatic immunity is much less important nowadays than in the past when the theories of exterritoriality and of the representative character of the ambassador were decisive for the correct formulation of such privileges and immunities and their definitive acceptance by civilized States. Although this problem has lost some of its importance one cannot ignore the fact that the acceptance of this or that theory may have far-reaching consequences in the interpretation of this or that immunity. Even though the Vienna Convention did lay down in a satisfactory manner the main privileges and immunities, quite a few of the provisions may still be applied restrictively or favourably. In such a case, the interpretation of a legal provision by a judge or by the ministry for foreign affairs must be made, according to the Vienna Convention, to ensure "the efficient performance of the functions of the diplomatic mission as representing States" and not to benefit the diplomatic agent. With this guiding principle, and in certain circumstances, a judge may refuse to admit the privileged situation of a diplomatic agent.

Even though it is no longer so important nowadays to determine the juridical bases of diplomatic immunities as it used to be, the problem was duly taken up in Vienna in 1961 when the preamble was considered by the conference. The wording finally accepted follows the guidance given by the International Law Commission, namely the functional necessity theory, but it is symptomatic that two suggestions put forward in which the theory was given a radical approach were rejected and the text finally adopted also takes into account the representative character theory.

In spite of the fact that modern international law no longer takes the exterritoriality theory into consideration there can be no doubt that in the past it had enormous influence in defining diplomatic privileges and immunities.

It is in the teaching of Grotius that we find the idea which was developed later on by doctrine. The crucial paragraphs are the following: "My unqualified conclusion, therefore, is that the rule has been accepted by the nations that the common custom, which makes a person who lives in foreign territory subject to that country, admits an exception in the case of ambassadors. Ambassadors as if by a kind of fiction are considered to represent those who sent them. In consequence, by a similar fiction they are is it were, *extra territorium*; and thus are not bound to the civil law of the State within which they are living".

It should be pointed out that Grotius insists that he only speaks figuratively, and that the idea is a fiction. The idea, however, took on, and was developed by future writers who were able to unite every privilege and im-

munity in a single theory and reconcile the principle of the territoriality of laws with the exceptional status of diplomats. Carlos Calvo, writing at the end of the nineteenth century, was able to say that this theory was adopted by almost every author. In the present century, however, it was realized that a new legal basis had to be found and the expression itself is gradually being abandoned, even though it is sometimes still used. Montell Ogdon, author of the most important work on the bases of diplomatic immunity, concludes that "with all deference to the rôle which the fiction of 'extra-territoriality' played in the formative period of the law, and recognizing that the term fairly aptly described the position of the seventeenth century ambassador, it may be safely concluded that the fiction does not furnish a sound reason for immunity, that it conflicts with recognized usage, produces undesirable results, is misleading and cannot be relied upon as a test in determining what the law is. Finally it may be added that it is of no value to States of today that are interested in molding the law to fit social and economis needs".[1]

The *representative character* theory bases the privileges and immunities on the idea that the diplomatic mission personifies the sending State. Originally it was linked to the theory of the ambassador as representative of his prince abroad, any injury he suffered being considered an affront to his sovereign. When the Russian ambassador in London was arrested in 1708 he complained that the offence committed against him amounted to an insult to the honour of the Czar, his master. Even nowadays, monarchies still cling to the idea that an ambassador represents the king or queen.

The representative character theory also springs from the aforementioned text of Grotius which mentions the fiction by which an ambassador represents the actual person of his sovereign. Later on this idea was modified and it began to be held that the ambassador represented the sending State. The preamble of the Havana Convention of 1928, recognizes that "diplomatic officers do not in any case represent the person of the chief of State but only their government".

None of the representative character theories provides an entirely satisfactory explanation since they are often illogical or inapplicable. But even though the International Law Commission was guided by the functional necessity it also bore in mind the representative character of the head of the mission and of the mission itself. The text finally adopted in Vienna did not completely discard this theory and the preamble recognizes the diplomatic mission "as representing States".

The *functional necessity theory* corresponds more closely to the present stage of international intercourse in which there is a marked attempt to reduce the number of diplomatic privileges granted to diplomatic agents and,

1. Montell Ogdon, "Juridical bases of diplomatic immunity", John Byrne & Co, Washington, D.C., 1936, pp. 103-104.

above all, to the other members of the diplomatic mission. By linking the granting of privileges and immunities to the performance of functions, and refusing them when no such link exists, doctrine and practice is able to avoid certain abuses.

The functional necessity theory however is not altogether satisfactory and can give rise to restrictive interpretations which might be detrimental to international relations. It need only be said that the theory which differentiates between the official and private activities of a diplomatic agent, refusing privileges and immunities in the latter case, springs from the functional necessity theory.

In spite of its shortcomings the functional necessity theory was considered to be the most suitable as a basis for an international multilateral convention designed to lay down the irreducible minimum of immunities which a diplomatic agent must enjoy. The International Law Commission was guided by this theory in solving problems on which practice was still unsatisfactory, and it was considered the basic theory by the Vienna Convention on Diplomatic Relations.

Examination of the various theories attempting to explain the *raison d'être* of diplomatic immunities will show that it is those which at a particular moment represented the consensus of opinion that should be considered the correct approach to the problem. As a result of the development of legal thought, a theory considered as valid may become obsolete, even though such a development does not mean that it was erroneous when formulated. On the other hand, it is a mistake to try to quote opinions and cases which no longer fit modern facts.

In 1925, Professor Mastny, writing on the subject in his capacity as a member of the Committee of Experts of the League of Nations for the Progressive Codification of International Law, said that in his opinion all diplomatic privileges are based on ancient tradition, the dignity and prestige of the State on one side and courtesy on the other, and Independence (the free exercise of functions). In other words he did not link diplomatic immunities to one exclusive theory but adopted a pragmatical and eclectic approach to the problem, and the same can be said of the draft of the International Law Commission. Such an approach should not come as a surprise when we consider that the three principal theories we have been discussing are based on the writings of Grotius.

Chapter XX

IMMUNITY FROM CIVIL JURISDICTION

Immunity from the civil and commercial jurisdiction of the receiving State is, in a certain sense, the most important privilege enjoyed by a diplomatic agent, owing to the high number of cases submitted to municipal courts.

Most jurists insist that civil immunity is not absolute, as it is in criminal suits, and the Vienna Convention on Diplomatic Relations endorses this theory, since it enumerates cases in which the diplomatic agents can be prosecuted in local courts. Existing national law and the rule of most courts, however, seem inclined to favour absolute exemption.

Historically, immunity from civil jurisdiction derives from the personal inviolability of the diplomatic agent. Suffice to recall that the Act of Anne (1708) was enacted as a consequence of the arrest of the Russian Ambassador in London on July 21, 1708, by officers of justice in the streets of London on the basis of a warrant of arrest obtained against him by several merchants to whom he owed about £300. He was forced from his carriage, and the officers tore his sword, his cane and his hat from him and led him through the streets as if he were an ordinary criminal. The incident was most embarrassing because arrest for debt was then lawful in England. Those responsible for the arrest were remanded before the privy council and condemned and the Court held that "by the law of nations, neither an ambassador nor any of his train or *comites*, can be prosecuted for any debt or contract in the courts of that kingdom wherein he is sent to reside".

Jurisprudence of the courts show that civil jurisdiction was in fact understood to be absolute, due to the difficulty of conciliating possible exceptions with the Grotian *omnis coactio abesse a legato debet*.

Abuses, however, provoked an understandable reaction, and writers at the end of the nineteenth Century defended the thesis that the necessity of granting diplomats a privileged status no longer existed and that their controversies could be decided by the local courts. According to this theory immunities would be strictly limited to the exercise of official duties, since exemption in the case of private acts was an unjust and unnecessary institution and good relations between States and the high standard of local justice no longer justified the privileged situation. The circumstance that P. Fiore should have adhered to this theory, together with Laurent, Esperson,

Bidau and Epitácio Pessoa, gave it a certain acceptance, so much so that the Rome Supreme Court of Cassation affirmed the principle in two judgements (1915 and 1921) that the immunity from jurisdiction in civil questions only extended to acts performed in the exercise of official functions, and accordingly did not apply to private transactions. The French Ambassador in Rome, acting in his capacity as Doyen of the Diplomatic Corps, protested against the latter judgements in a note addressed to the Italian Ministry for External Affairs in which he expressed doubts as to the juridical bases and to the future consequences of the adoption of the jurisprudence.

In January 18, 1940, the Court of Cassation reversed the decision of the Court of Rome and held that "for this reason, in the absence of provisions to the contrary in our municipal law and seeing that there are indications that we have adhered to the rule in question, it must be held that the principle that diplomatic agents accredited to our country are exempt from Italian civil jurisdiction applies in Italy even in respect of acts relating to the necessities of their private affairs. . .".

Be that as it may, the distinction between acts performed by the diplomatic agents in the exercise of their official functions and those relating to their private capacity would simply mean the negation of immunities to the diplomatic agent; in other words, when the diplomatic agent acts in his official capacity these acts must be attributed to the State he represents and the responsibility shall be of that State, in such a case the rules of international law that apply are those relating to the immunity of the State itself in foreign courts and not those which we find in the Vienna Convention on Diplomatic Relations.

Admitted that exceptions should be made to the principle of immunity from civil and commercial jurisdiction and considering the difficulties that arise from the adoption of a rule that takes into account the nature of the activity (public or private) of the diplomat the trend was in the sense of specifying the exceptions that should be made to the general rule of immunity from civil jurisdiction. In the characterization of these exemptions we find, however, considerable difference of opinion in doctrine and in the jurisprudence of national courts.

The project of the International Commission of American Jurists (1927) mentions six cases in which a diplomatic agent is liable to civil jurisdiction. When the Havana Convention on Diplomatic Officers was drafted, the Inter-american Conference using this project as the basis for its considerations, was of the opinion that if the article were adopted, the power of the local tribunal to accept jurisdiction might make it possible for the authorities of the receiving State to harass the diplomatic agent to the point of annuling the basic principle *ne impediatur legatio*. The fact is that the article which was finally adopted in Havana in 1928 is most unsatisfactory, since it only says that "Diplomatic officers are exempt from all civil and criminal jurisdiction of the

State to which they are accredited; they may not, except in the cases when duly authorized by their government, waive immunity, be prosecuted or tried unless it be by the courts of their own country".

When the International Law Commission took up the problem it decided that it was indispensable to spell out the cases in which exemption could not be invoked. The Vienna Conference fully endorsed this position so much so that the amendments submitted in 1961 aimed solely at completing the article. Article 31 of the Vienna Convention mentions the following three cases in which there is no immunity from civil, commercial an administrative jurisdiction:

a) a real action relating to private immovable property situated in the territory of the receiving State, unless the diplomatic agent holds it on behalf of the sending State for the purposes of the mission;

b) an action relating to succession in which the diplomatic agent is involved as executor, administrator, heir or legatee as a private person and not on behalf of the sending State;

c) an action relating to any professional or commercial activity exercised by the diplomatic agent in the receiving State outside his official functions.

These exemptions refer specifically to civil jurisdiction, since the general exemptions are equally relevant, such being the case of waivers of immunity, and the case of the beneficiary having the nationality of or being a permanent resident of the receiving State.

The most generally admitted exception to the rule of diplomatic immunity is with regard to real property owned by a diplomatic agent in his private capacity. In its observations on the 1957 draft of the International Law Commission the United States Government, while being of the opinion that the exceptions mentioned under paragraph 1 were "not presently recognized under international law" and therefore that the article should be revised to restate the existing principles on the subject, admitted the exception with respect to real property since, in this case, court proceedings are usually *in rem* rather than *in personam*.

As a general rule, States exercise exclusive jurisdiction with regards to immovable property situated in their territory, but admit that, exceptionally, foreign States may own the buildings or part of the buildings used for the purposes of their diplomatic missions, or consular offices. Professor Sandström's draft only made reference to "a real action relating to private immovable property situated in the territory of the receiving State". Taking into account the laws of certain countries that do not permit the ownership of land by foreign States, the phrase "unless he holds it on behalf of the sending State for the purposes of the mission" was adopted. Justifying the addition, Professor G. Tunkin pointed out that when local law did not permit a foreign State to own immovable property, the solution was to put it under the name of the head of mission and mentioned the case of property for the use of the

Soviet Mission to the United Nations in New York which had to be bought in the name of the head of the delegation.

The Netherlands Government in its observations to the 1957 draft was of the opinion that sub-paragraph *a* of paragraph 1 is tautological and that a "real action" in English law is not quite synonymous with an *action réelle* in continental law, and that the text should speak of an action *in rem* relating to immovable property.

The inclusion of actions relating to successions in which the diplomatic agent is involved as a private person is justified owing to the possibility of local justice considering itself incompetent to take cognizance of the case. Doubts as to its convenience were raised in the International Law Commission by Professor R. Ago since such an exception had not appeared either in the Harvard draft or in the 1929 resolution of the Institute of International Law. In his opinion, the matter could have been easily dealt with by inserting a reference to movable as well as to immovable property in sub-paragraph *a*.

The clause however was considered necessary by the International Law Commission and later on in Vienna. Should the diplomatic agent object to a decision regarding a succession in the receiving Stae he may initiate proceedings under article 32, paragraph 3, of the Vienna Convention; *contrariu sensu*, if a local inhabitant wished to contest the succession and the diplomatic agent should refuse to waive his immunity, the other part would be without any legal remedy.

The third exception to the rule of immunity from civil jurisdiction refers to the exercise of non-diplomatic activities by a diplomatic agent. The exception was included due to a suggestion by Professor Verdross who based his amendment on article 13 of the International Law Institute's 1929 resolution, which was akin to article 24, paragraph 2, of the Harvard draft. The amendment was received with mixed feelings by the International Law Commission. Professor J. P. A. François opposed the amendment as unnecessary since, in his opinion, diplomatic agents practically never engaged in any professional activity outside their official duties and if they did and the receiving State objected it could easily put an end to such activity by declaring him *persona non grata*. Sandström was still stronger in his objection saying that he regarded the whole idea of a diplomatic agent engaging in such activities "as repugnant".

The Government of Chile observed that the situation contemplated "appears very unusual and is in any case inadmissible by virtue of the very nature of diplomatic functions". In Vienna, the Colombian delegation tabled an amendment suggesting the delection of sub-paragraph *c* and the adoption of a new article reading "The staff of a diplomatic mission may not practise any liberal profession or commercial activity otherwise than in the performance of their official duties". The substance of the amendment was accepted by most of the delegations that commented on it, but drafting changes were suggested and the necessity of such an article was also raised.

The task of rewording the Colombian amendment was entrusted to the Drafting Committee where the point of view of the Brazilian representative finally prevailed, i.e. that the article should be as short and precise as possible, and that the inclusion of those activities which could be considered compatible with the functions of the diplomatic agent would only raise difficulties of interpretation in the future. Those doubts raised as to the convenience of the article still prevail. In the long run the receiving State is the sole authority competent to determine which activities are or are not compatible with the functions of the diplomatic agent. The sending State should also forbid its agents from exercising other functions incompatible with their privileged status, establishing the penalties for those who infringe them. Should the receiving State feel that the diplomatic agent has overstepped the limits permitted by international law, it can declare him *persona non grata*. In brief, article 42 merely creates a moral obligation and may be considered redundant, since it is in article 31 that we find the real operative article. Even though national legislations may forbid the exercise of professional or commercial activities incompatible with diplomatic functions, the agent may abusively take advantage of his privileged situation and in such a case it is necessary to consider the local courts competent.

During the course of the debates in Vienna and in the International Law Commission other exceptions to the rule of immunity were remembered and a special reference should be made to the trend towards giving the victims of automobile accidents in which diplomats are involved legal remedies to obtain reparation in local courts, i.e. in the courts of the country where the accident occurred. In Vienna two important amendements were tabled, respectively by the Netherlands and by Switzerland. The Dutch proposal was to include a new paragraph on the following lines: "The immunity from civil jurisdiction, in so far as it concerns an action for damages relating to a traffic accident in the receiving State in which the diplomatic agent is involved, is subject to the condition that such action can be brought directly against an insurance company before a court of the receiving State". The Swiss amendment had the same basis but was not so far reaching, since it only suggested the adoption of a new sub-paragraph, that is a fourth exception, in the sense that the diplomatic agent would not enjoy immunity in an administrative procedure for the issue or withdrawal of a driving license. Both amendments were considered just, but neither obtained the necessary votes.

Even though the Vienna Conference did not include in the Convention an unequivocal rule, it adopted a resolution is which it "Recommends that the sending State should waive the immunity of members of is diplomatic mission in respect of civil claims of persons in the receiving State when this can be done without impeding the performance of the functions of the mission, and that, when immunity is not waived, the sending State should use its best endeavours to bring about a just settlement of the claims".

Chapter XXI

IMMUNITY FROM CRIMINAL JURISDICTION

Immunity from criminal jurisdiction is universally recognized and derives from the diplomatic agent's inviolability. Since he is exempted from measures that would amount to direct coercion it would be useless to bring him to trial knowing beforehand that the local courts would be unable to mete out punishment for guilt duly proven.

Immunity from criminal jurisdiction is justified by the necessity for diplomatic agents to enjoy complete independence vis-à-vis the jurisdiction of the receiving State, in order to be able to exercise their functions freely.

When the Spanish Ambassador Mendonza was implicated in the plot against Queen Elizabeth in 1583-84, the question of his inviolability and immunity received careful attention, so much so that A. Gentili and Jean Hotman, two highly qualified jurists who happened to be in England at that time, were consulted. Ambassador Mendonza was summoned before the Council and given a fortnight to leave the country. With Grotius and Bynkershoek the principle of immunity became firmly established, the former pointing out that "the security of ambassadors outweights any advantage which accrues from a punishment".

According to generally recognized custom, immunity from criminal jurisdiction is complete, whereas in civil cases the diplomatic agent is subject to certain exceptions. The Vienna Convention endorses this doctrine, and the absolute nature of this immunity can be seen from a comparison of the provisions regarding criminal and civil jurisdiction. While article 31 is categorical as regards immunity from criminal jurisdiction ("A diplomatic agent shall enjoy immunity from criminal jurisdiction"), it employs a different language in dealing with civil and administrative matters and mentions specific cases in which local courts have competence.

The immunity of a diplomatic agent from criminal jurisdiction is recognized even in certain extreme cases, such as plotting against the security of the receiving State or of the members of its government and in cases of espionage in which responsibility is proven without any doubt. In 1654 De Bass, the French ambassador in England, conspired against the life of Cromwell and was ordered to leave the country within twenty-four hours; previously, in 1587, another French ambassador in England had conspired

against the life of Queen Elizabeth and was simply warned not to commit a similar act again.

Even though immunity from criminal jurisdictions is complete according to current practice, some textwriters, especially in the nineteenth century, reacted against the privileged position of diplomats in local law, in criminal and civil matters. Even nowadays, some judges, usually of the lower courts, refuse to admit their incompetence in cases in which the culpability of diplomats, as in cases of *flagrante delicto*, is clear.

Theoretically three different approaches to the problem can be mentioned. In the first place we have the overwhelming majority of writers that do not admit the smallest exception to the rule; secondly we can mention a few who are, or were, in favour of the abolition of diplomatic immunity; and, lastly, we have certain textwriters who have tried to present middle of the road theories i.e. recognize immunity as a rule, but admit some exceptions.

With respect to the first mentioned approach, we must not forget that in the case of a waiver of immunity or if the person is a national or a permanent resident of the receiving State, the local courts will normally be competent in criminal matters.

As regards the waiver of immunity, international practice demanded that it be express in criminal cases, admitting that in civil matters the waiver could be implied. Some authors went still further, teaching that there could be no renunciation of immunity in a criminal case. The Vienna Convention, however, modified the rule, putting criminal and civil matters on the same level and demanding an express waiver in both cases.

According to Sir Cecil Hurst, no example exists of a diplomatic agent being condemned by a criminal court. *Data venia* it would be more correct to say that no example can be cited of a criminal condemnation by a lower court being confirmed by a higher court. Jayme Eyzaguirre, for example, mentions in detail the case of a Second Secretary of the Brazilian Embassy in Santiago, Antonio Barroso Fernandes, who was sued by the German Transatlantic Bank in 1926, for issuing a cheque without funds. The judge did not take into account the existence of his immunities and condemned him to imprisonment. The Chief of Police, however, avoided taking such an extreme measure due precisely to the fact that the accused was a diplomat. The Court of Appel, on April 9, 1927 rejected the previous decision and refused to condemn him to prison. Soon after the decision of the lower court, the Brazilian Government dismissed the officer from its diplomatic service. A similar case occured in June 1961 in France where Judge Pierre David issued an order for the imprisonment of another Brazilian diplomat for the same crime, committed when he was serving in the Embassy in Paris, alleging that he no longer enjoyed immunity since his functions with the aforesaid diplomatic mission had ceased. Since the diplomat, who was subsequently dismissed from the career, was not in Paris, the order was not carried out and the plaintiff

dropped the charges.

The list of textwriters in favour of the abolition of diplomatic immunities in criminal matters is small but includes some outstanding authorities, such as Pasquale Fiore, Carnazza-Amari, Laurent, Esperon and Eduardo Bidau. Fiore makes a distinction between acts connected with diplomatic functions and those of a private nature, refusing immunity in the latter case. In his draft code of 1890 he writes that "diplomatic agents who, in the State where they reside, perform acts in no way connected with their character as public officers or representatives of a foreign government, but which, by their nature, must be considered as within the domain of civil or private relations, may, with respect to all the consequences of those acts, be rendered subject to the territorial courts, save for such concessions as are necessary to protect the dignity of the represented State" (Art. 347).

The third school of thought, as was pointed out, does not consider immunity from criminal jurisdiction as being absolute. In a certain sense, Fiore could be included in this list since he advocates immunity in cases connected with a diplomat's functions. But in this respect, it would be inconceivable that a State should send a diplomatic agent with instructions to violate the criminal laws of the receiving State.

Certain writers feel that local courts should have competence in cases of *flagrante delicto* but this opinion has received scant acceptance. Others are of the opinion that a distinction should be made between crimes of a certain gravity and lesser crimes. But this distinction should also be rejected since it would seem to be up to the local authorities to decide if the crime was or was not of such a seriousness as to justify actions by the territorial courts. In addition, certain acts may be punished severely in certain countries and not regarded as crime in others, as occurs with the legislation forbidding the sale of gold or foreign exchange.

Even though this distinction is considered unacceptable with respect to diplomatic relations, it has been admitted in consular affairs, so much so that the Vienna Convention on Consular Relations of 1963 adopted it in Article 41, which reads as follows: "1. Consular officers shall not be liable to arrest or detention pending trial, except in the case of a grave crime and pursuant to a decision by the competent judicial authority".

In spite of the fact that immunity from jurisdiction in criminal proceedings is absolute, this does not mean that a diplomat may do what he likes. Article 41 of the Vienna Convention of 1961 is categorical in this respect when it lays down that all persons enjoying privileges and immunities have the duty to respect the laws and regulations of the receiving State. If he behaves otherwise the receiving State may well request his recall.

Complaints are more generally felt with respect to violation of traffic laws, especially with regard to car parking. In 1963, letters were sent to all the ambassadors in London by Sir Harold Caccia, of the Foreign Office "on the

intractable subject of car parking", since they "have sometimes brought members of the Diplomatic Corp into direct dispute, if not conflict, with the Metropolitan Police; and I am anxious to do all I can to reduce possibilities of friction". In consequence, it was arranged that "every diplomatic mission with premises in an area where there are parking meters shall have a space reserved for one car outside the Embassy or Ambassador's residence". The note went on to mention the problem of casual parking and pointed out that "if a car is found to be holding up traffic, or to be in a place where, e.g., by obscuring a pedestrian crossing, it is a danger to the public, it is the duty of the police to see that the obstruction is removed". This note was sent in view of a rather violent and biased campaign in certain newspapers and even in the House of Lords, where Lord Carrington had the opportunity to say that "those who had experience abroad as Ambassadors would agree that it was necessary to protect diplomatic agents against pressure and subversion, in the interest of security".

In Washington, D.C., in the same year, Secretary of State Dean Rusk sent a circular note to the foreign ambassadors saying that the Department of State had requested the Board of Commissioners of the District of Columbia to publish a new regulation instructiong the Metropolitan Police Department to issue regular summonses for parking violations by vehicles bearing diplomatic licences. The note added that the Department expect that any charges imposed on account of parking violations would be promptly paid. Soon after, the Department of State revised its ruling, after witnessing some countermeasures against United States Embassies.

In November 1935, in the United States, the Iranian Minister, Ghaffar Djalal, while driving through Elkton, Maryland, was detained and charged with violating traffic regulations. The Minister and his chauffeur were arrested and taken before the Justice of Peace. The Minister lodged a protest with the Department of State. The Secretary of State, Cordell Hull, in his reply expressed apologies for the incident and informed the Minister that the offending officers had been tried and fined and were no longer in the public service. He pointed out, however, that the incident would not have occurred had the chauffeur observed the regulations. The Secretary concluded: "In this connection I may state that this Government has at all times impressed upon its own diplomatic officers in foreign countries that the enjoyment of diplomatic immunity imposes upon then the obligation and responsibility of affording scrupulous regard to the laws and regulations, both national and local, of the countries to which they are accredited. I feel confident that the Iranian Government will share the view that this Government is justified in expecting that foreign diplomatic officers accredited to the United States will manifest a similar regard for the laws and regulations in force in this country". Thirty days after M. Cordell Hull's public declaration, the Iranian Government recalled Minister Djalal to Teheran.

Chapter XXII

IMMUNITY FROM GIVING EVIDENCE

As a consequence of his immunity from local jurisdiction, a diplomatic agent cannot be obliged to give evidence either in civil or in criminal proceedings.

If a diplomatic agent could be compelled to be a witness – and this would consequently involve disrespect of his personal inviolability – a judge or a lawyer might be able to force him to disclose confidential documents or information.

As far as civil proceedings are concerned, the immunity from jurisdiction is relative, and, therefore, this should be taken into consideration. The International Law Commission, however, after having discussed the subject, reached the conclusion "that there is no obligation of a diplomatic agent to testify, i.e., to give evidence as a witness".

Even the functional necessity theory, which is considered the main basis of diplomatic privileges and immunities and usually tends to limit their application, was cited by the Secretary of the Commission, Mr. Yuen-li Liang, to prove that a diplomat's immunity from the obligation to give evidence was intimately connected with his functions in the sense that the giving of evidence would take up a great deal of his time.

Disregarding the two radical theses which say, on the one hand, that a diplomat cannot give evidence and on the other, that he may do so, two other approaches to the problem remain. The first, which has always been widely supported and accepted, considers that the diplomat cannot be compelled to give evidence, athough he can in certain circumstances agree to do so if he is invited to by the local authorities. According to the second approach the beneficiary of immunity can in certain circumstances be obliged to give evidence as a witness. Commenting the 1957 draft of the Commission the Italian Government proposed that the relevant part of the article should be amended to read: "A diplomatic agent is not obliged to give evidence concerning questions which are in any manner whatsoever connected with his duties. In other cases, he may not be summoned to appear before the judicial authority. If it should be necessary for the local judicial authority to take deposition from the diplomatic agent, the said authority shall proceed to his residence in order to receive his statement orally, or the said authority shall delegate a competent official for this purpose, or else shall request the agent

to make the statement in writing". Even though Professor Ago defended his Governemnt's position, pointing out that there was a certain inconsistency in the article as drafted, since a diplomatic agent's refusal to give evidence might hinder the settlement of the case, the Commission felt that the immunity should be absolute and not qualified. The Commission, however, taking into account the objections raised, decided that the language of the paragraph could be toned down and paragraph 2 of Article 31 reflects this opinion ("A diplomatic agent is not obliged to give evidence as witness").

In Vienna, the Italian Delegation re-introduced the idea and Professor R. Monaco explained that although the diplomatic agent did not have to give evidence about a matter connected in any way with his functions and that in other cases he could not be compelled to appear before a judicial authority, the re-draft provided that a court of law desiring a statement from him should submit a written list of questions. The Italian amendment was later withdrawn since in the long run it was only a half-measure and did not change the basic rule.

The Netherlands Government, however, suggested the redrafting of the paragraph with the object of establishing the cases in which the diplomatic agent could not refuse to collaborate. In its comments on the 1957 draft of the International Law Commission it suggested that the pertinent paragraph should be amended to read: "a diplomatic agent is not obliged to give evidence except in the cases coming under sub-paragraphs (a), (b) and (c) of paragraph 1".

Mr. Douglas L. Edmonds observed in the International Law Commission that it was clear from paragraph 1 that a diplomatic agent could, in addition to performing his official functions, also engage in private activities. Surely, he added, "the immunity could not extend to cases in which the diplomatic agent had been acting in his private capacity. If a diplomatic agent could not be compelled to give evidence in such cases, he would be able to escape the consequences of any transaction into which he entered in his private capacity".

If the rule suggested by the Netherlands Government had been accepted, it could be interpreted as meaning that any member of a diplomatic mission could be summoned to give evidence in all the cases in which the local courts are competent under paragraph 1 of Article 31. In order to eliminate such a possibility the Vienna Convention states clearly that "a diplomatic agent is not obliged to give evidence as a witness".

The presence or absence of a diplomatic agent as a witness can become important in criminal proceedings, especially if he was a witness in a serious crime or in a traffic accident. In such cases there is a moral obligation to co-operate with the local authorities. In some countries it is easy for the diplomatic agent to co-operate with them, since he can either make a statement to the competent authorities in the diplomatic mission or else send

them an affidavit. The question becomes more delicate in those countries where evidence is required to be given orally in a Court, in the presence of the accused and where he can be subjected to cross-examination.

John Bassett Moore mentions the case of the Netherlands Minister at Washington who, in 1856, was requested by the Secretary of State to appear in court to give evidence regarding a homicide committed in his presence. By the unanimous advice of his colleagues he refused. Representations were made to the Netherlands Government by that of the United Sates, which, while admitting that in virtue of international usage and the law of the United States, the Minister had the right of refusal, appealed to the general sense of justice of the Netherlands Government. The latter, however, declined to give the desired instructions, but authorized the minister to make his declaration under oath, and he accordingly offered to do so at the Department of State, adding that he could not be submitted to cross-examination. The offer was declined, as the district Attorney-General reported that such a declaration would not be admitted as evidence.[1] At the trial of Guiteau in the United States, in 1881, for the assassination of President Garfield, the Venezuelan Minister, Señor Comancho, was called as a witness for the prosecution. Under instructions from his Government, he was authorized to waive his rights and appear as a witness in the case.

The Havana Convention (1928) on Diplomatic Officers states clearly that diplomats "may refuse to appear as witnesses before the territorial courts" (Article 21). The Convention on Consular Agents, signed on the same day, is much more explicit and states that "in criminal cases the prosecution or the defence may request attendance of consular agents at the trial as witnesses".

The legislation of some States contains specific provisions on the subject. A Decree of 1932 of the Austrian Government says in Article 29 that "if testimony is to be taken from a person enjoying exterritorial status, the Federal Ministry of Justice shall be advised accordingly, with particulars of the parties, as to the subject of the evidence and the date on which the person is to testify (if at all). The Ministry shall arrange for the said person to be invited either to be present in court at the specified time for the purpose of testifying, or to state whether he is prepared to make a statement before a committee delegated by the court to take his testimony, or to make a statement in writing on the matter on which he is to be questioned".

The 1935 Colombian decree defining the privileges and immunities of foreign diplomatic agents provides that "if the testimony of a member of the diplomatic corps is necessary in a proceeding, the competent judicial authority shall transmit to him, through the Ministry for Foreign Affairs, a copy of the pertinent documents together with a note requesting him, if he consents,

1. John Bassett Moore, "A Digest of International Law", vol. IV (Washington, D.C., 1906), p. 643, § 662.

to make a statement in the from of a sworn declaration" (Article 6).

But as we have already seen, in some countries testimony, in order to be valid, must be given in court in the presence of the defendant. During the Vienna Conference, the U.S.S.R. submitted an amendment to include the following sentence: "If he agrees to give such evidence, he need not attend for that purpose any court or other authority of the receiving State". This amendement Mr. Cameron said he would vote against since, under the United States Constitution the defence had the right to require the appearance of witnesses in courts. Sir Francis Vallat said that it would give rise to difficulties of application in common-law countries, for in those countries witnesses were required to appear in court. He went on to add that the amendment was not sufficiently clear. "If it meant that the diplomat was under an obligation not to appear, his delegation would be unable to accept it since it would be incompatible with United Kingdom law. If on the other hand it meant simply that the diplomat had the option of submitting his evidence in some manner other than that laid down in the receiving State—and he considered that was the situation—the receiving State would none the less be entitled to interpret the diplomat's objections as a refusal to testify".

The attitude of the two common-law countries was, however, unfortunate, since the aim of the Conference was to codify international law on the matter and not to adapt it to the various national legislations. It must also be born in mind that a foreign diplomat will always have misgivings about appearing before a local court where he might be forced to answer insidious and violent questions in a language over which he has not sufficient command. In Vienna it was stressed that the testimony of the diplomatic agent could be read in court and in the absence of other depositions it might be of extreme value if, for example, he were the only witness to a crime.

The rule we find in the Vienna Convention corresponds to internationally accepted practice, according to which a diplomatic agent cannot be obliged to bear witness in court, even though he should whenever possible co-operate with the local authorities. Article 31 of the Convention recognizes the diplomatic agent's right not to give evidence, but Article 32 makes it possible for him to waive his immunity, thus permitting him to offer his collaboration in clearing up a problem.

Chapter XXIII

WAIVER OF IMMUNITY FROM JURISDICTION

Among the cases in which local courts are competent to judge persons entitled to immunity from jurisdiction, in civil as well as in criminal matters, we must mention the waiver by the sending State of that person's immunity.

Doctrine and universal practice are rather vague on some of the principal issues regarding waiver. In the first place there used to be a certain doubt about the right of a diplomatic agent to renounce his immunity; secondly, doubts existed as to the procedure to be adopted in civil and in criminal cases; and, thirdly, there were also doubts as to the competence of the head of mission to waive the immunity of the administrative, technical and service personnel, and of a diplomatic agent to waive the immunity of a member of his family.

The general opinion of writers was that a diplomatic agent could not, on his own initiative, waive his immunity, since such immunity is not granted in his personal interest, but exclusively in the interest of the sending State. This position was firmly endorsed by the Vienna Convention and is in harmony with the basic position adopted as regards privileges and immunities, namely that "The purpose of such privileges and immunities is not to benefit individuals but to ensure the efficient performance of the functions of diplomatic missions as representing States".

Article 32 of the Vienna Convention provides that "the immunity from jurisdiction of diplomatic agents and of persons enjoying immunity under article 37 may be waived by the sending State", settling this question once and for all.

The International Law Commission's draft was categorical as regards the waiver in criminal cases, but raised doubts as to the correct procedure in civil and administrative cases. As a result of the modifications introduced in Vienna in 1961, under which express waiver is necessary in every case, this question was also settled.

Even though the waiver must be express, doubts still linger as to the *modus faciendi*, since local courts might still have doubts, in a given case, if the waiver had been made in correct form.

Strictly speaking, if the head of mission renounces in the name of his government, one must presume that he was duly authorized to act in this manner; if no authorization was received the question must be presumed to

be purely an internal matter, between the head of mission and his government. In the opinion of Professor Ago the receiving State was entitled to regard a declaration by the head of mission as final; the sending State might regret the head of mission's action, but it could not repudiate it. Professor Spiropoulus, however, disagreed on this point and thought that the sending State could repudiate the waiver by the head of mission as long as the repudiation was made immediately.

In 1958, during the discussions in the International Law Commission Gilberto Amado pointed out that the head of a diplomatic mission must always be presumed to be speaking in the name of his Government. If a note from a head of mission was sufficient to produce the severance of diplomatic relations between two countries or even more serious consequences, he could not understand why it should not be sufficient to waive the immunity of a third secretary, for example. It was difficult to conceive—he went on to say—that a head of mission would not first have consulted his Government on a matter of such importance as a waiver of immunity, in which political issues out of all proportion to the person concerned might be involved.

Where it is a question of waiving the immunity of the head of the mission himself local courts should demand a formal document. The International Law Commission went into the problem but reached the conclusion that it would be wiser not to specify through whom the communication was to be made, whether through the prime minister, the minister for foreign affairs, or the ambassador. The question whether the Government should delegate power to its ambassador to decide in certain cases or not was a matter for the particular State. The question of the channel through which the communication was conveyed was immaterial.

As regards the other members of the staff of the mission there seems to be a certain consensus that the head of mission has power to waive the immunity. Such a right is still easier to accept with regard to the members of his family and the private staff. In 1958, the Italian Government proposed the addition of the following rule: "The head of mission may waive the immunity of members of his staff from jurisdiction on his own authority". The Swedish Government also was of the opinion that according to present international practice it is generally deemed enough that the head of mission waives the immunity of the other persons belonging to the mission.

In Vienna a joint amendment was submitted stating that, in addition to the diplomatic agent, other persons were entitled to diplomatic immunities. This amendment was accepted; the draft of the International Law Commision was amended accordingly, and the article as it now stands mentions also "persons enjoying immunity under article 37".

Paragraph 2 of article 32 is an innovation since it modifies the International Law Commission's draft by saying that "Waiver must always be express". The provision found in paragraph 2 of article 30 of the Inter-

national Law Commission's draft corresponded to prevailing international practice before the 1961 conference according to which a distinction was drawn between criminal and civil proceeding: in the former case, the waiver was to be express; in the latter case it might be express or implied. Doctrine taught that in civil proceedings a valid waiver could be inferred if the diplomatic agent brought an action in a civil court or if he contested an action brought against him in a civil court. In such a case he was not entitled to claim immunity later when it was brought before a higher court.

In almost every intervention in the International Law Commission its members called attention to the difference in procedure in civil and criminal jurisdiction. Explaining the rationale of this difference, Sir Gerald Fitzmaurice pointed out that criminal proceedings were never instigated by individuals, they constituted in a sense an act of State, and the immunity of the diplomatic agent was, at least in part, of a personal character, though there might be prior arrangements between him and his sending State regarding the waiver of it.

In Vienna however the Conference abandoned the traditional position and acting *de lege ferenda* decided to delete at the beginning of the paragraph the words "In criminal proceedings". Mr. Gasiorowski, introducing the Polish delegation's amendment, said that the deletion was the logical consequence of the fundamental principle on which the draft was based, namely that diplomatic immunities were established not for the diplomatic agent's benefit but by reason of the functions which he exercised, and hence for the sending State's benefit.

Even though the new text does not give rise to doubts, the necessity of an express waiver in every case may give rise to certain difficulties, namely in the contracts regarding the rent of premises for the private use of diplomats in which it is normal to include a clause saying that local courts will be competent in case of disagreement between the parties. When this point was raised in the International Law Commission, Professor Bartos said that in the United States, the United Kingdom and in France, for instance, case law was unanimous in the view that acceptance by diplomatic agents of the jurisdiction clause in leases and hire contracts implied that they thereby automatically waived their immunity from civil jurisdiction.

Paragraph 3 of article 32 provides that "the initiation of proceedings by a diplomatic agent or by a person enjoying immunity from jurisdiction under article 37 shall preclude him from invoking immunity from jurisdiction in respect of any counter-claim directly connected with the principal claim". The International Law Commission commenting on its draft article pointed out that "it goes without saying that proceedings, in whatever court or courts, are regarded as an indivisible whole, and that immunity cannot be invoked on appeal if an express or implied waiver was given in the court of first instance".

This paragraph was suggested by Professor François and gave rise to a prolonged discussion which went a long way towards clarifying the nature of a waiver by a diplomatic agent. Professor Roberto Ago, in view of the doubts raised as to the right of a diplomat to initiate an action, said that "the fact that a diplomatic agent enjoyed that immunity did not mean that the jurisdiction of the receiving State would never be able to operate with respect to that agent, even when he himself had recourse to that jurisdiction. Enjoying immunity from jurisdiction meant simply enjoying the right not to be object of judicial proceedings, in other words not being bound to appear as defendant in the courts in consequence of proceedings instituted against him. The immunity in question had never meant the inability to appear as a plaintiff before the same courts. Nor did the immunity mean that the courts were never competent to deal with cases in which a diplomatic agent was implicated. Later on, Professor Ago had the opportunity to stress that the question of implied waiver did not arise when the diplomatic agent had personally begun proceedings since "there could be no question of waiving immunity where it had never existed".

An apparent contradiction exists between the rule that waiver must always be express and come from the sending State and paragraph 3 under which a diplomatic agent may appear as a plaintiff, but in such a case it should be understood that the diplomatic agent must obtain previously his government's consent before entering into litigation in the receiving State.

When Professor Sandström's draft which contained a provision on the lines of paragraph 4 was brought up for consideration, Professor Jaroslav Zourek, Chairman of the International Law Commission in 1957 said that it laid down a principle that was universally recognized. No objection was raised then or in 1958. During the Vienna Conference, however, amendments were submitted in favour of its deletion. The delegate from Venezuela explained that there were two schools of thought on the question of separate waiver for the execution of judgement: in many countries, including his own, it was inconceivable that if diplomatic immunity had been waived for legal proceedings it was not automatically waived for the execution of judgement. In his opinion, it would be better to delete the paragraph, thus leaving each country to interpret the article according to its own law.

The various amendments to the paragraph were rejected and the text finally adopted reads as follows: "Waiver of immunity from jurisdiction in respect of civil or administrative proceedings shall not imply waiver of immunity in respect of the execution of the judgement, for which a separate waiver shall be necessary".

Even though from a theoretical point of view waiver of immunity from proceedings should imply waiver with regard to the execution of the judgement, practical considerations justify the maintenance of the distinction. In certain cases, the sending State may waive the immunity with the

intention of clarifying a question, especially in criminal cases, even though it might not wish to see executive measures adopted. On the other hand, the distinction which we find in article 32 is accepted by international law and there would be no advantage in abolishing a rule which had wide international acceptance. The standard case mentioned in this sense is *Suarez v. Suarez* (1917) in which the defendant, Bolivian Minister in London, had waived immunity and an order had been made by the court. Plaintiff issued summons for leave to proceed to execution, but the court held, after reviewing the authorities, that: "There is a consensus of opinion among textwriters, concurred by Astbury, J. (*in In re Republic of Bolivia Exploration Syndicate, Ltd.*), that any writ of execution directed against personal property is null and void under the statute (of 7 Anne, c. 12), and that it is immaterial that the Ambassador has up to that point in the action submitted to the jurisdiction, or even invoked it. . . I think the proper course is to make no order on the summons except that it does stand over generally, with liberty to restore in the event of the defendant ceasing to hold an office to which the immunity he asserts is attached".

With regard to the waiver of diplomatic immunity, one should also refer to the various amendments and speeches made during the Vienna Conference deploring the abusive use of immunity from jurisdiction, especially in the case of road traffic accidents, since it is hardly admissible that a person injured by the act of a diplomat or of a member of his family should have no effective redress. Various suggestions were put forward, but the conference feared that they all weakened the principle of absolute immunity in criminal proceedings. The solution finally reached was to adopt a special resolution recommending that "the sending State should waive the immunity of members of its diplomatic mission in respect of civil claims of persons in the receiving State when this can be done without impeding the performance of the functions of the mission, and that, when immunity is not waived, the sending State should use its best endeavours to bring a just settlement of the claims".

Chapter XXIV

EXEMPTION FROM TAXATION

It is a rule of international law that diplomatic missions and its members are exempt from dues and taxes in the receiving State. Even though national, provincial and municipal law are precise in determining their taxes, international law, on the contrary, is obliged to avoid going into details, due to the impossibility of conciliating the tax system and nomenclature of all countries.

Exemption is the word used to identify the non-submission of the diplomatic mission and of the diplomatic agent to the fiscal laws and the taxing authorities of the local government, even though the expression fiscal *immunities* is also to be found. The Vienna Convention, like the International Law Commission, speaks of exemption.

Writers as a general rule do not enter into details as to the tax exemptions acknowledging the rule in outline. The attempts at codification also avoided going into the matter. Professor Diena of the Committee of Experts for the Progressive Codification of International Law, established by the League of Nations, was of the opinion the "it must be admitted that these privileges are not suitable for any detailed regulation which could be adopted in the form of a collective treaty. . . Accordingly, it is only possible for States to conclude detailed agreements in this matter by means of bilateral conventions based on reciprocity. At the time, it is not necessary to exclude the possibility of a collective agreement, but this should constitute the minimum; i.e., it might be possible to obtain agreement to the adoption of certain universally accepted rules". The Harvard draft took an even more pessimistic approach, "since they vary greatly from state to state, it would seem impracticable to fix, by a study of national legislation, an absolute minimum of exemptions granted by every state which would not be so restrictive as to be unnacceptable to some".

The fact that the Vienna Convention should have been able to adopt rather complete articles on the fees and charges levied by the mission, exemptions of the diplomatic mission and of its members from dues and taxes and, finally, the exemptions from custom duties and taxes on objects for the use of the mission and of the members of the mission must be recognized as a remarkable demonstration of legal draftmanship.

The adoption of these articles puts an end to the discussion as to the

nature of the exemption from taxation, considered until recently as non-essential, based on international courtesy and not strictly necessary for the exercise of diplomatic functions. States linked to the Vienna Convention are obliged to grant the exemptions and as regards those that have not as yet ratified or adhered to it the commentary of the International Law Commission can be considered the yardstick in the matter: "although the degree varies from country to country, it may be regarded as a rule of international law that such exemptions exist, subject to certain exceptions".

Even though the articles of the Vienna Convention on Diplomatic Relations are quite explicit, as regards tax exemption it also contemplates, in Article 47, the possibility of a State applying its provisions restrictively because the other State acts likewise, that is on a basis of reciprocity; *contrariu sense*, nothing forbids a State from extending to another a more favourable treatment by custom or agreement. Such restrictive or liberal applications shall be decided by the ministry for external affairs in collaboration with the taxing authorities.

Fiscal exemptions of the diplomatic mission

The Vienna Convention on Diplomatic Relations established a clear distinction between the fiscal exemptions granted to the diplomatic mission and those of the diplomatic agent, and endorsed the International Law Commission's commentary that the granting of exemptions to the diplomatic mission "is generally regarded as a rule of international law".

In 1928 the Havana Convention on Diplomatic Officers had already recognized these exemptions as a right in sub-paragraph 2 of Article 18: "Diplomatic officers shall be exempt in the State to which they are accredited: ... 2. From all land taxes on the building of the mission, when it belongs to the respective government". Attention must be drawn to the bad drafting of the article, since the exemption contemplated is not that of the diplomatic agent (or officer) but of the sending State, that cannot be subject to local jurisdiction.

Article 23 of the Vienna Convention mentions the exemptions of the diplomatic mission in the following terms: "1. The sending State and the head of the mission shall be exempt from all national, regional or municipal dues and taxes in respect of the premises of the mission, whether owned or leased, other than such as represent payment of specific services rendered". Sub-paragraph 1 leaves no doubt as to the possibility of a mission renting a building or part of a building. In the interpretation of this article attention must be drawn to sub-paragraph *i* of Article 1 under which the premises of the mission are the buildings or parts of buildings and the land ancillary thereto, irrespective of ownership, used for the purposes of the mission including the residence of the head of the mission".

Even though the object of the article is to recognize the fiscal exemption of the mission, the article is quite clear in stating that there is no exemption with regard to dues or taxes which represent payment of specific services rendered. The terminology we find in Article 23 is the same used in sub-paragraph *e* of Article 34, on tax exemptions enjoyed by the diplomatic agent. The phrase "payment for specific services rendered" was adopted by the International Law Commission in 1958 in the place of the 1957 formula, "payment for service actually rendered". The Government of Luxembourg stressed the fact that the delimitation between taxes "as represent payment for services actually rendered and general taxes does not appear to be the same in all countries. Certain benefits (e.g. police protection, lighting or cleaning of public thoroughfares) are apparently considered in some countries as services which give rise to remuneration, whereas in other countries these measures are public services covered by the general tax. In such cases, therefore, it would seem that the criterion for making a distinction must be the specific nature of the services and not that of services *actually rendered*, since any public service is actually rendered".

As it was pointed out, owing to the complexity of determining which dues and taxes should be paid by the diplomatic mission, the solution is usually to grant or deny them on the basis of *reciprocity* or *courtesy*. An attempt to define *dues* and *taxes* could take into consideration the fiscal legislation of one particular country, since one finds enormous variety of expressions even between countries speaking the same language. The expressions "impôts et taxes" in the French version of the Vienna Convention which correspond *grosso modo* to the "impuestos y gravámenes" we find in the Spanish version are usually employed in a specific sense. Thus, when we speak of *taxes* or *gravámenes* we are thinking of certain services put at the disposal of the tax payer who may or may not avail himself of them, such as water, street lighting, sewers, fire brigade, police and others of the same nature. Be that as it may, the practice of national, regional and municipal governments is to grant exemption to diplomatic mission of those direct taxes or general rates in which there is a direct link between the fiscal authorities and the tax-payer (in this case the diplomatic mission) creating the possibility of an eventual enforcement in the case of non-payment. It is usually understood that the diplomatic mission must pay for certain services actually rendered which can be supplied by the local government or by private companies, as is the case with water, electricity, telephones, sewers etc. Out of courtesy the government may exempt the diplomatic mission from some of these rates and even postal services.

The situation becomes more complex when the municipal authorities levy all dues, taxes and rates together, that is they do not separate those specific services from the general administrative services. In London, the problem used to be solved in a practical manner: the diplomatic missions paid the local

rates and subsequently the so-called non-beneficial portion was refunded on application to the Foreign Office. The refunded portion amounted to approximately 2/3 of the rates paid, the part not refunded was charged for services rendered by the Municipality for street lighting, street cleaning, garbage removal and partial payment for the cost of providing police protection. When the Vienna Convention on Diplomatic Relations entered into force in the United Kingdom a new procedure was adopted: The British Government assumed the responsibility for the initial payment of all general rates levied on both official premises and on property occupied as residences by all members of Embassies (excluding servants), with the exception of water and garbage rates. The repayment of the beneficial portions of rates are normally requested twice yearly from the mission concerned and the residence of members of the mission.

Since the premises of a diplomatic mission may not be the property of the foreign State but merely leased, the question arises as to the right of the mission to enjoy tax exemption in such a case. Article 23 of the Vienna Convention envisages both situations, but does not offer a satisfactory solution, that can be found in the comments of the International Law Commission to Article 21 of its draft: "the provision does not apply to the case where the owner of leased premises specifies in the lease that such taxes are to be defrayed by the mission. This liability becomes part of the consideration given for the use of the premises and usually involves, in effect, not the payment of taxes as such, but an increase in the rental payable". In other words, if the premises are occupied at rentals which are inclusive of rates, the mission cannot be regarded as qualifying for rating relief.

Tax exemption of the diplomatic agent

Diplomatic agents in the exercise of their functions enjoy certain tax exemptions, especially upon their persons, their income and their personal property. The evolution from 1928 to 1961 is quite remarkable. If one compares Article 18 of the Havana Convention, which merely states that the diplomatic officer shall be exempt "from all personal taxes, either national or local" with Article 34 of the Vienna Convention, one realizes the progress made in this field. The article lays down that:

> "A diplomatic agent shall be exempt from all dues and taxes, personal or real, national, regional or municipal, except:
> (a) indirect taxes of a kind which are normally incorporated in the price of goods or services;
> (b) dues and taxes on private immovable property situated in the territory of the receiving State, unless he holds it on behalf of the sending State for the purposes of the mission;
> (c) estate, succession or inheritance duties levied by the receiving State,

subject to the provisions of paragraph 4 of Article 39;

(d) dues and taxes on private income having its source in the receiving State and capital taxes on investments made in commercial undertakings in the receiving State;

(e) charges levied for specific services rendered;

(f) registration, court or record fees, mortgage dues and stamp duty, with respect to immovable property, subject to the provisions of Article 23".

It should be noted that the Vienna Convention also contains articles on customs exemptions (Article 36), exemption from militairy contributions (Article 35), and from social security provisions (Article 33).

Jurists usually present a cursory enumeration of those taxes which the diplomatist is not liable to. Raoul Genet, however, prefers to formulate his theory as follows: "in principle, the diplomatic agent is exempt from every direct personal tax; he is liable to remunerative administrative taxes; and, finally he enjoys a very wide import and export custom franchise".[1] This enumeration corresponds to the general theory governing the matter and to the provisions laid down in the Vienna Convention. Even though a precise distinction between direct and indirect taxation is lacking it fulfils a useful purpose in international law: exemption is recognized with regard to direct taxation since there is no doubt as to whom the tax-payer is and the fiscal onus cannot be transferred to a third party; in the indirect taxes, the sums are assessed impersonally. In the first case there would be the power of enforcement and a coaction in the act of collection of the dues or taxes; in the indirect taxes the diplomatic agent is free to buy or not the merchandise that has been levied.

The payment of a direct tax is unjustifiable and, in the long run, the exemption does not mean the non-payment of taxes since the diplomatic agent continues liable to the sending State and, as far as the treasury is concerned, there is no serious loss since the diplomatists of the receiving State enjoy the same exemption abroad but continue liable to its taxing authorities.

If the receiving State had the power of enforcement in regard to sums paid by the sending State such a faculty would represent an infringement of the rule *par in parem non habet jurisdictionem* since such a payment is an act of State.

Exemption from direct taxation, especially income tax, is aimed at the salaries received from the sending State as well as other sources of revenue from abroad. In this sense, Article 18 of the Havana Convention is open to abuse and it would have been better to adopt an enumeration of those taxes from which the diplomatic agent is exempt. The Vienna Convention is far

1. Raoul Genet, "Traité de Diplomatie et de Droit Diplomatique" vol. I (Paris, 1931), n. 396, p. 424.

more precise since it spells out two important exceptions to the general rule in sub-paragraph *b* and *d*.

The national legislation of many countries exempt foreign diplomats explicitly from the payment of income tax and even in those in which no such provision exists it is tacitly granted. Such exemptions are normally granted on a reciprocal basis and in many countries the rule is that the exemption does not apply to members of the embassy who are nationals of the receiving State. In some cases, the obligation to pay such taxes, including income tax, applies equally to foreigners who are permanently resident in the receiving State. The legal justification for the collection in these two cases (nationals of or permanent residents of the State) is doubtful since the source of revenue is the treasury of a foreign sovereign State that cannot be obliged to disclose the sums paid to the members of its staff, even if they are nationals of the receiving State. The assessment in such a case is difficult since the embassy is under no obligation to hand over a statement on such salaries and may even consider the disclosure as undesirable. Be that as it may, the Vienna Convention lays down in Article 38 that a diplomatic agent who is a national of or a permanent resident of the receiving State "shall enjoy only immunity from jurisdiction, and inviolability, in respect of official acts performed in the exercise of his functions". This article can be construed affirmatively or negatively; the general idea seems to be to consider such persons as subject to local legislation, but in a restrictive interpretation it would be equally valid to point out that the article only mentions immunity from jurisdiction and inviolability, and is silent as regards exemptions from dues and taxes.

The situation of the other members of the mission who are not nationals of or permanent residents of the receiving State is regulated in Article 37; members of the administrative and technical staff enjoy the exemptions enumerated in Article 34; members of the service staff and private servants of members of the mission enjoy "exemption from dues and taxes on the emoluments they receive by reason of their employment".

In principle, local authorities should not assess revenues derived from sources outside the receiving State and sub-paragraph *d* can be construed in this sense, since it obligates the diplomatic agent to pay dues and taxes on private incomes that have their source in the receiving State. If such is the case, incomes derived from abroad should be exempt. It is a well-known fact that the ambassadors of some countries must have a personal revenue since their salaries are insufficient. The Harvard draft mentions incomes "derived from sources outside the receiving State" among those that cannot be taxed by the local authorities. The provision we find in the Vienna Convention is more complex since it also speaks of investments in commercial undertakings in the receiving State, due to an unnecessary amendment tabled and accepted during the Conference.

The Vienna Convention also exempts the diplomatic agent from "all

personal services, from all public services of all kind whatsoever, and from military obligations such as those connected with requisitioning, military contributions and billeting". This article can also be considered superfluous and it should be remembered that neither Sandström's draft nor the International Law Commission's 1957 draft mentioned it. It was included owing to a suggestion of the Soviet Government, but the points raised were already covered by other provisions of the Convention. Articles 22 and 29 in proclaiming the inviolability of the premises of the mission and of the private residence of diplomatic agents had already excluded them from military requisitioning and billeting. When it admits fiscal exemption of the diplomatic mission and of the diplomatic agent in Articles 23 and 34 it also covers those contributions which can be levied in public emergencies and in case of militairy necessity.

Customs duties

Sixteenth-century writers, such as Octavian Maggi, already held that the ambassador and his suite need not pay customs duties on any baggage and goods brought into the country. In practice, during the sixteenth and seventeenth century ambassadors in England were definitely regarded as exempt from customs duties on goods accompanying them or consigned to them; indeed the customs searchers did not seem normally to have interfered with such property at all.[2] Later writers on the subject were in almost general agreement that the privilege of entry for articles destined for the use of the diplomatic mission or for the personal use of diplomatic agents rested upon international courtesy alone, and not upon any mandatory rule of international law. Some authors went even further and concluded that diplomatic agents did not enjoy exemption from customs duties. The International Law Commission in its commentaries on Article 34 adopted a pragmatical approach to the problem showing that "articles for the use of the mission are in practice exempted from customs duties, and this is generally regarded as a rule of international law". As regards articles destined for the personal use of diplomatic agents the Commission adopted another point of view saying "this exemption has been regarded as based on international comity. Since, however, the practice is so generally current, the Commission considers that it should be accepted as a rule of international law". With the entry of the Vienna Convention into force, this question lost all academic interest, since nowadays there can be no doubt as to the legal obligation of the receiving State to grant the exemption, subject however to the various limits laid down in the Convention.

2. E. R. Adair, "Exterritoriality of Ambassadors in the Sixteenth and Seventeenth Centuries". p. 95.

In practice, the principle of reciprocity plays an important role in this matter, so much so that in Vienna the French delegation was of the opinion that the granting of exemption should be expressly conditioned to reciprocity. This point was also raised more than once in the International Law Commission but it was considered necessary to formulate a basic rule of international law that might serve as a guide for States. But even though the article does not mention reciprocity specifically, it can be considered as covered by the opening statement that the free entry is subject to such laws and regulations as the receiving State may adopt. This interpretation is in harmony with Article 47 which gives States the right to apply the Convention restrictively or liberally.

The question of terminology was also raised in Vienna on more than one occasion with regard to this article, since some delegations were of the opinion that the expression *customs duties* was not sufficiently clear. The United States, for example, tabled an amendment since in that country there were both customs duties and import taxes. The opinion that finally prevailled was that the Convention should only lay down the general principle without going into details since an attempt to include every peculiarity would only create confusion. As regards the expression *customs duties* the commentary of the International Law Commission clarifies that it "means all duties and taxes chargeable by reason of import or export".

The Vienna Convention in Article 36 mentions in first place "articles for the official use of the mission". This exemption often figures in national legislations since the beneficiary is a foreign State and not an individual. The Brazilian legislation which grants customs exemptions subject to reciprocity, makes an exception in this case since no reference to reciprocity is made in the case of objects imported directly by a diplomatic mission.

The draft of the International Law Commission spoke of "articles for the use of a diplomatic mission". The word *official* resulted from a French amendment, the usefulness of which can be doubted since the possibility of an embassy importing an article for a non-official use seem highly improbable.

The Vienna Convention codified the most generally accepted rule as regards articles imported for personal use in sub-paragraph *b*, that grants customs exemptions on "articles for the personal use of a diplomatic agent or members of his family forming part of his household including articles intended for his establishment". In this sense, it must be remembered that a diplomatic agent is the head of mission or a member of the diplomatic staff of the mission (Article 1, sub-paragraph *e*). In certain countries, the exemption was only granted to the head of mission. The Vienna Convention puts all the members of the mission having diplomatic rank on the same footing, leaving the question as to who must request the exemption to the laws or regulation of the receiving State which may insist that the request

must be signed by the head of mission, or in his name.

The delicate question that had to be solved was regarding the situation of the administrative and technical staff. The 1958 International Law Commission's draft granted them the same privileges and immunities as those of the diplomatic staff. This position was strongly attacked in Vienna where, finally, the Conference rejected the innovation and their situation was regulated in paragraph 2 of Article 37, under which the member of the administrative and technical staff only enjoy the exemption in respect of articles imported at the time of first installation.

Certain countries that limit the number of articles that can be imported by embassies and diplomatists, attempted to introduce a provision in this sense. The best example is the amendment submitted by India that gave the receiving State the right to restrict the quantity of goods imported; to designate the period during which the import of articles for the establishment of the diplomatic agent must take place; and to specify a period within which goods imported duty free must not be re-sold. This question had already been clarified by the International Law Commission which had pointed out that it was covered by the phrase included in the *caput* of Article 36 "in accordance with such laws and regulations as it (*the receiving State*) may adopt", since these laws and regulations "cannot be regarded as inconsistent with the rule that the receiving State must grant the exemption in question".

The question of the examination of the personal luggage of diplomats is the object of paragraph 2 of Article 36 which provides: "The personal baggage of a diplomatic agent shall be exempt from inspection, unless there are serious grounds for presuming that it contains articles not covered by the exemptions mentioned in paragraph 1 of this Article, or articles the import or export of which is prohibited by the law or controlled by the quarantine regulations of the receiving State. Such inspection shall be conducted only in the presence of the diplomatic agent or of his authorized representative".

Even though an amendment by Switzerland saying that the exemption from customs duties did not apply "to articles in which the law of the receiving State expressly prohibits traffic for reasons of morality, security, health or law and order", was rejected, it does not mean that the embassy or the diplomatic agent is free to import articles the import of which is strictly forbidden.

The paragraph also forbids the export of articles of high historical, artistic or archaeological value, taking into account a number of abuses by diplomats in the past.

Following an Australian amendment, the receiving State may also forbid the entry of animals or plants in violation of its quarantine regulations.

Should the customs authorities have reason to suspect that the luggage contains objects the entry or exit of which is prohibited they may conduct an inspection. In such a case, the inspection must be in the presence of the agent or of his authorized representative.

Chapter XXV

PERSONS ENTITLED TO DIPLOMATIC PRIVILEGES AND IMMUNITIES

The general practice is to accord to members of the diplomatic staff of the Mission and their families the same privileges and immunities as are enjoyed by heads of missions, and as the International Law Commission points out, "this is a rule of international law". The legal situation of the other members of the mission has, however, been far from clear not only in State practice but also in the writings of jurists.

The uncertainties in this field find a very satisfactory solution in the Vienna Convention, and a comparative study of the Havana Convention of 1928, the Harvard Draft, Professor Sandström's first draft and the final draft of the International Law Commission shows how the matter has evolved over a relatively short period.

In the International Law Commission and at Vienna in 1961 the principal difficulty consisted precisely in determining the legal situation of the administrative and technical staff. It is symptomatic that in this very controversial matter the Conference did not accept the position advocated by the Commission, as a progressive step, that the administrative and technical personnel should enjoy the same privileges and immunities as the members of the diplomatic staff. The Vienna Conference, while recognizing the present importance of the duties of the administrative and technical personnel, finally decided that it was as yet premature to grant them those same privileges.

Article 37 as drafted represents an important step in the evolution of international law and is the result of very hard and conscientious examination of the problem and in it we find four paragraphs dealing with the privileges and immunities of four categories of persons entitled to them.

To understand the development that has taken place it is enough to say that Professor Sandström's draft was in favour of granting privileges and immunities to the "personnel of the mission, including the administrative and service personnel". In paragraph 3 the draft went on to grant these privileges and immunities to "private servants of foreign nationality". In other words, full privileges and immunities were to be granted not only to the members of the diplomatic staff and their families, but also to the administrative and technical staff, the service staff and even to foreign private servants, thus creating an undesirable legal situation under which a very large number of

persons would not be subject to the local courts. Even though the International Law Commission was of the opinion that privileges and immunities should be granted in relation to the work of the mission as an organic whole, it was unable to go so far with regard to the service staff, which it though should enjoy immunity only in respect of acts performed in the exercise of their duties, and exemption from dues and taxes on emoluments they received by reason of their employment.

Taking into account Article 37 and its precedents we feel that it is necessary to study separately not four categories but six: 1) the head of mission; 2) diplomatic personnel of the mission; 3) members of the family of a diplomatic agent; 4) members of the administrative and technical staff of the mission and the members of their families; 5) service staff; 6) private servants.

Nowadays, the position of the head of mission and that of the other members of the diplomatic staff is almost identical. Previously, however, the situation was different and even recently a great number of countries still used to establish a distinction between the status of the head of mission and that of the other diplomats, in connection with customs exemptions. The articles of the Vienna Convention regarding privileges and immunities employ a wider expression—diplomatic agent—which includes both categories. But this proviso does not mean that the receiving State is obliged to grant diplomatic status to all the officials appointed by the sending State; in view of its interest in avoiding the recognition of such privileges and immunities to an excessive number of persons it may limit the list of beneficiaries.

The civil and military attachés enjoy the same rights as secretaries of embassies of legations. The increase of the diplomatic functions made it necessary to appoint all kinds of officials with the title of *attachés*, in order that they could be included in the diplomatic list.

The receiving State has the right to refuse such attachés diplomatic status. In other words, it is up to the receiving State to decide which persons may be included in the diplomatic list.

Great Britain for a long time refused to accept the nomination of cultural and labour attachés. Accordingly the foreign office refused in 1925 to accord diplomatic status to the members of the United States Treasury, who were in London at that time collecting financial data, on the ground that their functions were merely of an internal nature.

In principle, inclusion in the diplomatic list means that that person enjoys diplomatic immunities, but this formality must not be considered as a *sine qua non* condition for the enjoyment of immunities. Conversely, the inclusion of a name does not automatically give the right to diplomatic privileges.

In Great Britain "a statement made to the Court by the Secretary of State for Foreign Affairs or by the Attorney-General on the instructions of the

Foreign Office, as to the status of a person claiming diplomatic immunity, whether as ambassador or as a member of an ambassador's staff, is accepted by the Court as being conclusive (Engelke v. Mussman); and in any case of uncertainty the Court will apply to the Foreign Office for information (Duff v. Kelantan Government). It is usual for a list of persons attached to an embassy to be furnished to the Secretary of State for Foreign Affairs, but inclusion in or omission from the list is not conclusive as to the status of a person claiming privilege".

A similar practice exists in the United States of America, where the reply of the Department of State is often conveyed to the Court by the medium of a procedural device known as a *Suggestion*. The suggestion is a formal document which sets out the facts in issue and it comments thereon, sometimes at length. The Suggestion however does not seem to be as conclusive as the Foreign Office Certificate, even though the American courts have considered themselves bound by, and will accord great respect to a Suggestion of the Executive recognizing and allowing a claim of immunity, so long as it is not concerned too obviously with questions of pure law.

Article 37 of the Vienna Convention mentions in the first place members of the family of a diplomatic agent forming part of his household. The privileges and immunities are not applicable to all members of the family but only to those who actually live with the diplomatic agent and are under his responsibility. If by chance a diplomat's son sets himself up and practises any professional activity or lives apart from his father, he will not enjoy privileges or immunities.

Only the members of the families of the diplomatic staff of the Mission enjoy full privileges and immunities, while the status of the families of the other members of the Mission is subject to certain restrictions.

The Vienna Convention did not suceed in defining the word *family*, and although such a definition was considered necessary it was not possible to reconcile the countless suggestions put forward. The Convention finally adopted the expression "members of the family of a diplomatic agent forming part of his household", which corresponds to the formula adopted in Havana in 1928 by the Bustamante Code. The interpretation of the expression "forming part of his household" will be up to the local protocol.

There have been attempts to limit the scope of the expression "members of the family". The International Law Commission studied, but did not accept, a proposal which limited the privileges and immunities to the wives and children under the age of 18.

Article 37 does not accord privileges and immunities to members of the diplomat's family who are nationals of the receiving State. According to the Vienna Convention, an ambassador or minister's wife will continue subject to the local courts and may even be arrested if she is a national of the receiving State. It is obvious that in such circumstances the inviolability and the im-

munity of the diplomatic agent will be fictitious since he will be vulnerable through his wife.

With regard to the immunities granted to the members of the family of a diplomatic agent it is worth examining the legal situation of his wife apart from that of the other members of his family. There is no doubt that the immunities granted to the diplomatic agents are extended to their wives.

Even though the Vienna Convention says that the wife must form part of the diplomatic agent's household it has been admitted that she can have a different residence or domicile from that of her husband.

Which other members of the diplomatic mission enjoy immunity from jurisdiction? An increase in the member of persons who are entitled to diplomatic immunity is an evil from the point of view of the local administration.

When the International Law Commission began to study which persons were entitled to diplomatic privileges and immunities, the first serious problem raised was the adoption of a clear definition of the various categories. Up till then, the principal problem was the granting of such privileges and immunities to the auxiliary staff, which embraced secretaries, stenographers, archivists, mission chauffeurs etc, and to the non-official staff (private secretaries or servants). The question which was to create the greatest difference of opinion in Vienna, namely the status of the administrative and technical personnel, only arose after the Second World War.

As has been pointed out earlier, the International Law Commission in its draft put the administrative and technical personnel and their families on the same footing as the diplomatic agents and their families for the reasons summarized as follows. "It is the function of the mission as an organic whole which should be taken into consideration, not the actual work done by each person. Many of the persons belonging to the services in question perform confidential tasks which, for the purposes of the mission's functions, may be even more important than the tasks entrusted to some members of the diplomatic staff. . . For these reasons, and because it would be difficult to distinguish between the various members or categories of the administrative and technical staff, the Commission recommends that the administrative and technical personal should be accorded not only immunity from jurisdiction in respect of official acts performed in the course of their duties but, in principle, all the privileges and immunities granted to the diplomatic staff".

The Vienna Conference, however, did not accept this course which was presented as a progressive step in the development of international law. The provision finally adopted (Article 37, paragraph 2) is most satisfactory since it places, in principle, the members of the administrative and technical staff on the same footing as the diplomatic personnel, but subjects them to certain restrictions. In other words, they enjoy personal inviolability and immunity from criminal jurisdiction. In civil matters they enjoy immunity in respect of official acts; but they do not enjoy immunity with respect to acts performed

outside the course of their duties. They are granted the same tax exemptions accorded to diplomats, but only enjoy customs exemption on articles imported at the time of the first installation.

There are three main conceptions concerning the privileges and immunities of the service personnel and of private servants. The first is that held by Great Britain and the United States, by both of which substantially the same privileges and immunities granted to diplomats are extended to the non-official personnel, subject to restrictive interpretations. The Diplomatic Privileges Act of 1708 (7 Anne, c. 12) which, as far as the United Kingdom is concerned, is the corner-stone of all diplomatic privileges and immunities, had already foreseen such an assimilation.

Italy and Brazil adopted up to 1961 a totally different policy and simply denied the non-official personnel such privileges and immunities.

Finally there is the middle solution with seemed to have the widest acceptance, recognizing that the privileges and immunities should be granted to the members of the service staff and private servants, provided they are not nationals of the receiving State. This solution was adopted explicitly in Article 19 of the German law of 1898, which recognized in the Reich immunity from jurisdiction to persons in the service of a foreign diplomatic agent, provided that they were not of German nationality.

The Vienna Convention gave a definite and satisfactory solution to the problem. Initially it established a distinction between the members of the service staff of the Mission and the private servants. The duties of these two categories can be similar and what distinguishes one from the other is that the wages of the service staff of the mission are paid by the sending State, while those of the private servants are paid directly by the members of the mission for whom they work.

The difficulty we run across in considering Article 37 is to establish the limits between the administrative and technical personnel and the service staff, since they are all functionaries of the sending State and, in consequence, paid by it. The difference lies, in the nature of their functions. The Rapporteur of the International Law Commission had occasion to explain that the term covered the subordinate official staff, such as messengers and chauffeurs, engaged in ancillary duties, in other words, what were known as *employés d'ambassade*. In many cases, the functions carried out may be similar to those of private servants, since chauffeurs, servants, waiters, *maîtres d'hôtel* and even cooks can be enlisted on the staff of an embassy, provided that they are included in the official pay-roll.

Article 24 of Professor Sandström's draft put the members of the service staff on the same footing as the administrative and technical personnel, and during the discussions on that subject this position was widely supported. In justifying his opinion Professor Sandström pointed out that he did not consider the question of the privileges and immunities from the individual

point of view of the beneficiaries, but viewed the mission as an integral whole.

The Vienna Convention endorsed the Commission's conclusion that it would be sufficient to accord the service staff immunities in respect of acts performed in the performance of their duties, and exemption from dues and taxes on their emoluments.

According to the 1961 Vienna Conference, private servants have a juridical position inferior to that of the members of the service staff.

It must be noticed, however, that there are many historic precedents for the granting of diplomatic privileges and immunities to the private servants of the head of the mission. We must not forget, however, that in the past the organization of the diplomatic mission was different.

In 1957, Sir Gerald Fitzmaurice said that the International Law Commission would not be innovating if it recognized private servants as entitled to certain privileges and immunities. Referring to the Diplomatic Privileges Act of 1708 he concluded that "the majority of the States accorded without any doubt to the private servants many immunities, although they did not consider themselves obliged to do it".

The Vienna Convention accepted the principle according to which private servants do not enjoy privileges and immunities, except exemption from income-tax. It also recognizes that the interests of the mission are satisfactorily protected if the receiving State exercises its jurisdiction over such persons without interfering unduly in the performance of the functions of the mission.

Paragraph 4 of Article 37 mentions the private servants of the *members of the mission*, widening therefore the roll of privileged servants, since general international law only occupied itself with the servants of the diplomatic personnel of the mission.

A special reference must be made to the status of the service staff and of the private servants under the labour laws of the receiving State. The draft of the International Law Commission was silent on this point. In Vienna a reference to Article 33 was added at the end of paragraph 3 of Article 37, although it would have been more appropriate to include this problem in Article 33 itself. As the service staff is generally hired locally, it is up to the mission to pay the dues imposed upon employers.

The situation of the private servants is covered by Article 33, which lays down that they are exempt from social security provisions as long as they are not nationals or permanently resident in the receiving State and that they are protected by the social security provisions in force in the sending State or in a third State. Although the *caput* of the Article grants exemption, the conditions enumerated transform the rule into the exception, since private servants are usually either nationals or permanent residents of the receiving State.

Part V

Protocol

Chapter XXVI

PROTOCOL

The idea of protocol is implicit in that of diplomacy. Protocol plays an important part in diplomatic intercourse, but it is merely a regulating function, a matter of method, aimed at making diplomatic intercourse easier, and it is usually only laymen who attach excessive importance to it.

Protocol or ceremonial is, above all, simply common sense applied to concrete cases in order to prevent confusion and disregard of the rights of others. It has been stated that one of the aims of protocol is to have the legal equality of all States respected and prevent local authorities from giving preferential treatment to the envoys of great powers or of particulary friendly countries in flagrant contrast to the way in which the ambassador of other countries are treated. Thus it may safely be said that the basic rules of protocol spring from the principle of the legal equality of States and that in these rules some of the most important manifestations of that equality are to be found. In this connection Article 14 § 2 of the Vienna Convention on Diplomatic Relations, may be quoted: "Except as concerns precedence and etiquette, there shall be no differentiation between heads of mission by reason of their class". Although the Article seems to distinguish between protocol and etiquette, its content is clear: the only distinctions tolerated in the treatment of foreign diplomats shall be those due to the category of the head of the mission; in other words, ambassadors will take precedence over ministers plenipotentiary, and protocol can lay down different norms for the presentation of the credentials of each.

Protocol differs from country to country, but nowadays certain practices and customs are universal. In general, the Ministry for Foreign Affairs lists local practices and customs as a guide for foreign diplomats.

Other important sources of protocol are found in multilateral treaties, as, for example, in the Franco-Ottoman Capitulation of 1740, in which the Sultan recognized the precedence of the Emperor of France over the Emperor of Spain and other sovereigns.

In dealing with the sources of protocol, we need to make special reference to comity (*Courtoisie Internationale* or *comitas gentium*) which plays such an important part in allowing more liberal and elastic interpretations of strict

legal norms and in making concessions that tend to improve the relations between States.

Another important factor in the application of protocol is that of reciprocity, which also leads to liberal or restrictive interpretations of the norms of protocol.

Almost every country has a so-called Protocol or Ceremonial Department which usually forms part of the Ministry for Foreign Affairs. Its task is to see that the accepted norms of protocol are respected both by the authorities of its own country and by the foreign Diplomatic Corps.

Ceremonial or Protocol is perhaps the part of diplomatic law that is most open to criticism and derision. But those who criticize it, and see in all that it does an opportunity for mockery and jibes, are exactly those who are most sensitive themselves when there own personal situation is at stake.

The truth is that Protocol is not a special attribute of diplomacy alone: rules for proper procedure and order are adopted as a matter of course in all professions and organizations where the absence of them would lead to misunderstandings and disagreements that might eventually prevent any effective work being done. In this respect, it should be noted that the system of ceremonial in the armed forces is far more rigid and formal than diplomatic ceremonial. To sum up, the rules of protocol are simply the product of common sense, which means that although they are expected to be obeyed, they must be applied without excessive formalism.

Chapter XXVII

CREDENTIALS

The most important document the head of a mission takes with him is his letter of credence or credentials (French: *lettre de créance*, Portuguese: *credenciais*, Latin: *litterae fidei*).

It is the document by which the head of the mission is accredited by his Sovereign or President to the Head of the State in which he is to exercise his functions. In it are indicated his name, his category and his mission, and the document invariably ends with a request to give entire credence to all his statements.

The letter of credence is entrusted to the ambassador or minister closed and sealed, and must be presented in that state to the Sovereign or President it is intended for. Together with the letter of credence, the agent also receives a true copy (*copie figurée*) of it, which, unlike the original, is handed to him open for him to convey to the Minister for Foreign Affairs on his first audience.

A diplomat may be the bearer of a letter recalling his predecessor. In such a letter of recall (*lettre de rappel*) the Head of State explains the reason for the termination of the mission. In theory the document should be presented by the outgoing diplomat, but in practice this is becoming less and less common.

The credentials of a chargé d'affaires *ad hoc* (i.e. permanent chargé d'affaires) are in the form of a note addressed by the Minister for Foreign Affairs of the sending State to his couterpart in the receiving State.

A chargé d'affaires *ad interim* (i.e. a temporary chargé d'affaires) is usually accredited by a note from the head of the outgoing mission, either definitively or provisionally. If the chargé d'affaires is entrusted with opening the Embassy or Legation he may be given a note addressed from Minister to Minister.

The solemn ceremony of presenting letters of credence has survived to our own times, but with embassies growing more numerous and increasing in size, the pomp and circumstance surrounding it has diminished a little. At present there are variations in the ceremony from one country to another, for a number of different influences are at work affecting the particular form of protocol. At Courts the ceremony is more ostentatious. Climate may influence the style of dress worn; hot countries are gradually giving up their

former insistence on the wearing of uniform, full dress coat or morning dress. The physical extent of the great capitals, in which embassies are frequently situated in new residential areas a long way from government offices, has led to the use of carriages with an escort of mounted horsemen being given up in favour of motor-cars with a motor-cycle escort. However, despite all the variations in the ceremonies adopted by the different countries, most of them do in general follow a common set of practices.

The head of a mission only officially begins to be considered as such from the moment he presents his credentials. This is the rule, but nowadays it is becoming more and more common to follow the practice accepted by Article 13 of the Vienna Convention, namely, that the head of a mission is considered as having taken up his functions in the receiving State either when he has presented his credentials or when a true copy of his credentials has been presented to the Minister for Foreign Affairs. The object of this second practice is to prevent it happening that a head of mission has to remain for a long time without being able to take up his functions when circumstances have made it impossible for him to present his credentials to the Head of the State.

The Foreign Office considers the head of a mission as taking up his functions, being able to sign treaties and be invited to receptions at Court, from the moment of the presentation of the true copies of his credentials. Though a pragmatic solution obviously aimed at simplifying diplomatic intercourse, this practice has no solid basis in law.

H. Accioly considers that if the letters of credence were signed by a head of State who has since ceased to exercise his functions, such letters ought not, in principle, to lose their value, for it should be borne in mind that the granter of the credentials is not properly the Head of the State but rather the actual government of the country, which is impersonal, the Head of State being merely the authority who represents the State in its external relations. This conclusions seems doubtful. It is the receiving State that will have to decide whether to accept or not such letters of credence signed by an ex-Head of State.

Generally speaking, the principal legal consequence of the presentation of credentials is the full recognition of the status of the ambassador or minister. But the acceptance or presentation of letters of credence and of the statements made in them may have important consequences. The acceptance of the credentials of an envoy of a country whose *de facto* government is not recognized by the receiving State implies recognition of that government, and, conversely, the presentation of credentials to the head of a *de facto* government would signify that the government was now recognized.

Similarly, a sovereign may refuse to receive credentials in which not all his titles are enumerated, for the deliberate exclusion of one will be interpreted as non-recognition of it. The most important example of this came about on

9 may 1936 when King Victor Emmanuel III of Italy assumed the title of Emperor of Ethiopia, which implied not only the recognition of the title of Emperor, but also, and this was much more serious, the legitimacy of Italy's annexation of Ethiopia. The problem thus raised had to be faced immediately, for the French Government had recalled its embassador and had already appointed his successor, Ambassador de St. Quentin. The Italian Government made it known that if the King's new title was not used in the letter of credence, the ambassador would not be received; its being used, on the other hand, would *ipso facto* imply recognition of the conquest of Ethiopia. France chose to be represented in Rome by a chargé d'affaires, and when a year had passed without the new ambassador being appointed, Italy granted indefinite leave to its ambassador at Paris. During 1938 a number of States recognized the King of Italy as Emperor and on 14 October 1938 the Italian Chargé d'affaires at Paris was informed of the French Government's decision to send an ambassador and to recognize the King as Emperor of Ethiopia. M. François Poncet was designated three days later and his name was at once accepted; Italy, in turn, designated a new ambassador to Paris.

Chapter XXVIII

DIPLOMATIC PRECEDENCE

Precedence consists in the right to occupy the place of honour at a ceremony or an official meeting. Since 1815 the legal and diplomatic problems of precedence has lost its importance with the adoption of the regulation approved by the Congress of Vienna on 19 March of that year, which states that "the precedence of diplomatic agents of the same class shall be determined in accordance with the date of the official notification of their arrival" (art. 4). Up to the adoption of the rule, which is now observed without dispute, the fixing of precedence was the most delicate of diplomatic problems, owing to the presence of different diplomatic missions and agents in one State at the same time.

The thesis put forward by Martin de Lodi at the beginning of the fifteenth century that the envoy of a greater prince should take precedence over the envoy of a lesser one inevitably led to a series of clashes since no ambassador was prepared to allow another to rank higher than himself.

From an early period the Popes alloted themselves the right to fix the precedence of sovereigns and other Heads of States. They themselves, *ipso facto*, took precedence over everybody else, with the Emperor of the Holy Roman Empire in the second place. When the "Embassy of Obedience" from the king of England was received by Pope Julius II on 12 May 1504, the order adopted was considered as having been laid down by the Pope himself and was consequently from then on observed as such.

Most writers who have dealt with the Pope's list state that it has no legal value, but it can be fairly safely asserted that normally the order of precedence thus established must have been the one accepted by Papal ceremonial. with, of course, variations imposed by changing circumstances and by the course of history itself. Igino Cardinale reproduces it as an authentic document, which seems to settle the matter beyond dispute.

At a later period the Papacy had occasion to express itself officially on the question of the precedence of kings, with a view to clearing up disputes that had arisen.

During the negotiations at Carlowitz at the end of the seventeenth century, which culminated in peace between Turkey, Austria, Poland and Venice, the question of the precedence of ambassadors was solved in a different way. A

large round pavilion was erected with as many doors as there were plenipotentiaries. The plenipotentiaries all entered at exactly the same moment and sat down at a round table at the places exactly facing their respective doors. Later on this round table system had to be given up, it having been decided that the place of honour was that facing the main door.

It is not suprising, then, that courts tried to limit the number of envoys "of a representative character" to as few as they could. By this time various systems had been proposed in an attempt to find an *a priori* solution for the problem, and Pradier Fodéré puts before us the nine most important ones adopted.

On the wedding of the Princess of Brazil, the heiress presumptive to the Portuguese throne, and her uncle the Infante Dom Pedro, the Marquis of Pombal sent a circular letter to the foreign representatives giving them information about the ceremony and also stating that in future the ambassadors to the court at Lisbon, with the exception of the papel nuncio and the ambassador of the Holy Roman Empire, would, whenever they were paying visits or having audiences granted to them, have their precedence determined in accordance with the date on which they had presented their credentials.

In view of the poor welcome given to the Portuguese proposal, no one would ever have dreamt that it would not only be accepted by the Congress of Vienna in 1815 but would also prove to be the definitive solution for the problem.

The Regulation on precedence dated 19 March 1815 divided envoys into three classes and then laid down that "Diplomatic officials shall rank in each class according to the date on which their arrival was officially notified. The present regulations shall not in any way modify the position of the Papal representative". In Article 6 the Regulation adds that "ties of relationship or family alliances between courts shall not confer any rank on their diplomatic officials. The same shall be the case with political alliances".

Later on the rule laid down in Article 4 of the Vienna Regulation was altered in some countries to follow Pombal's circular, which had said that the precedence of ambassadors and ministers would be fixed in their respective classes by the date on which credentials were delivered and not by the date of the official notification of arrival.

The whole matter is regulated today by Article 16 of the Vienna Convention, the first paragraph of which says, "Heads of Mission shall take precedence in their respective classes in the order of the date and time of taking up their functions in accordance with Article 13".

The draft of the Article by the International Law Commission of 1958 stipulated that "Heads of Mission shall take precedence in their respective classes in the order of date either of the official notification of their arrival or of the presentation of their letters of credence, according to the practice prevailling in the receiving State, which must be applied without discrimin-

ation". The Brazilian delegation to the Vienna Conference considered that this Article was not in harmony with Article 13, which dealt with the taking up of functions of heads of mission, and judged it to be better to say purely and simply that "heads of mission shall take precedence in their respective classes according to the date when they take up their function as provided in Article 12". The Brazilian amendment, which soon won general acceptance, suffered a few slight formal changes and was approved as a joint amendment.

The expression "in their respective classes" is used in the Convention to establish a distinction between ambassadors and ministers plenipotentiary, the former always ranking before the latter, even if their seniority at post is less.

The reference to the date and the time has in view the very frequent occurring case of various credentials being presented on the same day. When this happens, the time in the deciding factor. When more than one head of mission presents his credentials on the same day, the one who arrived in the receiving State first becomes the first to be received.

Article 16 of the Vienna Conference also lays down, in its second paragraph, that "alterations in the credentials of a head of mission not involving any change of class shall not affect his precedence". This clause has in view the case of a head of mission who has already presented his credentials to the Head of the State he is accredited to and now presents new credentials. This is most likely to occur where the head of mission has been raised in category from minister to ambassador. In this case, which involves a change of class, the length of his stay as minister will not be taken into account and the head of the mission will now figure in the list of precedence of ambassador from the moment he presents his new credentials, i.e. he will take the last place.

In monarchies which regard the ambassador or minister as being the representative of the person of the Sovereign, new credentials are by custom required if the Sovereign dies, abdicates or is deposed. In any of these three cases the head of mission of the sending Sovereign is provided with new credentials; but there is usually no solemn handing over of the credentials: they are simply delivered to the Ministry for Foreign Affairs. Although nowadays no point of law or protocol is raised by the presentation of credentials in such circumstances, doubts have been given rise to in the past.

In the same way, a government which has suffered the death, abdication or deposition of the Sovereign may demand new credentials. In this case there will also be no change in the order of precedence, the presentation of the new letters of credence being carried out in accordance with the existing precedence. In 1958, on the occasion of the Coronation of Pope John XXIII, the Secretary of State of the Holy See made it known that the new credentials would be presented in accordance with the order of precedence, thus preventing, in principle, the possibility of this order being changed. As the Polish Ambassador, whose credentials had been handed over on 24 July 1939, could

not present new ones, the German Ambassador was the first to present his credentials and so took over the position of doyen of the Diplomatic Corps accredited to the Pope.

The general rule determining the precedence of heads of mission also applies to chargés d'affaires: it is fixed by the date on which the *lettre de cabinet* is presented to the Minister for Foreign Affairs or on which a note is sent communicating the fact that he has taken up the direction of the mission. The commonest usage is for this precedence to be determined within each class of chargés d'affaires, in the first place coming permanent chargés d'affaires (*en pied*), in the second place those who are temporarily in charge of an embassy, and in the third place the chargés d'affaires of legations.

Precedence within diplomatic missions is laid down by the laws or regulations of the sending State. In drawing up its diplomatic list the receiving State limits itself to asking the heads of mission for a statement of the names of the members of their missions, and in the list the order of precedence is followed.

Generally speaking, diplomatic staff take precedence over technical staff, but this rule may be modified, owing to the tendency, which is becoming more and more general, of States to appoint highranking officers belonging to other ministries to exercise technical functions abroad.

The Vienna Convention deals with this question in a very superficial way when it states in Article 17 "The precedence of the members of the diplomatic staff of the mission shall be notified by the head of the mission to the Ministry for Foreign Affairs or such other ministry as shall be agreed". In commentaries on the draft of the International Law Commission we see that body was of the opinion that it was not within its competence to deal with the specific rank of members of a mission.

The Vienna Convention has nothing to say about the order of precedence to be followed in ceremonies attended by members of two or more diplomatic missions. There is no doubt as to the position of diplomatic agents, however; in their case the deciding factor is their rank, minister-counsellors coming before counsellors, and counsellors before Secretaries. Where two or more diplomatic agents of the same rank are concerned, the rule is that it is the precedence of their respective heads of mission that decides, irrespective of the seniority at post of the guests.

At a diplomatic ceremony at which foreign military, naval and air attachés appear, precedence is to be determined by the general criteria of rank and length of time at post of their respective heads of mission. This does not exclude the possibility of some other criteria being followed in the case of formal occasions or meetings specifically for attachés. Thus, at the Association of Naval Attachés in London, "the Naval officer who has been in London the longest time as Naval attaché is the Doyen of the Association, irrespective of his rank or seniority in rank". The regulation also lays down

that the Naval Attaché is always senior to Assistant Naval Attachés whatever their rank.

The growing practice of appointing women to be in charge of embassies and legations created certain difficulties in the beginning, but these have now been solved in a reasonable manner. Whenever an ambassadress, woman ambassador (in Portuguese *Embaixadora*) appears among men at an official ceremony her precedence is regulated purely and simply by the date on which she took up her official functions as shown by the presentation of her credentials or of a true copy of them. At a *cercle diplomatique* or in a procession in which the other foreign ambassadors are present with their wives, a woman ambassador will come after any of her colleagues who took up their functions before she did. Doubts begin to arise when it is a question of seating a woman ambassador at table at an official banquet at which foreign ambassadors and their wives are present. In this case the a woman ambassador will take precedence over the ambassadors' wives, even if their husband presented their credentials before she did (and in this case, too, it may happen that the woman ambassador, as a result of the convention which seats men and woman alternately at table, may find herself seated higher up than the ambassador who has precedence over her). In this respect it should be noted that a woman ambassador enjoys preprogatives *de jure*, whereas the position of an ambassador's wife is ill-defined and depends on a question of etiquette, so much so, in fact, that if the husband of one is temporarily absent from his post, invitations to official ceremonies are addressed to the chargé d'affaires and his wife.

A more delicate problem is that of determining the place to be occupied by the husband of a woman ambassador when both are present together at an official banquet. In 1950 the Danish Government, after consulting the Diplomatic Corps, decided that Mr. Anderson, husband of the United States Ambassadress, should come below the foreign ambassadors and ministers plenipotentiary. Three years later, Italian protocol also decided that Mr. Henry R. Luce, husband of Mrs Clare Boothe Luce, Head of the American Embassy in Rome, should come below the ministers plenipotentiary. In both cases the husband were given the most important position after the permanent foreign representatives accredited to the local government.

On the occasion of the coronation of a sovereign, the inauguration of a president, the funeral of a Head of State, or the wedding of a sovereign or of members of his family, it is the practice to send special missions to attend them.

When for some imperative reason the sending State cannot in fact send a special mission, it usually designates the head of the ordinary mission Ambassador Extraordinary to the ceremony in question, the granting of the title of Ambassador *ad hoc* being held to be a question of international courtesy. The head of the ordinary mission and the other members of the mission may also

be included in the special mission if an ambassador *ad hoc* is sent.

If it is wanted to show special deference to the receiving State, it is common to send a mission headed by a personality of higher rank than that possessed by the ambassadors; thus, at the funerals of sovereigns the appearance of a number of heads of State is quite usual.

The present tendency is to give precedence to the highest ranking personalities and to determine a system of precedence within each class, basing it, perhaps, on the official notification of the mission.

In such cases the determining of rules for precedence has shown fluctuations even in the most tradition-bound courts, which only shows the difficulties that exist. The usual principle, based on the interpretation of Article 3 of the Vienna Regulation of 1815, is that precedence shall be determined by the presentation of credentials, but as the International Law Commission notes, "in practice it is almost impossible for this rule to be carried out".

For the funeral of Sir Winston Churchill in January 1965, which was attended by representatives from a hundred and eleven countries, protocol adopted a system based on the rule mentioned above, but in which the position in each class was quite arbitrary. The highest places were reserved for sovereigns, and the precedence adopted for them was the date on which they had ascended the throne. Even so, King Baudouin of Belgium (crowned 1951) was placed before Queen Juliana of the Netherlands (crowned in 1948). Presidents of Republics came next, though they were apparently placed in alphabetical order, which allowed General de Gaulle to sit with the sovereigns and before the president of Iceland, Israel, Uruguay and Zambia. Despite the arbitrary nature of the placing, few complaints were made and those that were made mostly concerned the decision of the British Government to limit the number of those invited to three from each of the three big Allies, two from each member of the Commonwealth, and one from each of the other countries. Crowned sovereigns were not included in these quotas, but Presidents of Republics were.

During the Solemn Mass for the soul of Pope Pius XII celebrated on 19 October 1958, Vatican ceremonial did not concern itself with the question of precedence: the special mission took their seats on the tribunes as they arrived. This criterion seems to have given rise to complaints, there being a certain disparity between the heads of the various missions.

It was possibly with such complaints in mind that the Secretary of State adopted quite a different criterion for the order of precedence of the heads of the extraordinary missions at the Coronation of Pope John XXIII on 4 November 1958. According to the circular note issued, a criterion for precedence was adopted which took into consideration the rank of the heads of the extraordinary missions and not the date on which the communication arrived, obviously an unimportant point. Thus the order of precedence laid down was (a) Heads of State to occupy a special tribune; (b) royal princes to

occupy the tribune reserved for princely families; (c) the third place to be occupied in order by Heads of Government, Ministers for Foreign Affairs, other ministers and finally the other Heads of missions according to the alphabetical order as shown in the Diplomatic List.

The same criterion was again followed in 1961 for the coronation of Pope Paul VI.

The Convention on Special Missions, signed at New York on 8 December 1969, deals with the problem in Article 16, where it states: "1. Were two or more special missions meet on the territory of the receiving state or of a third state, precedence among the missions shall be determined, in the absence of a special agreement, according to the alphabetical order of the names of the states used by the protocol of the state on whose territory the mission are meeting. 2. Precedence among two or more special missions which meet on a ceremonial or formal occasion shall be governed by the protocol in force in the receiving state. 3. Precedence among the members of the same special mission shall be that which is notified to the receiving state or to the third state on whose territory two or more special missions are meeting".

The place to be occupied by diplomats at ceremonies attended by members of the local government is another question which may create difficulties.

Generally speaking, ambassadors are given one of the highest places. In monarchies they usually come after members of the reigning families, perhaps in recognition of the principle accepted by most Courts, that they represent the person of their Sovereign.

In republics, ambassadors mostly take third place. Brazil and the United States have similar orders of precedence, and foreign ambassadors in both countries come immediately after the Vice-President of the Republic.

In Great Britain there are no written norms for public ceremonials, practice being governed by traditional precedence and customs, and doubtful cases being solved by Foreign Office protocol or by the Marshal of the Diplomatic Corps. The present order of precedence generally is as follows: the Sovereign, the Duke of Edinburgh, the Prince of Wales, the Duke of Gloucester, the Duke of Windsor, the Archbishop of Canterbury, the Lord High Chancellor, the Archbishop of York, the Prime Minister, the Lord President of the Council, the Speaker of the House of Commons, the Lord Privy Seal, the High Commissioners for the Commonwealth Countries and Foreign Ambassadors, Dukes, Ministers and Envoys.

Chapter XXIX

THE DIPLOMATIC CORPS

The diplomatic corps is a body *sui generis*, devoid of independent legal standing, which comprises all the heads of mission permanently accredited to a particular Government.

In a wider sense it also includes the members of all the diplomatic missions serving in the receiving State whose names figure in the diplomatic list, i.e. the heads of mission, all the members of the diplomatic staff, and some members of the administrative and technical staff and their wives.

The expression can also be used to include all the diplomatic officials of a particular country wherever they may be, and in this sense one can speak of a national diplomatic corps as opposed to the foreign diplomatic corps, using the expression in the wide sense given above to mean all the foreign diplomats serving in a particular capital.

The diplomatic corps has certain inherent protocol functions. Except in connection with matters affecting it alone as a whole, its decisions must be taken unanimously. In other words, the diplomatic corps may meet to standardize the mode of individual procedure of its members in a particular question of protocol, and in this case the majority vote is not binding on any one of its members, who may freely act in his own way.

Meetings of the diplomatic corps are usually held for the purpose of discussing questions of etiquette, precedence, prerogatives and, in certain countries, problems in connection with food and petrol rationing, and so on.

The problems debated by the diplomatic corps are not important ones, but in exceptional cases, such as in time of war or civil war, or in periods of civil disturbance, the diplomatic corps may act as a body and assume significant attitudes in defence of the local populations.

It is up to the receiving State to fix its own protocol and the way it is to be interpreted, but it may on occasion, especially in questions of precedence, request the diplomatic corps to put forward an opinion on exceptional cases or may accept a solution already proposed by them.

Although it is true that in certain circumstances statements made by the diplomatic corps, or attitudes taken by them may assume special importance, it should be remembered that such occasions are very exceptional.

The 1961 Vienna Convention makes no reference to the diplomatic corps.

In its comments on the 1957 draft, the Italian Government proposed (unsuccessfully) that a specific article should be included as follows: "The heads of mission accredited to the same State form the diplomatic corps. The diplomatic corps performs the functions which it is recognized to possess by international usage, and it is represented for all purposes by its doyen. The doyen is the senior head of mission or, in countries in which precedence is granted to the Holy See, the Apostolic Nuncio".

Sir Gerald Fitzmaurice was of the opinion that the concept of a diplomatic corps was one of the best known and should receive recognition in the draft since it also dealt with etiquette, usage and privileges. The opinion that prevailed was, however, contrary to the adoption of such an article. As Mr. Gilberto Amado pointed out, the proposed new article was superfluous; it attached an incorrect meaning to the term *diplomatic corps* and it did not sufficiently define its functions.

The question was raised again in Vienna by the Italian Delegation and a special working party was appointed to draft a clause concerning the diplomatic corps. The group subsequently proposed the following text: "The heads of mission accredited to the same State, together with the members of the diplomatic staff, form the diplomatic corps, which shall be presided over by its doyen". As a definition it was satisfactory but it was rejected since it did not add anything and, therefore, it was agreed that it would be better not to mention the diplomatic corps in the Convention.

The proposed formula adopts the idea that the diplomatic corps embraces not only the heads of mission but also the other members of the mission included in the diplomatic list.

The *diplomatic list* mentions in alphabetical order the representatives of foreign States accredited to a given country with the names and designations of the persons returned as composing the establishment of their respective offices. It also contains the order of precedence of the heads of mission and the national days of the countries represented.

The publication of the diplomatic list is a usual practice of countries in the conduct of foreign affairs, although no obligation is involved. The names of duly accredited officers are submitted by the foreign missions and it is usually the local Protocol that prepares the diplomatic list.

One can say that the principal object of the diplomatic list is to make known to diplomatic and social circles the names of the members of the various embassies, their ranks, addresses whether they are married or single, if they are accompanied by their daughters, and also whether they are or not, at the time of the printing of the list, in the country.

In certain countries the inclusion of a name in the diplomatic list has a certain importance, since it may mean that that person has a right to diplomatic privileges and immunities. The Diplomatic Privileges Act of 1708 provides "that no person shall be preceeded against as having arrested the servant

of an ambassador or public minister, by virtue of his act, unless the name of such servant be first registered in the office of one of the principal secretaries of state, and by such secretary transmitted to the sheriffs or deputies of London and Middlesex for the time being, or their under sheriffs or deputies, who shall, upon the receipt thereof, hang up the same in some public place in their offices, whereto all persons may resort, and take copies thereof, without fee or reward". Nowadays, however, the inclusion in or the omission of a name from the list is not conclusive as to the legal status of the person claiming such privileges and immunities. Even though the authorities of the receiving State may refuse to include a given name in the diplomatic list, they will usually avoid taking such a drastic step. *Contrariu sensu*, the privileges and immunities accorded by international law are not limited to those whose names are contained in the diplomatic list, but are extended to all those persons who are officially recognized as belonging to the diplomatic mission. In certain countries the diplomatic list is not published frequently and, therefore, those persons who are accepted and whose names will be included in the future list obviously have a right to every privilege and immunity.

The diplomatic corps is presided over by the *doyen*, whose functions are chiefly of a ceremonial character.

As a general rule, the doyen is the senior head of mission of the highest category. The title of doyen may, however, be assigned, by treaty or custom, to the ambassador of a given country. In those States in which there is an Apostolic Nuncio he is *de jure* considered doyen of the diplomatic corps, even though he may the last head of mission to have presented his credentials.

The privileged situation for the nuncios goes back to the period in which the precedence of the heads of mission was fixed by the precedence of the Heads of State and when the Pope ranked above all emperors and kings.

The Regulation of Vienna of 1815 says that "the present regulation shall not in any way modify the position of the Papal representative". With the occupation of the Papal States certain States and authors contended that the nuncios should no longer be automatically regarded as the doyens of the diplomatic corps. In those countries were the Papal representative is not accepted as the doyen, the Holy See used to send internuncios, but since 1965 it has been represented by pro-nuncios who may, eventually, be doyens should they become the senior heads of mission.

The draft of the International Law Commision contained a paragraph on the lines of the 1815 Regulation: "The present article is without prejudice to any existing practice in the receiving State regarding the precedence of the representative of the Pope".

In Vienna, Monsigneur Casaroli of the Holy See said that the words "any existing practice in the receiving State" might mean that the exception in favour of representatives of the Pope would be restricted to the States applying the rule at the time of ratification or acceptance of the Convention

and that some States which had not yet recognized the practice might wish to adopt it in the future. He stressed that the Conference should codify current practices and rules rather than introduce new ones and that his delegation's amendment did not in any way restrict or impose upon States, which would remain entirely free to follow or reject the very long-standing custom followed in so many other States. Lastly, the amendment met the criterion of equality between the older States, which had already been able to choose, and the new or future States.

Professor G. Tunkin, commenting on the proposed amendment of the Holy See, said that an old rule of international law could be considered from two points of view: either it was of long standing and conformed to a venerable tradition, or it was out of date and obsolete. The Conference had met because the Regulation adopted at Vienna in 1815 had become out-dated. He also pointed out that of the eight countries taking part in the Congress of Vienna, four had been Catholic, and at that time religious freedom had not been at all secure. In his opinion, paragraph 3 contradicted the principle of the equality of States and hence he asked for a separate vote on the paragraph and abstained.

The rule finally adopted, in which the word "Pope" was replaced by "Holy See" was adopted by 59 votes to 1.

The doyen has duties *vis-à-vis* the receiving State and in regard to the other members of the diplomatic corps.

In the first case, he represents the diplomatic corps on certain public occasions, such as at State banquets to which all the heads of mission cannot be invited. Certain public ceremonies such as those at the beginning or the end of the year, the funeral of a colleague or of a personality linked to the diplomatic corps or at other ceremonies of a similar nature, he is the spokesman for his colleagues. If the occasion should have a certain significance he must submit his speech previously to the other heads of mission for approval. Exceptionally, the doyen may be called to speak on very solemn occasions. On March 9, 1929, the Brazilian Ambassador to the Holy See pronounced the historic speech in which the Catholic nations conveyed to the Pope their congratulations on the signature of the Lateran Treaties.

The doyen's duties towards the diplomatic corps might be considered as of an internal nature. The doyen, on his own initiative or at the request of another head of mission, convenes the diplomatic corps, gives advice to the new heads of mission on local protocol and etiquette, transmits instructions on diplomatic privileges and immunities to the diplomatic corps at the request of the local government and requests interpretation of the rules of precedence.

The doyen is always the head of mission of a given State, but we must not confuse these two capacities: that of doyen and that of head of mission. The distinction can be important, as in the case of two countries that do not

maintain diplomatic relations with each other. In such a case, the head of mission may not have official contacts with the other head of mission, but must recognize and obey him if he is the doyen of the diplomatic corps. In these circumstances he can avoid unnecessary contacts, but must participate in the meetings of the diplomatic corps under his chairmanship and accept those of a ceremonial description which are adopted.

The wife of the senior married diplomatic head of mission of ambassadorial category is called the *doyenne* and usually has certain honorific and ceremonial duties established by local custom, and may be, for example, expected to accompany newly-arrived wives of heads of mission on their first call on the queen or the wife of the Head of State or of the Minister for Foreign Affairs.

Part VI

Termination of the Mission

Chapter XXX

EXTINCTION OF THE DIPLOMATIC MISSION

The extinction of a diplomatic mission is a very serious measure which must be avoided and used only as a last resort. It is quite different from the mere termination of the diplomatic agent's functions, which is a normal event that occurs when the head of mission is removed to another post or called back to the Ministry for Foreign Affairs of his country. The extinction of the diplomatic mission automatically implies the termination of the diplomatic agent's functions, while the termination of ambassadorial functions does not affect the diplomatic mission itself.

The termination of a diplomatic mission may occur as a consequence of the extinction either of the sending State or of the receiving State, in which cases the right of legation disappears. In all the other cases of extinction, what occurs in practice is the temporary withdrawal of the mission, which can be re-established when the causes that led to its closing cease to exist.

The following cases of extinction can also be mentioned: a) declaration of war, with the consequent severance of diplomatic relations: b) severance of diplomatic relations in peace time for an indefinite period; c) withdrawal of recognition and consequent closing down of the diplomatic mission; d) non-recognition, for a long period, of a particular government; e) closing down of a diplomatic mission for reasons of economy, as a result of the lack of political or economic interest.

In practice, the definitive extinction of the mission only occurs in the case of loss of the right of legation. If the birth of a State implies the existence of the right of legation, which is a result of the mere existence of the State, the extinction of the State also implies the end of international relations and, consequently, of the diplomatic missions.

The short union of Egypt and Syria in 1958 meant the closing down of all the diplomatic missions of the two countries, although in practice the missions *ipso facto* became the representatives of the new United Arab Republic. When there were two missions in one capital, such as occurred in Rio de Janeiro, the new Government merely chose one of the two buildings. Simultaneously, all the diplomatic missions in Cairo and in Damascus were extinguished; those of Cairo became accredited to the new Republic and those in Damascus were transformed into consulates-general.

In 1946, when the union of Tanganyka and Zanzibar gave birth to the Republic of Tanzania, the new Government announced that the embassies in Zanzibar would have to be transformed into consulates.

There are cases in which the extinction of a State may not have as an immediate consequence the extinction of its diplomatic mission in one or more States. We can, for instance, mention the case of the Baltic countries, which were annexed by the USSR in 1940 and whose international personalities and right of legation continue to be recognized by the United States.

In principle, only sovereign States have the right of legation and when a *capitis diminutio* occurs, this right of legation disappears.

War is incompatible with the maintenance of diplomatic relations; once it has been declared, diplomatic relations cease, although the closing of the mission may occur after the declaration of war. The severance of diplomatic relations with the consequent closing of embassies and legations should precede the declaration of war, but if it does not, relations must cease, regardless of a formal notification.

In the International Law Commission, however, the prevailing opinion was that diplomatic relations do not cease *ipso facto* with the declaration of war and it was recalled that there were cases in which armed conflict had lasted for a certain period without severance of diplomatic relations.

Article 45, in its opening sentence, only refers to the breaking off of diplomatic relations between two States, but subparagraph *a* mentions the "case of armed conflict". It was argued that this expression should appear in the introductory part of the Article, since it might seem that the case of armed conflict only applied to the above-mentioned sub-paragraph. This expression was included to give more emphasis to the rule contained in sub-paragraph *a*, but there can be no doubt that the whole Article also refers to the breaking off of diplomatic relations in case of war.

Sub-paragraph *a* of Article 45 of the Vienna Convention lays down that "the receiving State must, even in case of armed conflict, respect and protect the premises of the mission together with its property and archives". This provision can be linked to Article 22 which deals with the inviolability of diplomatic missions.

The aim of this Article is to leave no doubt as to the duty of the receiving State to protect the premises of the mission and its archives, which does not cease with the breaking off of diplomatic relations, especially when this step precedes the declaration of war or coincides with it.

When diplomatic relations are severed, States usually entrust the protection of their interests and those of their nationals in the receiving State to a third State. This practice is a relatively modern one, the first instance occurring during the Franco-Prussian war of 1870, when Switzerland was entrusted with such functions.

Professor Sandström's draft did not mention the protection of the interests

of the State in the case of severance of diplomatic relations, but in 1957 the International Law Commission adopted the following rule: "The sending State may entrust the protection of the interests of its country to the good offices of the mission of a third State acceptable to the receiving State". In the following year, the Italian Government suggested the deletion of the expression *good offices*.

Sub-paragraph *b* of Article 45 of the Vienna Convention says that such a State must be *acceptable*. In its comments on the 1957 draft of the International Law Commission, the Finnish Government suggested that it would be preferable to use in the text the clear and accurate formula *accepté par* (and not *acceptable pour*). When the suggestion was brought up, Sir Gerald Fitzmaurice recalled that the conclusion reached at the previous meeting had been that the third State must be acceptable to the receiving State, in the sense that the receiving State was entitled to object to the sending State's choise. This interpretation is based on logic and endorsed by international practice.

The third State exercises various function. If it has been accepted as such before the departure of the members of the diplomatic mission and consular office of the sending State it must guarantee their safe departure from the country. Another function, especially in time of war, is the protection of the nationals and their property, as well as assistance to prisoners of war.

The premises of the mission, together with its property and archives, are likewise entrusted to the third State. When the severance of diplomatic relations occurs the receiving State has the duty to protect the premises and archives of the mission, since the right of the sending State to entrust them to a third State may not be exercised at once, especially in the case of a sudden departure of the mission.

The severance of diplomatic relations may be the result of a collective or of an individual decision of States. Thus, diplomatic relations may be broken off in two ways: the first consists of a sanction voted in a group; the second occurs when a State tries to impose its will on another in a given matter.

The severance of diplomatic relations, which is a step taken by one State when its relations with another worsen, may simultaneously occur with a declaration of war.

The severance of diplomatic relations used to be individual, but nowadays it is included in Article 41 of the United Nations Charter as one of the measures that can be taken by the Security Council not involving the use of armed forces, to give effect to its decisions. On December 12, 1946, the General Assembly of the United Nations adopted a resolution by which all Member-States were invited to severe relations with Spain, whose regime was considered as contrary to the principles of the United Nations Charter.

A similar sanction exists in the Interamerican Treaty of Reciprocal Assistance (Treaty of Rio de Janeiro), signed on September 2, 1947.

In the unilateral severance of diplomatic relations, a State tries to impose its will on another; either it assumes the role of judge and condemns the other for a real or fictitious violation of international law; or it tries to force the other to change its foreign policy, which it regards as incompatible with existing ties of friendship. In some cases, this severance of relations may have an altrustic basis—or an apparently altrustic basis—such as the condemnation of measures against human rights or the adoption of racial, ethnic or religious discriminatory laws.

The only judge of the convenience of discontinuing relations is the State which desires to do so. Such a measure is not a violation of international Law since no State is compelled to establish or maintain diplomatic relations with another.

An important difference between the breaking off of diplomatic relations and the declaration of war consists in the fact that the severance does not extinguish existing treaties among the two States except those regarding diplomatic relations and even so temporarily.

Relations between the two States in question do not cease completely with the breaking off of diplomatic relations, even in the case of a declaration of war, since certain indirect links are created through the action of the third States which are invited to protect the interests of the sending States. An example of complete severance of relations, at least in theory, occurred when the Foreign Minister of Indonesia asked the British Government to stop representing the Netherlands interests, saying that this action was "merely implementing the Government's decision calling for the total liquidation of all remnants and interests of the Dutch in Indonesia". The Foreign Minister of Indonesia added that "for us it is not necessary that the interests of one country must be served by another country after diplomatic ties have been severed". This decision was taken when the Conference on Diplomatic Intercourse and Immunity was being held in Vienna, where most of the delegates considered this measure as being contrary to international law.

Among the other reasons which may lead to the termination of diplomatic relations we have the withdrawal by one State of recognition of the government of another State. In this case there are usually two factions contending for that government and the withdrawal affects the faction that up to then was recognized as such by the majority of States. The present Chinese situation is typical. When the United Kingdom decided to recognize the People's Republic of China, the Chinese Embassy in London ceased to be that of Nationalist China. A rather similar decision was taken by France in 1965 when it closed down its Embassy in Taipeh and informed the Chinese Embassy in Paris of the establishment of diplomatic relations with the Government of Peking. The Nationalist Government thereupon decided to transform its Embassy into its representation to UNESCO, thus creating a deadlock which was finally solved only when the Paris Police occupied the

premises *manu militari*.

If a political upheaval occurs involving an unconstitutional change of government, the other States will recognize the new *de facto* government as soon as certain conditions proving its stability and intention to fulfil its international obligations have been taken. The sending State is perfectly free to delay such recognition and in such a case it may close down the diplomatic mission. The usual procedure, however, it is to recall the ambassador, and hand over the direction of the embassy to an acting chargé d'affaires, who must avoid maintaining official diplomatic relations with the receiving State, since they might be interpreted as being a tacit recognition of the new regime.

Finally we can mention those cases in which the closing down of an embassy was not motivated by political considerations but merely by the desire of the sending State to cut down on expenses, once the reasons that justified the opening of the diplomatic mission have ceased. Sometimes such a measure may create a certain amount of ill-feeling and have the closing down of the other diplomatic mission as a result. In this case, the interests of the sending State may also be entrusted to a third State, on the conditions established in Article 46 of the Vienna Convention.

Some recent examples of the closing down of diplomatic missions for reasons of economy can be mentioned. In January 1964, the Embassy of Cambodia in London sent a circular note to the other diplomatic missions in London informing them that its offices would be closed for an indefinite period. A few months later, in July 1964, the Ambassador of Gabon sent a circular note in similar terms but adding that the Ambassador in Paris would also be accredited to the Court of Saint James. Brazil in 1968 and 1969 closed down its Embassies in Colombo and Saigon but instructed its Ambassador to convey to the Governments of Ceylon and Vietnam the assurance that the measure should in no way affect their good relations with Brazil.

In September 1970, the Belgian Minister for Foreign Affairs, Mr. Pierre Harmel, declared that the Embassy of Belgium in Montevideo would be closed, as a mere routine matter, and that the Ambassador, who was also accredited to Assunción, would establish the mission in the Capital of Paraguay. It leaked out in the press, however, that in his interview with the Uruguaian Ambassador in Brussels, Mr. Harmel had stressed that the provisions of the Vienna Convention regarding the security of diplomatic missions were not being observed.

Chapter XXXI

END OF THE FUNCTION OF THE DIPLOMATIC AGENT

The functions of a diplomatic agent usually come to an end when the sending State decides to give him another assigment or, exceptionally, when the receiving State requests his recall. Normally, the end of his function is a mere routine matter and, therefore, it is out of place to study this question simultaneously with that of the extinction of a diplomatic mission, which is a serious measure.

The Vienna Convention on Diplomatic Relations covers the two cases in Article 43: "The function of a diplomatic agent comes to an end, *inter alia*: a) on notification by the sending State to the receiving State that the function of the diplomatic agent has come to an end; b) on notification by the receiving State to the sending State that, in accordance with paragraph 2 of Article 9, it refuses to recognize the diplomatic agent as a member of the mission".

The expression *inter alia* means that the Convention bears in mind other ways in which the function may come to an end. Strictly speaking, the expression only covers a third case: the death of the diplomatic agent.

The functions are usually terminated on the initiative of the sending State, which may decide that its diplomatic agent will fulfil his functions better elsewhere. His transfer may also be the result of rules or regulations which limit the stay of diplomats in foreign posts. The period replacement of the members of embassies and legations is a routine matter. Although the experience acquired by a diplomat in a given post may be very valuable, experience shows that the compulsory rotation of the members of the foreign service is advisable.

From an international point of view the functions end when the sending State sends a note to the Ministry for Foreign Affairs of the receiving State informing it of its decision. From the administrative point of view there are various reasons for terminating the functions. Usually the diplomat is sent to a new post or else recalled to serve in the Ministry of Foreign Affairs. The transfer may be mere routine, but may also be motivated by the diplomatic agents behaviour in the receiving State, which may mean he is being recalled in order to be punished or even expelled from the career.

In exceptional cases, the removal of a diplomat may be the result of a

suggestion on the part of the receiving State implying that his removal would be advisable. But from a legal point of view, a transfer in this case would come under sub-paragraph *a* of Article 43, that is in the absence of a formal note asking for the removal of the diplomatic agent in question. The hypothesis we find in sub-paragraph *b* only occurs when the receiving State formally requests the withdrawal of a diplomatic agent. Such a request might have a negative effect on the relations between the two States and is only used in extreme cases.

The end of the function of a diplomatic agent can occur automatically if there should be a law or regulation establishing a fixed limit for each assignment. In certain republics, with the expiration of the term of office of the president, all the ambassadors are expected to tender their resignation, in order to give the new Head of State a free hand in making his own choise. Sometimes, even though no resignation has been tendered, it is considered as implied. In monarchies the heads of mission are usually regarded as the personal representatives of the monarch and their functions cease when he dies, abdicates or is deposed. In this case, the new monarch may maintain the ambassador, and usually does so, but fresh credentials will be issued.

Just as the receiving State is perfectly free not to accept a given diplomatic agent it can equally demand the recall of a diplomat whose presence in its territory is deemed detrimental to the good relations between the two States. Sub-paragraph *b* is the pertinent proviso and in it we find a cross-reference to Article 9, which completes the rule: "The receiving State may at any time and without having to explain its decision, notify the sending State that the head of the mission or any member of the diplomatic staff is *persona non grata* or that any other member of the staff of the mission is not acceptable". It goes on to add that a person may be considered *non grata* or not acceptable even before arriving in the territory of the receiving State.

Should the receiving State consider a diplomatic agent *persona non grata* the sending State must see to his transfer to a new assignment. If friendly relations exist between the two States and this extreme step was taken owing to the bad behaviour of the diplomatic agent, who will normally be subjected to some disciplinary measure, no special difficulty arises. Sometimes, however, the diplomatic agent may have been acting on instructions and possibly fulfilled them correctly. In this case, the sending State may be loath to proceed as requested. But if the diplomatic agent should remain in the receiving State he is liable to have his status as a member of the diplomatic mission cancelled, thus forfeiting his privileges and immunities and becoming liable to legal proceedings and even imprisonment. Nowadays it is normal practice to give a person declared *non grata* or not acceptable a period of time in which to leave the country, and in certain serious cases the limit may even be of 24 or 48 hours.

The Vienna Convention uses two expressions: *persona non grata* or *not*

acceptable. In the first case it has in view the diplomatic agent, and the second the other members of the staff of the mission, without diplomatic status.

The reasons which may lead the receiving State to declare a member of the diplomatic staff *persona non grata* are innumerable, the most frequent being a default in professional conduct. Nowadays, however, it may be difficult in certain cases to determine precisely whether the decision of the receiving State is aimed directly at the foreign diplomat or if its principal object is to demonstrate its displeasure with the sending State, in which case the diplomat is an innocent victim.

In other cases, the diplomatic agent, in acting on instructions, may have done something which amply justifies his removal from the country, as in the cases of espionage or if he interferes in the internal affairs of the receiving State. In April 1959, Nikolai A. Belous, Counsellor of the Soviet Embassy, was expelled from Argentina for having participated in the violent manifestations against the government of that country which resulted in death and injuries. On the same occasion two other members of the Soviet Embassy and one from the Roumanian Embassy were also declared *persona non grata*. On September 24, 1968, the President of Uruguay declared that three members of the Soviet Embassy had been declared *persona non grata* and invited to leave the Country due to their close relations with the local Communist Party, which was responsible for the violent agitation among the working classes of that country.

A number of cases of foreign diplomats who had to leave on account of unbecoming professional conduct can be mentioned and are to be found in the principal books on diplomacy. In this connection, the reprimand sent in 1846 by the Secretary of State to the United States chargé d'affaires at Lima, Mr. Jewett, who had behaved in an impolite way to the local government deserves to be reproduced: "If diplomatic agents render themselves so unacceptable as to produce a request for their recall from the government to which they are accredited, the instance must be rare indeed in which such a request ought not to be granted. To refuse it would be to defeat the very purpose for which they are sent abroad, that of cultivating friendly relations between independent nations. Perhaps no circumstances would justify such a refusal unless the national honour were involved".

In most cases, a mere hint will be sufficient and will spare the receiving State the displeasure of notifying the sending State of its desire. If a written note becomes necessary it must be couched in appropriate terms and set out, if possible, the reasons why the recall is requested. But we must observe that the Vienna Convention following in the footsteps of the Havana Convention of 1928 (Article 8), lays down in Article 9 that the receiving State is not obliged "to explain its decision". In other words, it adopts the same rule with regard both to the non-acceptance and to the request for recall of a diplo-

matic agent. In our opinion, the circumstances are not the same, since in the latter case the diplomat was duly accepted and an explanation, even if verbal, can only be construed as an act of friendship aimed at avoiding a misunderstanding.

In 1952, the Brazilian Government distributed a press release in which it said that the Brazilian Minister to Teheran had been recalled to Rio de Janeiro because the Iranian Government had asked for his recall on the grounds of incompatibility. The press release added that "it is international practice that a government is not obliged to disclose its reason for having declared a diplomatic agent *persona non grata*. Therefore, the Brazilian Government promptly complied with the request of the Iranian Government". It should be added that some years later the Shah personally decorated the aforementioned Minister.

The request for the recall of a foreign diplomat may be prompted by acts of a certain importance, such as participating in a plot to overthrow the government or aimed at jeopardizing national security, but may also result from acts of a moral order or ones capable of reflecting discredit on the diplomat. The constant disregard by a diplomatic agent or a member of his family of local laws and regulations, such as the traffic laws dealing with parking and speed-limits, may be sufficient to justify a request for recall.

Furthermore, an experienced diplomat, especially should he belong to a great power, will avoid making remarks which may be misinterpreted, thus giving rise to misunderstanding and explanations that could have been avoided.

The Vienna Convention specifically mentions the situation of members of the staff of the mission (as distinct from that of the members of the diplomatic staff) who may be considered not acceptable to the receiving State. In this connection Article 9 makes a neat distinction since it also says that sending States "shall, as appropriate, either recall the person concerned or terminate his functions with the mission". In the case of some members of the administrative and technical staff, and most members of the service staff and private servants, the person concerned are admitted locally, that is, they are usually nationals of or permanent residents of the receiving State and, therefore, once their functions with the embassy come to an end, they remain in the territory of the receiving State and are not recalled. This means that, after a given period, they will be deprived of any privilege or immunity to which they had a right and will be treated like the rest of the inhabitants of the country. In other words, they may eventually be brought to trial and sentenced should they have violated any law.

In the case of a diplomatic agent, the fact that he has been declared *persona non grata* does not mean the immediate loss of his privileges and immunities. Paragraph 2 of Article 39 of the Vienna Convention is quite precise on this point: "When the functions of a person enjoying privileges and immunities have come to an end, such privileges and immunities shall normally cease at

the moment when he leaves the country, or on expiry of a reasonable period in which to do so, but shall subsist until that time, even in case of armed conflict. However, with respect to acts performed by such a person in the exercise of his functions as a member of the mission, immunity shall continue to subsist". But his name can be removed from the diplomatic list.

During the Vienna Conference, Mr. Glasse of the United Kingdom observed that Article 43 should contain an exhaustive list of the circumstances in which a diplomatic agent's functions might be brought to an end. The reference books on legal practice—he added—contained very complete catalogues of such circumstances, and the article ignored a very important one, namely, the death, abdication or deposition of the sovereign head of the State to which the diplomatic agent is accredited. We have already pointed out that current international law no longer endorses this rule, even though monarchies still demand new credentials in the case of the death or abdication of a king or reigning queen and supply new credentials to their respective ambassadors in such circumstances. The Holy See also proceeds on these lines. But this practice is a mere vestige of the theory of the representative character of the head of mission, no longer accepted today. Even though new credentials may be presented, they do not in any way change the order of precedence of the heads of mission.

Appendices

FINAL ACT OF THE VIENNA CONFERENCE ON DIPLOMATIC INTERCOURSE AND IMMUNITIES

1. The General Asembly of the United Nations, by resolution 1450 (XIV) of 7 December 1959, decided to convene an international conference of plenipotentiaries to consider the question of diplomatic intercourse and immunities and to embody the results of its work in an international convention, together with such ancillary instruments as might be necessary. The General Assembly, accepting an invitation extende by the Federal Government of Australia, also asked the Secretary-General to convoke the conference at Vienna not later than the spring of 1961.

2. The United Nations Conference on Diplomatic Intercourse and Immunities met at the Neue Hofburg in Vienna, Austria, from 2 March to 14 April 1961.

3. The Governments of the following eighty-one States were represented at the Conference: Albania, Argentina, Australia, Austria, Belgium, Brazil, Bulgaria, Burma, Byelorussian Soviet Socialist Republic, Cambodia, Canada, Central African Republic, Ceylon, Chad, Chile, China, Colombia, Congo (Leopoldville), Cuba, Czechoslovakia, Denmark, Dominican Republic, Equador, El Salvador, Ethiopia, Federal Republic of Germany, Federation of Malaya, Finland, France, Ghana, Greece, Guatemala, Haiti, Holy See, Honduras, Hungary, India, Indonesia, Iran, Iraq, Ireland, Israel, Italy, Japan, Lebanon, Liberia, Libya, Liechtenstein, Luxembourg, Mali, Mexico, Morocco, Netherlands, Nigeria, Norway, Pakistan, Panama, Peru, Philippines, Poland, Portugal, Republic of Korea, Republic of Viet Nam, Romania, Saudi Arabia, Senegal, Spain, Sweden, Switzerland, Thailand, Tunisia, Turkey, Ukrainian Soviet Socialist Republic, Union of South Africa, Union of Soviet Socialist Republics, United Arab Republic, United Kingdom of Great Britain and Northern Ireland, United States of America, Uruguay, Venezuela, Yugoslavia.

4. At the invitation of the General Assembly, the following specialized agencies were represented by observers at the Conference:

International Labour Organisation;

Food and Agriculture Organization of the United Nations;

United Nations Educational, Scientific and Cultural Organization.

5. At the invitation of the General Assembly, the International Atomic

Energie Agency and the following intergovernmental organizations were also represented by observers at the Conference:

League of Arab States;

Asian-African Legal Consultative Committee.

6. The Conference elected Mr. Alfred Verdross (Austria) as President.

7. The Conference elected as Vice-Presidents the representatives of the following participating States: Argentina, Canada, Chile, China, Colombia, Czechoslovakia, France, Iran, Iraq, Italy, Liberia, Mexico, Nigeria, Philippines, Romania, Spain, Union of Soviet Socialist Republics, United Kingdom of Great Britain and Northern Ireland, United States of America, Yugoslavia.

8. The following committees were set up by the Conference:

General Committee

Members:

The President of the Conference, the Vice-Presidents, and the Chairman of the Committee of the Whole.

Chairman:

The President of the Conference.

Committee of the Whole

Chairman:

Mr. A. S. Lall (India)

Vice-Chairmen:

Mr. H. Birecki (Poland)

Mr. N. Iriniz Casas (Uruguay)

Rapporteur:

Mr. W. Riphagen (Netherlands)

Drafting Committee

Members:

Mr. Geraldo Eulalio Nascimento Silva (Brazil)

Mr. Hu Ching-Yu (China)

Mr. Jacques Patey (France)

Mr. E. K. Dadzie (Ghana)

Mr. Endre Ustor (Hungary)

Mr. Alfonso de Rosenzweig Diaz (Mexico)

Mr. Rudolf L. Bindschedler (Switzerland)

Mr. G. I. Tunkin (Union of Soviet Socialist Republics)

Mr. Abdullah El-Erian (United Arab Republic)

Mr. F. A. Vallat (United Kingdom of Great Britain and Northern Ireland)

Mr. Warde M. Cameron (United States of America)

Chairman:

Mr. R. S. S. Gunewardene (Ceylon)

Credentials Committee

Members:

Austria, El Salvador, Haiti, Mali, Philippines, Spain, Union of Soviet Socialist Republics, United Arab Republic, United States of America.

Chairman:

Mr. J. C. G. Kevin (Australia).

9. The Committee of the Whole set up the following sub-committee:

Sub-Committee on Special Missions

Members:

Ecuador, Iraq, Italy, Japan, Senegal, Union of Soviet Socialist Republics, United Kingdom of Great Britain and Northern Ireland, United States of America, Yugoslavia.

Chairman:

Mr. N. Ponce Miranda (Ecuador).

10. The Secretary-General of the United Nations was represented by Mr. C. A. Stavropoulos, the Legal Counsel. Mr. Yven-li Liang, Director of the Codification Division of the Office of Legal Affairs of the United Nations, was appointed Executive Secretary.

11. The General Assembly, by its resolution 1450 (XIV) convening the Conference, referred to the Conference chapter III of the Report of the International Law Commission covering the Work of its Tenth Session as the basis for its consideration of the question of diplomatic intercource and immunities. The General Assembly, by its resolution 1504 (XV) of 12 December 1960, also referred to the Conference the draft articles on special missions contained in chapter III of the Report of the International Law Commission covering the Work of its Twelfth Session, so that they might be considered together with the draft articles on diplomatic intercourse and immunities included in the Commission's report on its tenth session.

12. The Conference also had before it observations submitted by Governments on the drafts prepared by the International Law Commission during successive stages of its work, preparatory documentation prepared by the Secretariat of the United Nations, the text of the final report of the Asian-African Legal Consulative Committee on functions, privileges and immunities of diplomatic envoys or agents, adopted at the Committee's third session, and the text of the Convention regarding diplomatic officers adopted by the Sixth International American Conference and signed at Havana, 20 February 1928.

13. On the basis of the deliberations, as recorded in the records and report of the Committee of the Whole and in the records of the plenary meeting, the Conference prepared the following Convention and Protocols:

Vienna Convention on Diplomatic Relations;

Optional Protocol concerning Acquisition of Nationality;

Optional Protocol concerning the Compulsory Settlement of Disputes.

The foregoing Convention and Protocols, which are subject to ratification,

were adopted by the Conference on 14 April 1961, and opened for signature on 18 April 1961, in accordance with their provisions, until 31 October 1961 at the Federal Ministry for Foreign Affairs of Austria and subsequently, until 31 March 1962, at the United Nations Headquarters in New York. The same instruments were also opened for accession, in accordance with their provisions, and will be deposited with the Secretary-General of the United Nations.

14. In addition the Conference adopted the following resolutions which are annexed to this Final Act:

Resolution on Special Missions;

Resolution on Consideration of Civil Claims;

Resolution expressing a tribute to the International Law Commission;

Resolution expressing a tribute to the Government and people of the Republic of Austria.

IN WITNESS WHEREOF the representatives have signed this Final Act.

DONE AT VIENNA this eighteenth day of April, one thousand nine hundred and sixty-one, in a single copy in the Chinese, English, French, Russian and Spanish languages, each text being equally authentic. By unanimous decision of the Conference the original of this Final Act shall be deposited in the archives of the Federal Ministry for Foreign Affairs of Austria.

VIENNA CONVENTION ON DIPLOMATIC RELATIONS

The States Parties To The Present Convention

RECALLING that peoples of all nations from ancient times have recognized the status of diplomatic agents,

HAVING IN MIND the purposes and principles of the Charter of the United Nations concerning the sovereign equality of States, the maintenance of international peace and security, and the promotion of friendly relations among nations,

BELIEVING that an international convention on diplomatic intercourse, privileges and immunities would contribute to the development of friendly relations among nations, irrespective of their differing constitutional and social system,

REALIZING that the purpose of such privileges and immunities is not to benefit individuals but to ensure the efficient performance of the functions of diplomatic missions as representing States,

AFFIRMING that the rules of customary international law should continue to govern questions not expressly regulated by the provisions of the present Convention,

HAVE AGREED as follows:

Article 1

For the purpose of the present Convention, the following expressions shall have the meaning hereunder assigned to them:

a) the "head of the mission" is the person charged by the sending State with the duty of acting in that capacity;

b) the "members of the mission" are the head of the mission and the members of the staff of the mission;

c) the "members of the staff of the mission" are the members of the diplomatic staff, of the administrative and technical staff and of the service staff of the mission;

d) the "members of the diplomatic staff" are the members of the staff of the mission having diplomatic rank;

e) a "diplomatic agent" is the head of the mission or a member of the diplomatic staff of the mission;
f) the "members of the administrative and technical staff" are the members of the staff of the mission employed in the administrative and technical service of the mission;
g) the "members of the service staff" are the members of the staff of the mission in the domestic service of the mission;
h) a "private servant" is a person who is in the domestic service of a member of the mission and who is not an employee of the sending State;
i) the "premises of the mission" are the buildings or parts of buildings and the land ancillary thereto, irrespective of ownership, used for the purpose of the mission including the residence of the head of the mission.

Article 2

The establishment of diplomatic relations between States, and of permanent diplomatic missions, takes place by mutual consent.

Article 3

1. The functions of a diplomatic mission consist *inter alia* in:
a) representing the sending State in the receiving State;
b) protecting in the receiving State the interests of the sending State and of its nationals, within the limits permitted by international law;
c) negotiating with the Government of the receiving State;
d) ascertaining by all lawfull means conditions and developments in the receiving State, and reporting thereon to the Government of the sending State;
e) promoting friendly relations between the sending State and the receiving State, and developing their economis, cultural and scientific relations.

2. Nothing in the present Convention shall be construed as preventing the performance of consular functions by a diplomatic mission.

Article 4

1. The sending State must make certain that the *agrément* of the receiving State has been given for the person it proposes to accredit as head of the mission to that State.

2. The receiving State is not obliged to give reasons to the sending State for a refusal of *agrément*

Article 5

1. The sending State may, after it has given due notification to the receiving States concerned, accredit a head of mission or assign any member of the diplomatic staff, as the case may be, to more than one State, unless there is express objection by any of the receiving States.

2. If the sending State accredits a head of mission to one or more other States it may establish a diplomatic mission headed by a *chargé d'affaires ad interim* in each State where the head of mission has not his permanen seat.

3. A head of mission or any member of the diplomatic staff of the mission may act as representative of the sending State to any international organization.

Article 6

Two or more States may accredit the same person as head of mission to another State, unless objection is offered by the receiving State.

Article 7

Subject to the provisions of Articles 5, 8, 9 and 11, the sending State may freely appoint the members of the staff of the mission. In the case of military, naval or air attachés, the receiving State may require their names to be submitted beforehand, for its approval.

Article 8

1. Members of the diplomatic staff of the mission should in principle be of the nationality of the sending State.

2. Members of the diplomatic staff of the mission may not be appointed from among persons having the nationality of the receiving State, except with the consent of that State which may be withdrawn at any time.

3. The receiving State may reserve the same right with regard to nationals of a third State who are not also nationals of the sending State.

Article 9

1. The receiving State may at any time and without having to explain its decision, notify the sending State that the head of the mission or any member of the diplomatic staff of the mission is *persona non grata* or that any other member of the staff of the mission is not acceptable. In any such case, the sending State shall, as appropriate, either recall the person concerned or terminate his functions with the mission. A person may be declared *non grata* or not ac-

ceptable before arriving in the territory of the receiving State.

2. If the sending State refuses or fails within a reasonable period to carry out its obligations under paragraph 1 of this Article, the receiving State may refuse to recognize the person concerned as a member of the mission.

Article 10

1. The Ministry for Foreign Affairs of the receiving State, or such other ministry as may be agreed, shall be notified of:

a) the appointment of members of the mission, their arrival and their final departure or the termination of their functions with the mission;

b) the arrival and final departure of a person belonging to the family of a member of the mission and, where appropriate, the fact a person becomes or ceases to be a member of the family of a member of the mission;

c) the arrival and final departure of private servant in the employ of persons referred to in sub-paragraph (a) of this paragraph and, where appropriate, the fact that they are leaving the employ of such persons;

d) the engagement and discharge of persons resident in the receiving State as members of the mission or private servants entitled to privileges and immunities.

2. Where possible, prior notification of arrival and final departure shall also be given.

Article 11

1. In the absence of specific agreement as to the size of the mission, the receiving State may require that the size of a mission be kept within limits considered by it to be reasonable and normal, having regard to circumstances and conditions in the receiving State and to the needs of the particular mission.

2. The receiving State may equally, within similar bounds and on a non-discriminatory basis, refuse to accept officials of a particular category.

Article 12

The sending State may not, without the prior express consent of the receiving State, establish offices forming part of the mission in localities other than those in which the mission itself is established.

Article 13

1. The head of the mission is considered as having taken up his functions in the receiving State either when he has presented his credentials or when he

has notified his arrival and a true copy of his credentials has been presented to the Ministry for Foreign Affairs of the receiving State, or such other ministry as may be agreed, in accordance with the practice prevailing in the receiving State which shall be applied in a uniform manner.

2. The order of presentation of credentials or of a true copy thereof will be determined by the date and time of the arrival of the head of the mission.

Article 14

1. Heads of missions are divided into three classes, namely:

a) that of ambassador or nuncios accredited to Heads of State, and other heads of missions of equivalent rank;

b) that of envoys, ministers and internuncios accredited to Heads of State;

c) that of *chargés d'affaires* accredited to Ministers for Foreign Affairs.

2. Except as concerns precedence and etiquette, there shall be no difference between heads of missions by reason of their class.

Article 15

The class to which the heads of their missions are to be assigned shall be agreed between States.

Article 16

1. Heads of mission shall take precedence in their respective classes in the order of the date and time of taking up their functions in accordance with Article 13.

2. Alterations in the credentials of a head of mission not involving any charge of class shall not affect his precedence.

3. This article is without prejudice to any practice accepted by the receiving State regarding the precedence of the representative of the Holy See.

Article 17

The precedence of the members of the diplomatic staff of the mission shall be notified by the head of the mission to the Ministry for Foreign Affairs or such other ministry as may be agreed.

Article 18

The procedure to be observed in each State for the reception of heads of mission shall be uniform in respect of each class.

Article 19

1. If the post of head of the mission is vacant, or if the head of the mission is unable to perform his functions, a *chargé d'affaires ad interim* shall act provisionally as head of the mission. The name of the *chargé d'affaires ad interim* shall be notified, either by the head of the mission or, in case he is unable to do so, by the Ministry for Foreign Affairs of the sending State to the Ministry for Foreign Affairs of the receiving State or such other ministry as may be agreed.

2. In cases where no member of the diplomatic staff of the mission is present in the receiving State, a member of the administrative and technical staff may, with the consent of the receiving State, be designated by the sending State to be in charge of the current administrative affairs of the mission.

Article 20

The mission and its head shall have the right to use the flag and emblem of the sending State on the premises of the mission, including the residence of the head of the mission, and on his means of transport.

Article 21

1. The receiving State shall either facilitate the acquisition on its territory, in accordance with its laws, by the sending State of premises necessary for its mission or assist the latter in obtaining accommodation in some other way.

2. If shall also, where necessary, assist missions in obtaining suitable accommodation for their members.

Article 22

1. The premises of the mission shall be inviolable. The agents of the receiving Stat may not enter them, except with the consent of the head of the mission.

2. The receiving Stat in under a special duty to take all appropriate steps to protect the premises of the mission against any intrusion or damage and to prevent any disturbance of the peace of the mission or impairment of its dignity.

3. The premises of the mission, their furnishings and other property thereon and the means of transport of the mission shall be immune from search, requisition, attachment or execution.

Article 23

1. The sending State and the head of the mission shall be exempt from all national, regional or municipal dues and taxes in respect of the premises of the mission, whether owned or leased, other than such as represent payment for specific services rendered.

2. The exemption from taxation referred to in this Article shall not apply to such dues and taxes payable under the law of the receiving State by persons contracting with the sending State or the head of the mission.

Article 24

The archives and documents of the mission shall be inviolable at any time and wherever they may be.

Article 25

The receiving State shall accord full facilities for the performance of the functions of the mission.

Article 26

Subject to its laws and regulations concerning zones entry into which is prohibited or regulated for reasons of national security, the receiving State shall ensure to all members of the mission freedom of movement and travel in its territory.

Article 27

1. The receiving State shall permit and protect free communication on the part of the mission for all official purposes. In communicating with the Government and the other missions and consulates of the sending State, wherever situated, the mission may employ all appropriate means, including diplomatic couriers and messages in code or cipher. However, the mission may install and use a wireless transmitter only with the consent of the receiving State.

2. The official correspondence of the mission shall be inviolable. Official correspondence means all correspondence relating to the mission and its functions.

3. The diplomatic bag shall not be opened or detained.

4. The packages constituting the diplomatic bag must bear visible external marks of their character and may contain only diplomatic documents or articles intended for official use.

5. The diplomatic courier, who shall be provided with an official document indicating his status and the number of packages constituting the diplomatic bag, shall be protected by the receiving State in the performance of his functions. He shall enjoy personal inviolability and shall not be liable to any form of arrest or detention.

6. The sending State or the mission may designate diplomatic couriers *ad hoc*. In such cases the provisions of paragraph 5 of this Article shall also apply, except that the immunities therein mentioned shall cease to apply when such a courier has delivered to the consignee the diplomatic bag in his charge.

7. A diplomatic bag may be entrusted to the captain of a commercial aircraft sheduled to land at an authorized port of entry. He shall be provided with an official document indicating the number of packages constituting the bag but he shall not be considered to be a diplomatic courier. The mission may send one of its members to take possession of the diplomatic bag directly and freely from the captain of the aircraft.

Article 28

The fees and charges levied by the mission in the course of its officials duties shall be exempt from all dues and taxes.

Article 29

The person of a diplomatic agent shall be inviolable. He shall not be liable to any form of arrest or detention. The receiving State shall treat him with due respect and shall take all appropriate steps to prevent any attack on his person, freedom or dignity.

Article 30

1. The private residence of a diplomatic agent shall enjoy the same inviolability and protection as the premises of the mission.

2. His papers, correspondence and, except as provided in paragraph 3 of Article 31, his property, shall likewise enjoy inviolability.

Article 31

1. A diplomatic agent shall enjoy immunity from the criminal jurisdiction of the receiving State. He shall also enjoy immunity from its civil and administrative jurisdiction, except in the case of:

a) a real action relating to private immovable property situated in the territory of the receiving State, unless he holds it on behalf of the sending

State for the purposes of the mission;
b) an action relating to succession in which the diplomatic agent is involved as executor, administrator, heir or legatee as a private person and not on behalf of the sending State;
c) an action relating to any professional or commercial activity exercised by the diplomatic agent in the receiving State outside his official functions.

2. A diplomatic agent is not obliged to give evidence as a witness.

3. No measure of executions may be taken in respect of a diplomatic agent except in the cases coming under sub-paragraph (a), (b) and (c) of paragraph 1 of this Article, and provided that the measures concerned can be taken without infringing the inviolability of his person or of his residence.

4. The immunity of a diplomatic agent from the jurisdiction of the receiving State does not exempt him from the jurisdiction of the sending State.

Article 32

1. The immunity from jurisdiction of diplomatic agents and of persons enjoying immunity under Article 37 may be waived by the sending State.

2. Waiver must always be express.

3. The initiation of proceedings by a diplomatic agent or by a person enjoying immunity from jurisdiction under Article 37 shall preclude him from invoking immunity from jurisdiction in respect of any counterclaim directly connected with the principal claim.

4. Waiver of immunity from jurisdiction in respect of civil or administrative proceedings shall not be held to imply waiver of immunity in respect of the execution of the judgment, for which a separate waiver shall be necessary.

Article 33

1. Subject to the provisions of paragraph 3 of this Article, a diplomatic agent shall with respect to services rendered for the sending State be exempt from social security provisions which may be in force in the receiving State.

2. The exemption provided for in paragraph 1 of this Article shall also apply to private servants who are in the sole enploy of a diplomatic agent, on condition:
a) that they are not nationals of or permanently resident in the receiving State; and
b) that they are covered by the social security provisions which may be in force in the sending State or a third State.

3. A diplomatic agent who employs persons to whom the exemption

provided for in paragraph 2 of this Article does not apply shall observe the obligations which the social security provisions of the receiving State impose upon employers.

4. The exemption provided for in paragraph 1 and 2 of this Article shall not preclude voluntary participation in the social security system of the receiving State provided that such participation is permitted by that State.

5. The provisions of this Article shall not affect bilateral or multilateral agreements concerning social security concluded previously and shall not prevent the conclusion of such agreements in the future.

Article 34

A diplomatic agent shall be exempt from all dues and taxes, personal or real, national regional or municipal, except:

a) indirect taxes of a kind which are normally incorporated in the price of goods or services;

b) dues and taxes on private immovable property situated in the territory of the receiving State, unless he holds it on behalf of the sending State for the purpose of the mission;

c) estate, succession or inheritance duties levied by the receiving State, subject to the provisions of paragraph 4 of Article 39;

d) dues and taxes on private income having its source in the receiving State and capital taxes on investments made in commercial undertakings in the receiving State;

e) charges levied for specific services rendered;

f) registration, court or record fees, mortgage dues and stamp duty, with respect to immovable property, subject to the provisions of Article 23.

Article 35

The receiving State shall exempt diplomatic agents from all personal services, from all public service of any kind whatsoever, and from military obligations such as those connected with requisitioning, military contributions and billeting.

Article 36

1. The receiving State shall, in accordance with such laws and regulations as it may adopt, permit entry of and grant exemption from all customs duties, taxes and related charges other than charges for storage, cartage and similar sevices, on:

a) articles for the official use of the mission;

b) articles for the personal use of a diplomatic agent or members of his

family forming part of his household, including articles intended for his establishment.

2. The personal baggage of a diplomatic agent shall be exempt from inspection, unless there are serious grounds for presuming that it contains articles not covered by the exemptions mentioned in paragraph 1 of this Article, or articles the import or export of which is prohibited by the law or controlled by the quarantine regulations of the receiving State. Such inspection shall be conducted only in the presence of the diplomatic agent or of his authorized representative.

Article 37

1. The members of the family of a diplomatic agent forming part of his household shall, if they are not nationals of the receiving State, enjoy the privileges and immunities specified in Article 29 to 36.

2. Members of the administrative and technical staff of the mission, together with members of their families forming part of their respective households, shall, if they are not nationals of or permanently resident in the receiving State, enjoy the privileges and immunities specified in Articles 29 to 35, except that the immunity from civil and administrative jurisdiction of the receiving State specified in paragraph 1 of Article 31 shall not extend to acts performed outside the course of their duties. They shall also enjoy the privileges specified in Article 36, paragraph 1, in respect of articles imported at the time of first installation.

3. Members of the service staff of the mission who are not nationals of or permanently resident in the receiving State shall enjoy immunity in respect of acts performed in the cource of their duties, exemption from dues and taxes on the emoluments they receive by reason of their employment and the exemption contained in Article 33.

4. Private servants of members of the mission shall, if they are not nationals of or permanently resident in the receiving State, be exempt from dues and taxes on the emoluments they receive by reason of their employment. In other respects, they may enjoy privileges and immunities only to the extent admitted by the receiving State. However, the receiving State must exercise its jurisdiction over those persons in such a manner as not to interfere unduly with the performance of the functions of the mission.

Article 38

1. Except insofar as additional privileges and immunities may be granted by the receiving State, a diplomatic agent who is a national of or permanently resident in that State shall enjoy only immunity from jurisdiction, and inviolability, in respect of official acts performed in the exercise of his functions.

2. Other members of the staff of the mission and private servants who are nationals of or permanently resident in the receiving State shall enjoy privileges and immunities only to the extent admitted by the receiving State. However, the receiving State must exercise its jurisdiction over those persons in such a manner as not to interfere unduly with the performance of the functions of the mission.

Article 39

1. Every person entitled to privileges and immunities shall enjoy them from the moment he enters the territory of the receiving State on proceeding to take up his post or, if already in its territory, from the moment when his appointment is notified to the Ministry for Foreign Affairs or such other ministry as may be agreed.

2. When the functions of a person enjoying privileges and immunities have come to an end, such privileges and immunities shall normally cease at the moment when he leaves the country, or on expiry of a reasonable period in which to do so, but shall subsist until that time, even in case of armed conflict. However, with respect to acts performed by such a person in the exercise of his functions as a member of the mission, immunity shall continue to subsist.

3. In case of the death of a member of the mission, the members of his family shall continue to enjoy the privileges and immunities to which they are entitled until the expiry of a reasonable period in which to leave the country.

4. In the event of the death of a member of the mission not a national of or permanently resident in the receiving State or a member of his family forming part of his household, the receiving State shall permit the withdrawal of the movable property of the deceased, with the exception of any property acquired in the country the export of which was prohibited at the time of his death. Estate, succession and inheritance duties shall not be levied on movable property the presence of which in the receiving State was due solely to the presence there of the deceased as a member of the mission or as a member of the family of a member of the mission.

Article 40

1. If a diplomatic agent passes through or is in the territory of a third State, which has granted him a passport visa if such visa was necessary, while proceeding to take up or to return to his post, or when returning to his own country, the third State shall accord him inviolability and such other immunities as may be required to ensure his transit or return. The same shall apply in the case of any members of his family enjoying privileges or immunities who

are accompanying the diplomatic agent, or traveling separately to join him or to return to their country.

2. In circumstances similar to those specified in paragraph 1 of this Article, third States shall not hinder the passage of members of the administrative and technical or service staff of a mission, and of members of their families, through their territories.

3. Third States shall accord to official correspondence and other official communications in transit, including messages in code or cipher, the same freedom and protection as is accorded by the receiving State. They shall accord to diplomatic couriers, who have been granted a passport visa if such visa was necessary, and diplomatic bags in transit the same inviolability and protection as the receiving State in bound to accord.

4. The obligations of third States under paragraphs 1, 2 and 3 of this Article shall also apply to the persons mentioned respectively in those paragraphs, and to official communications and diplomatics bags, whose presence in the territory of the third State is due to force majeure.

Article 41

1. Without prejudice to their privileges and immunities, it is the duty of all persons enjoying such privileges and immunities to respect the laws and regulations of the receiving State. They also have a duty not to interfere in the internal affairs of that State.

2. All officials business with the receiving State entrusted to the mission by the sending State shall be conducted with of through the Ministry for Foreign Affairs of the receiving State or such other ministry as may be agreed.

3. The premises of the mission must not be used in any manner incompatible with the functions of the mission as laid down in the present Convention or by other rules of general international law or by any special agreements in force between the sending and the receiving State.

Article 42

A diplomatic agent shall not in the receiving State practise for personal profit any professional or commercial activity.

Article 43

The function of a diplomatic agent comes to an end, *inter alia*:
a) on notification by the sending State to the receiving State that the function of the diplomatic agent has come to an end;
b) on notification by the receiving State to the sending State that, in accor-

dance with paragraph 2 of Article 9, it refuses do recognise the diplomatic agent as a member of the mission.

Article 44

The receiving State must, even in case of armed conflict, grant facilities in order to enable persons enjoying privileges and immunities, other than nationals of the receiving State, and members of the families of such persons irrespective of their nationality, to leave at the earliest possible moment. It must, in particular, in case of need, place at their disposal the necessary means of transport for themselves and their property.

Article 45

If diplomatic relations are broken off between two States, or if a mission is permanently or temporarily recalled:
a) the receiving State must, even in case of armed conflict, respect and protect the premises of the mission, together with its property and archives;
b) the sending State may entrust the custody of the premises of the mission, together with its property and archives, to a third State acceptable to the receiving State;
c) the sending State may entrust the protection of its interests and those of its nationals to a third State acceptable to the receiving State.

Article 46

A sending State may with the prior consent of a receiving State, and at the request of a third State not represented in the receiving State, undertake the temporaty protection of the interests of the third State and of its nationals.

Article 47

1. In the application of the provisions of the present Convention, the receiving State shall not discriminate as between States.

2. However, discrimination shall not be regarded as taking place:
a) where the receiving State applies any of the provisions of the present Convention restrictively because of a restrictive application of that provision to its mission in the sending State;
b) where by custom or agreement States extend to each other more favourable treatment than is required by the provisions of the present Convention.

Article 48

The present Convention shall be open for signature by all States Members of the United Nations or of any of the specialised agencies or Parties to the Statute of the International Court of Justice, and by any other State invited by the General Assembly of the United Nations to become a Party to the Convention, as follows: until 31 October 1961 at the Federal Ministry for Foreign Affairs of Austria and subsequently, until March 31 1962, at the United Nations Headquarters in New York.

Article 49

The present Convention is subject to ratification. The instuments of ratification shall be deposited with the Secretary-General of the United Nations.

Article 50

The present Convention shall remain open for accession by any State belonging to any of the four categories mentioned in Article 48. The instruments of accession shall be deposited with the Sevretary-General of the United Nations.

Article 51

1. The present Convention shall enter into force on the thirtieth day following the date of deposit of the twenty-second instrument of ratification or accession with the Secretary-General of the United Nations.
2. For each State ratifying or acceding to the Convention after the deposit of the twenty-second instrument of ratification or accession, the Convention shall enter into force on the thirtieth day after deposit by such State of its instrument of ratification or accession.

Article 52

The Secretary-General of the United Nations shall inform all States belonging to any of the four categories mentioned in Article 48:
a) of signatures to the present Convention and of the deposit of instruments of ratification or accession, in accordance with Articles 48, 49 and 50;
b) of the date on which the present Convention will enter into force, in accordance with Article 51.

Article 53

The original of the present Convention, of which the Chinese, English, French, Russian and Spanish texts are equally authentic, shall be deposited with the Secretary-General of the United Nations, who shall send certified copies thereof to all States belonging to any of the four categories mentioned in Article 48.

IN WITNESS WHEREOF the undersigned Plenipotentiaries, being duly authorised thereof by their respective Govenrments, have signed the present Convention.

DONE AT VIENNA, this eighteenth day of April one thousand nine hundred and sixty-one.

HAVANA CONVENTION ON DIPLOMATIC OFFICERS

The Government of the Republics represented at the Sixth International Conference of American States, held in the city of Habana, Republic of Cuba, the year 1928, being aware that one of the most important matters in the field of international relations is that pertaining to the rights and duties of diplomatic officers, which should be regulated in accordance with the conditions of economic, political and international life of nations;

Realizing the desirability that such regulation be effected pursuant to the new trends on the matter;

Recognizing that diplomatic officers do not in any case represent the person of the chief of State but only their Governments and that they must be accredited to a recognized Government, and acknowledging the fact that diplomatic officers represent their respective States and should not claim immunities which are not essential to the discharge of their official duties, and acknowledging also that it would seem desirable that either the officer himself or the State represented by him renounce diplomatic immunity whenever touching upon a civil action entirely alien to the fulfillment of his mission;

There being no possibility, nevertheless, at the present moment, of agreeing to general stipulations which although formulating a well-defined trend in international relations sometimes conflict with the established practices of various States in a contrary sense;

Therefore and until a more complete regulation of the rights and duties of diplomatic officers can be formulated;

Have decided to conclude a Convention incorporating the principles generally accepted by all nations, and have designated the following Plenipotentiaries: (Here follows the list of Plenipotentiaries)

Who, after having deposited their full powers, found to be in good and due form, have agreed on the following provisions:

General Provision

Article 1. States have the right of being represented before each other through diplomatic officers.

Section I. Chiefs of Mission

Article 2. Diplomatic officers are classed as ordinary and extraordinary.

Those who permanently represent the Government of one State before that of another are ordinary.

Those entrusted with a special mission or those who are accredited to represent the Govenrment in international conferences and congresses or other international bodies are extraordinary.

Article 3. Except as concerns precedence and etiquette, diplomatic officers, whatever their category, have the same rights, prerogatives and immunities.

Etiquette depends upon diplomatic usages in general as well as upon the laws and regulations of the country to which the officers are accredited.

Article 4. In addition to the functions indicated in their credentials, ordinary officers possess the attributes which the laws and decrees of the respective countries may confer upon them. They should exercise their attributes without coming into conflict with the laws of the country to which they are accredited.

Article 5. Every State may entrust its representation before one or more governments to a single diplomatic officer.

Several States may entrust their representation before another to a single diplomatic officer.

Article 6. Diplomatic officers, duly authorized by their governments, may, with the consent of the local government, and upon the request of a State not represented by an ordinary officer before the latter Government, undertake the temporary or accidental protection of the interests of the said State.

Article 7. States are free in the selection of their diplomatic officers; but they may not invest with such functions the nationals of a State in which the mission must function, without its consent.

Article 8. No State may accredit its diplomatic officers to other States without previous agreement with the latter.

States may decline to receive an officer from another or, having already accepted him, may request his recall, without being obliged to state the reasons for such a decision.

Article 9. Extraordinary diplomatic officers enjoy the same prerogatives and immnunities as ordinary ones.

Section II. Personnel of Missions

Article 10. Each mission shall have the personnel determined by its Government.

Article 11. When diplomatic officers are absent from the place where they exercise their functions or find it impossible to discharge them, they shall be substituted for temporarily by persons designated for that purpose by their Government.

Section III. Duties of Diplomatic Officers

Article 12. Foreign diplomatic officers may not participate in the domestic or foreign politics of the State in which they may exercise their functions.

Article 13. Diplomatic officers shall, in their official communications, address themselves to the Minister of Foreign Relations or Secretary of State of the country to which they are accredited. Communications to other authorities shall also be made through the said Ministry or Secretary.

Section IV. Immunities and Prerogatives of Diplomatic Officers

Article 14. Diplomatic officers shall be inviolate as to their persons, their residence, private or official, and their property. This inviolability covers:

a) All classes of diplomatic officers;
b) The entire official personnel of the diplomatic mission;
c) The members of the respective families living under the same roof;
d) The papers, archives and correspondence of the mission.

Article 15. State should extend to diplomatic officers every facility for the exercise of their functions and especially to the end that they may freely communicate with their governments.

Article 16. No judicial or administrative functionary or official of the State to which the diplomatic officer is accredited may enter the latter, or of the mission, without his consent.

Article 17. Diplomatic officers are obliged to deliver to the competent local authority that requests it any person accused or condemned for ordinary crimes, who may have taken refuge in the mission.

Article 18. Diplomatic officers shall be exempt in the State to which they are accredited:

1. From all personal taxes, either national or local;
2. From all land taxes on the building of the mission, when it belongs to the respective government;
3. From customs duties on articles intended for the official use of the mission, or for the personal use of the diplomatic officer or of his family.

Article 19. Diplomatic officers are exempt from all civil or criminal juris-

diction of the State to which they are accredited; they may not, except in the case when duly authorized by their government, waive immunity, be prosecuted or tried unless it be by the courts of their own country.

Article 20. The immunity from jurisdiction survives the tenure of office of diplomatic officers insofar as regards actions pertaining thereto; it may not, however, be invoked in respect to other actions except while discharging their diplomatic functions.

Article 21. Persons enjoying immunity from jurisdiction may refuse to appear as witnesses before the territorial courts.

Article 22. Diplomatic officers enter upon the enjoyment of their immunity from the moment they pass the frontier of the State where they are going to serve and make known their position.

The immunity shall continue during the period that the mission may be suspended, and even after it shall be terminated, for the time necessary for the officer to be able to withdraw with the mission.

Article 23. Persons belonging to the mission shall also enjoy the same immunities and prerogatives in the State which they cross to arrive at their post or to their own country, or in a State where they may casually be during the exercise of their functions and to whose Government they have made known their position.

Article 24. In case of death of the diplomatic officer, his family shall continue to enjoy the immunities for a reasonable term, until they may leave the State.

Section V. Termination of the Diplomatic Mission

Article 25. The mission of the diplomatic officer ends:

1. By the official notification of the officer's Government to the other Government that the officer has terminated his functions;
2. By the expiration of the period fixed for the completion of the mission;
3. By the solution of the matter, if the mission had been created for a particular question;
4. By the delivery of passports to the officer by the Government to which he is accredited;
5. By the request for his passport made by the diplomatic officer to the Government to which he is accredited.

In the above mentioned cases, a reasonable period shall be given the diplomatic officer, the official personnel of the mission, and their respective families to quit the territory of the State; and it shall be the duty of the Government to which the officer was accredited to see that during this time none of them is molested nor injured in his person or property.

Neither the death or resignation of the head of the State nor the change of government or political régime of either of the two countries shall terminate

the mission of the diplomatic officers.

Article 26. The present Convention does not affect obligations previously undertaken by the contracting parties through international agreements.

Article 27. (Provides for ratification).

BIBLIOGRAPHY

Accioly, Hildebrando, "Tratado de Direito Internacional Público", 2nd ed., 3 vols., Rio de Janeiro, 1956-1957.

Adair, E.R., "The exterritoriality of Ambassadors in the Sixteenth and Seventeenth Centuries", London, 1929.

Antokoletz, Daniel, "Tratado teorico y pratico de derecho diplomatico y consular", Buenos Ayres, 1948.

Anzilotti, Dionisio, "Cours de Droit International", vol. I, Paris, 1929.

Bevilaqua, Clovis, "Direito Público Internacional", 2nd ed., 2 vols., Rio de Janeiro, 1939.

Bluntschli, J.G., "Le Droit International Codifié", 5th ed., Paris, 1895.

Borchard, Edwin M., "The Diplomatic Protection of Citizens abroad or the Law of International Claims", New York, 1928.

Busk, Sir Douglas, "The Craft of Diplomacy", New York, 1967.

Cahier, Philippe, "Le Droit Diplomatique Contemporain", 2nd ed., Geneva, 1964.

Calvo, Charles, "Le Droit International Théorique et Pratique", 5th ed., 6 vols., Paris, 1888-1896.

Cambon, Jules, "Le Diplomate", Paris, 1926.

Cardinale, Igino, "Le Saint-Siège et la Diplomatie", Tournai, Belgium, 1962.

Cavaré, Louis, "Le Droit International Public Positif", 2nd ed., 2 vols., Paris, 1962.

Chazelle, Jacques, "La Diplomatie", Paris, 1962.

Colliard, Claude-Albert, "Droit International et Histoire Diplomatique", 2nd ed., Paris, 1950.

Contuzzi, F.P., "Trattato Teorico-Practico di Diritto Consulare e Diplomatico", Torino, 1910.

De Conde, Alexander, "The American Secretary of State, an interpretation", New York, 1962.

Fauchille, Paul, "Traité de Droit International Public", 4 vols., Paris, 1922-1926.

Fiore, Pasqualle, "Le Droit International Condifié et sa sanction jurisdique", Paris, 1890.

Florio, Franco, "Nozioni di Diplomazia e Diritto Diplomatico", Milano, 1962.

Foster, John W., "The Practice of Diplomacy", New York, 1906.

Genet, Raoul, "Traité de Diplomatie et de Droit Diplomatique", 3 vols., Paris, 1931-1932.

Grotius, Hugo, "De Jure Belli ac Pacis Libri Tres", in *Classics of International Law*, New York, 1913-1925.

Guggenheim, Paul, "Traité de Droit International Public", 2 vols., 1953-1954.

Hackworth, Green Heywood, "Digest of International Law", 8 vols., Washington, D.C., 1940-1944.

Hardy, Michael, "Modern Diplomatic Law", Manchester, 1968.

Hartmann, Frederick, "The Relations of Nations", 3rd edition, New York, 1967.

Harvard Law School, Research in International Law–"Diplomatic Privileges and Immunities", in *The American Journal of International Law*, vol. 26, 1932, *supplement.*

Hurst, Sir Cecil, "Les Immunités Diplomatiques", in *Recueil des Cours de l'Académie de Droit International*, vol. 12, 1926-II.

Hayter, Sir William, "The Diplomacy of Great Powers", New York, 1961.

International Law Commission, "Yearbook of the International Law Commission".

Jessup, Phillip C., "Parliamentary Diplomacy", in *Recueil des Cours de l'Académie de Droit International*, vol. 89, 1956-I.

Jusserand, Jean J., "L'Ecole des Ambassadeurs", Paris, 1934.

Kahn, David, "The Codebreakers", New York, 1968.

Kennedy, A.L., "Old Diplomacy and new", London, 1922.

Korovin, Y.A., "Derecho Internacional Publico", México, 1963.

Lauterpacht, Hersh, "Oppenheim's International Law", vol. I, 8th ed. London, 1955.

Lisboa, Henrique C.R., "Les Fonctions Diplomatiques en Temps de Paix", Santiago, 1908.

Maresca, Adolfo, "La Missione Diplomatica", Milano, 1959.

Mattingly, Garrett, "Renaissance Diplomacy", London, 1966.

Mello, Rubens Ferreira de, "Tratado de Direito Diplomático", 2 vols. 2nd ed., Rio de Janeiro, 1949.

Moncada, H. Cabral de, "O Asilo Interno em Direito Internacional Público", Coimbra, 1946.

Moussa, Farag, "Bibliographie de Droit Diplomatique", Geneva, 1963.

Nascimento e Silva, Geraldo Eulálio do–"Manual de Derecho Consular", Rosario (Argentina), 1952.

– "Organizaçao Diplomática e Consular Brasileira", Rio de Janeiro, 1959.

– "A Convençao de Viena sobre Relaçoes Diplomáticas", Rio de Janeiro, 1967.

– "The Vienna Conference on Consular Relations", in *The International and Comparative Law Quarterly*, Oct., 1964.

– "Diplomacia e Protocolo", Rio de Janeiro, 1969.

– "A Missao Diplomática", Rio de Janeiro, 1971.

Nicolson, Harold, "Diplomacy", 3rd ed., 1965.

– "The Evolution of Diplomacy", New York, 1962.

Numelin, Ragnar, "Les Origines de la Diplomatie", Paris 1945.

Nussbaum, Arthur, "A concise History of the Law of Nations", New York, 1947.

Nys, Ernest, "Les Origines de la Diplomatie et le Droit d'Ambassade jusqu'à Grotius", Brussels, 1884.

O'Brian, William Vincent, "The New Nations in Internatinal Law and Diplomacy", Washington, D.C., 1965.

Ogdon, Montell, "Juridical Bases of Diplomatic Immunity", Washington, 1936.

Oppenheim, L., "International Law: a treatise", 2 vols., 1952 and 1955, London-New York.

Pessoa, Epitácio, "Projeto de Código de Direito Internacional Público", Rio de Janeiro, 1911.

Phillipson, Coleman, "The International Law and Custom of Ancient Greece and Rome", 2 vols., London, 1911.

Plowden, Lord, "Report of the Committee on Representational Service Overseas appointed by the Prime Minister under the chairmanship of Lord Plowden", 1962-1963, London, 1964.

Potemkin, Vladimir Petrovitch, "Histoire de la Diplomatie", 3 vols., Paris, 1946-1947.

Pradier-Fodéré, R., "Cours de Droit Diplomatique", 2 vols., 2nd ed., Paris, 1899.

Raux, Jean, "Les rélations exterieures de la Communauté Economique Européenne", Paris, 1966.
Redslob, Robert, "Histoire des grands principes du droit des gens", Paris, 1923.
Regala, Roberto, "The Trends in Modern Diplomatic Practice", Milano, 1959.
Renouvin, Pierre et Jean-Baptiste Duroselle, "Introduction to the History of International Relations", London, 1967.
Ruiz Moreno, Isidoro, "El Derecho Internacional Público antes de la Era Cristiana", Buenos Ayres, 1946.
Sá Valle, Raymundo de, "Des Agents Diplomatiques", Geneva 1875.
Sandström, A.E.F., "Diplomatic Intercourse and Immunities", in *Yearbook of the International Law Commission*, 1955, vol. II.
Satow, Sir Ernest, "A Guide do Diplomatic Practice", 4th ed. (by Sir Neville Bland), London, 1957.
Sebastian de Erice, José, "Normas de Diplomacia y Derecho Diplomatico", 2 vols., Madrid, 1945.
Sereni, Angelo Piero, "Diritto Internazionale", 4 vols., Milano, 1957-1965.
– "The Italian Conception of International Law", New York, 1943.
Serres, Jean, "Manuel Pratique de Protocole", 2nd ed., Vitry-le-François (Marne), 1960.
Sibert, Marcel, "Traité de Droit International Public", 2 vols., Paris, 1951.
Staffa, Dino, "Le Delegazioni Apostoliche", Rome, 1959.
Strang, Lord, "The Foreign Office", London, 1957.
– "The Diplomatic Career", London, 1962.
Stuart, Graham Henry, "American Diplomatic and Consular Practice", New York, 1952.
– "The Department of State", New York, 1949.
Szilassy, Baron J. de, "Traité Pratique de Diplomatie Moderne", Paris, 1928.
Taube, Baron Michel de, "L'apport de Byzance au développement du droit international occidental", in *Recueil des Cours de l'Académie de Droit International*, vol. 67, 1939-I.
Thayer, Charles W., "Diplomat", New York, 1959.
Vattel, Emerich, "Le Droit des Gens ou Principes de la Loi Naturelle appliqués à la conduite et aux affaires des nations et des souverains", Paris 1863.
Verdross, Alfred, "Derecho Internacional Publico", 2nd ed., Madrid, 1966.
Vidal y Saura, Ginés, "Tratado de Derecho Diplomatico", Madrid, 1925.
Walsh, Edmund A., "L'evolution de la diplomatie aux Etats Unis", in *Recueil des Cours de l'Academie de Droit International*, vol. 69. 1939-III.
Waters, Maurice, "The *ad hoc* diplomacy: a study in municipal International Law", The Hague, 1963.
Whiteman, Marjorie M., "Digest of International Law", 11 volumes, Washington, D.C., 1963-1968.
Wicquefort, A. van, "L'Ambassadeur et ses Fonctions", London, 1840.
Williams, K.C., Vaughan, "Les Méthodes de Travail de la Diplomatie", in *Recueil des Cours de l'Académie de Droit International*, vol. 4, 1924-III.
Wolgast, Ernst, "Le Diplomate et ses Fonctions", in *Recueil des Cours de l'Académie de Droit International*, vol. 60, 1937-II.
Wood, John, R. and Jean Serres, "Diplomatic Ceremonial and Protocol", London, 1970.

INDEX